Nehru and the Language Politics of India

Nehru and the Language Politics of India

Robert D. King

DELHI
OXFORD UNIVERSITY PRESS
CALCUTTA CHENNAI MUMBAI
1998

Oxford University Press, Great Clarendon Street, Oxford OX2 6DP

Oxford New York
Athens Auckland Bangkok Calcutta
Cape Town Chennai Dar es Salaam Delhi
Florence Hong Kong Istanbul Karachi
Kuala Lumpur Madrid Melbourne Mexico City
Mumbai Nairobi Paris Singapore
Taipei Tokyo Toronto

and associates in

Berlin Ibadan

Oxford India Paperbacks 1998

ISBN 0 19 564804 8

Typeset by Rastrixi, New Delhi 110 070
and published by Manzar Khan, Oxford University Press
YMCA Library Building, Jai Singh Road, New Delhi 110 001

To Sarvepalli Gopal
In homage and friendship . . .

Acknowledgements

It is the custom in books of this nature to thank the people who have aided the project to its completion. Normally I should obey this code and endeavour to list everyone who has helped me as this book took shape. But there have been many, and I do not like to risk inadvertent omission.

I should like to thank by name only seven people. Two are Audre and Bernard Rapoport. Their extraordinary generosity in endowing the Audre and Bernard Rapoport Chair of Jewish Studies at the University of Texas has given me freedom and opportunity that are the dreams of scholars. My debt to them is profound, as is my affection for them. That debt can never be repaid in full, but only in small instalments, of which this book is one.

I also thank my colleague W. Roger Louis — historian of the British Empire, comrade in intellectual enterprise, critic, and friend, who persuaded me to make a book out of my musings about Nehru and language.

Finally there is my family: my children Irene, Kevin, and Michael — interested, bemused, affectionate observers of my days and ways — and my wife Karen, whose intelligence, grasp of things, and always sunny disposition have brightened my life for the past twenty-five years.

Acknowledgements

Preface

This book was conceived over the past decade as I reflected upon the linguistic battles that had accompanied the first years of India's independence. The better I grasped the deeper meanings of the language controversies that had pushed India to the brink of instability during that period, the more I came to admire Nehru's handling of the situation. The judgment that Nehru acquitted himself well in the language wars is not widely shared, indeed will be thought eccentric in some quarters, yet I, as an historical linguist by training and academic discipline, have not been able to see it in any other way.

Language is no longer the threat to the national unity of India that it was once considered to be. A scholarly study written in the 1980s puts the case with an assurance that I hope will not prove misplaced: '[L]anguage no longer poses a threat to national integration.'[1] I concur with this assessment. Nothing has happened over the last decade to undermine seriously or for long my optimism that the worst of India's language problems have receded into history, neutralized now as forces for national disequilibrium. Nehru played no small role in this; rather he played, by some distance, the leading role.

In any country with as many different established languages as India, language will never not be a problem. We must learn to live with it, as India has by and large done. It is however one thing to have a major illness with a bleak prognosis; altogether another for that illness to have been downgraded to a condition that is irritating and occasionally painful, but not life-threatening.

For much of the first two decades after Independence in 1947, language politics pushed India in the direction of serious disorder. A disproportionately large amount of political energy was expended during the language controversies of the 1950s and 1960s, but the advantages of hindsight now suggest more strongly than ever before that those struggles were the birth pangs of a new India, not harbingers of a permanent fragility.

Though language in India today is not the burning issue that it was, it does remain and will ever remain a problem — but limited now in its ability to infect the national body politic. There were terrible scenes of communal rioting in Badaun on 28 September 1989 following the decision of the Uttar Pradesh government to make Urdu the second official language of the state. Hindi remained the official language of U.P., as it always had been, but Muslims had fought for greater recognition of themselves and their Islamic culture through recognition for their language, which was Urdu. Language was here, as elsewhere, a symbol — an icon — concealing a deeper perception of injury to ethnic and religious self-respect. The salient fact, however, and one overriding all others in this sad but not uncommon incident, is that the Badaun linguistic infection — the rioting, the killing — did not spread beyond the borders of U.P.

The India of today is an India in which language is something less of a problem than it is, say, in Belgium or eastern Canada. In these countries language tensions (which conceal vast social, religious, and ethnic differences) have careered between full boil and a steady simmer for decades and more, and it would be foolhardy indeed to predict the eventual outcomes. At the present time the language–culture tensions in Belgium between the Flemish-speaking north and the French-speaking south are ominous and threaten the fragile unity of this weakly fused country created in 1830;[2] the language war in Canada between French-speaking Quebec and the largely English-speaking remainder of Canada was in unquiet remission for most of the decades preceding the 1980s, but the secession of Quebec is currently a very real possibility.[3] Quebec's separatist yearning is largely emotional rather than economic or political; it centres on the protection and preservation of French culture and the French language in North America; it is an affirmation of national identity.

Language as a source of public discontent rises and falls in India, though it now sits low on the scale of events in Indian official life. All the indicators are that the language condition of India will continue to improve, which is to say that language will not be a greater problem in the future than it is at present, and far less of a problem than it was during Nehru's day.

Moreover, it is my view that this improvement in the Indian linguistic scene will continue largely independently of what governments do or do not do. It is no longer a matter of government policy (if it ever was), and the less Indian governments, central or state, do with regard to language the better. The ability of governments to effect fundamental changes in the linguistic habits of those they govern is greatly overestimated. From this truism derives a good part of my admiration for Nehru's skill in his disposition of the language issues.

Nehru was fond of bestowing names on his initiatives — Panch Sheela comes to mind — but he never gave a name to his approach to the language problems. A wag could provide one: 'Operation Muddle', the phrase of course modelled after the Churchillian 'Operation Scuttle'.[4] It is facetious to call Nehru's conduct of language policy 'Operation Muddle', but I am not being facetious when I say that a certain amount of grey imprecision and misdirection, an insouciant forcelessness — muddle — is what India needed most during its time of greatest linguistic distress. To do nothing or to do as little as possible is never congenial to politicians, and almost never garners praise. Doing as little as possible, and that little slowly, is, however, often the best rule of state when it comes to contagious and highly divisive questions of policy. Nowhere is this truer than in the legislation of linguistic usage. Benign neglect is not always a bad thing; it is almost always the wisest policy in regard to language.

'History', according to a man who knew, Napoleon, 'is a fable agreed upon.' One such fable is that Nehru let his country down during its time of most redoubtable language tension by lack of aggressive leadership. Another fable is the belief that a democratic government, given the will, can do very much to significantly change the language usage and practices of its subjects. There are no ideal solutions in language-troubled countries. The perfect is the enemy of the good, here no less than anywhere else. Linguistic–political equilibrium in a multilingual country like India will always be measured not by victories but by the absence of disasters; by the lack of contentiousness and strife; by all the monstrous things that did not happen though wise observers warned that they would.

So it has gone with India's language problems since the great linguistic battles of the 1950s and 1960s. Because time attenuates most passions, it is possible to discuss the period following Independence with greater detachment than most observers could have summoned at mid-century when language issues seemed to threaten to destroy India's newly acquired freedom and its unity. History gets thicker, the historian A.J.P. Taylor said, as it approaches recent times. Percival Spear wrote in the early 1960s: 'Our proximity to the tossing waves of events since 1947 is far too close for an appraisal of the deeper currents and the underlying groundswell. One cannot measure Atlantic currents and storm patterns from a rowboat close to the shore.'[5] We are, I believe, far enough removed from the dark language storms of Nehru's India to see whole many of their patterns and to better appreciate his motives for acting as he did.

The linguistic problems of India have been studied, analysed, reanalysed, discussed, and commented upon almost to excess, and I am not interested in reworking the entire ground. It is not my wish to 'analyse' the whole of India's linguistic terrain, though there is much here to be analysed: how language interacts with nationalism, how language conflicts are so frequently surrogates for greed, malice, hatred, and rapaciousness. 'Language' problems are almost never what they appear to be: they are very often camouflage to hide agendas that are linked only tenuously to language and linguistics.

However, from the initial conception of this book my interest was and always has remained first and foremost Nehru: why he dealt with the language issues as he did, what he thought about language, how he came by his (as we shall see) sophisticated views on language matters and linguistic policies. It is however impossible to appreciate Nehru's accomplishment without knowing the historical context of language against which he had to act. I have therefore provided background material consisting primarily of my views of language and nationalism, as well as an account of the two major language issues facing Nehru as leader of independent India, the linguistic–state movement and the national language.

My principal goal in this book is to narrate the history of Nehru's involvement with language from early childhood to his death in 1964. That narrative alone is worth the telling: it throws new light on hitherto recessed areas of the mind and thought of the sensitive, intelligent, subtle figure of Jawaharlal Nehru; a man whose innermost being was concealed and to this day remains concealed under layer upon layer of veils. There was a splendour in his presence that reflects back the light of analysis by sober academics.

The book also has a thesis, however: that Nehru did a far better job of joining battle in India's language conflicts than he is customarily given credit for. His biographers have not given him high marks for his handling of the language issues, usually holding that he was tentative, ineffective, overcautious, and dilatory. Common opinion is that it was almost always a case of too little too late whenever Nehru could be induced, reluctantly and waspishly, to turn his mind away from thoughts of higher purpose — nonalignment, for example, or Chinese–Indian relations or India's economy — to the turgid and dispiriting commonplaces of language politics which is like all politics, only more so. Nehru was invariably ill-natured when forced to wrestle with intractable domestic problems such as the movement for linguistic provinces and the drive to make Hindi the national language.

It is correct that Nehru dragged his feet in regard to the language issues that plagued India's electoral politics after Independence. True, he resented the energy that these divisive but to him inconsequential controversies consumed, and the pain they caused when they estranged him from some of his closest associates and fellow freedom warriors from the campaign to rid the country of British domination. He stalled, contrived dodges, sought to avoid decisive action, pleaded for time. It cannot be denied that he was indecisive and often querulous about the language controversies, loath to join the fray. But delay in the political process is not always a vice, nor is feverish activism always a virtue. And when Nehru did engage the language controversies, he was usually effective in getting his way.

It is because of these qualities in him that I once considered giving this book the subtitle *Arjuna of the Linguistic Wars*. Arjuna is of course the central actor in the *Bhagavadgita*, who shrank before his duty to lead the armies of the Pandava brothers against their cousins, the hundred sons of Dhritarashtra. It is a cliché to say that Nehru was Hamlet-like in his private persona and not infrequently also in his public persona. In some beliefs he never wavered, for instance that religious and class or caste strife must be fought tooth and nail no matter what the cost or how daunting the opposition; or the belief that nothing ever could be allowed to threaten the unity of India. He believed in tolerance. He acquiesced in a wide range of demands made by Indian interest groups; but his tolerance of centrifugal forces ceased at the banks of Indian unity. Unity at all costs, unity all the time, always; never, never give up on Indian unity. Apart from bedrock beliefs such as these on which he never hesitated, Nehru constantly put to himself the disabling 'To be or not to be' question: is this the time to take up arms against a sea of troubles? Can this fight not be postponed to a more favourable time for resolution, when passions are banked and tempers cooled?

Arjuna asks of Krishna, his charioteer: why must I fight? Can you not see the horrible destruction that will follow?

> Saying this in the time of war,
> Arjuna slumped into the chariot
> and laid down his bow and arrows,
> his mind tormented by grief.
> (*Bhagavadgita* 1: 47)

However, one remembers that Arjuna did in the end put his irresolution behind him and lead the Pandavas to victory on the plains of Kurukshetra. Arjuna prevailed, and so did Nehru — though how much easier it would have been if Nehru had had as his charioteer a Krishna not only wise and courageous but also well endowed with a linguistic sophistication beyond the normal. In the event, there was no one in Nehru's circle who was 'reliable' on the language issues; almost anyone he might have consulted was either uninformed, uninterested, prejudiced, or committed in advance to one side or the other. Nehru had no one to whom he could turn for disinterested advice on how to manoeuvre through the lines of battle drawn up by the parties in India bent on achieving linguistic goals post-haste and the devil take the consequences. He had no Krishna whose counsel he could seek in time of language war. Where language politics was concerned, Nehru was marooned on an island of perpetual loneliness.

Jawaharlal Nehru was in one sense a man shipwrecked by history. His high hopes for Chinese–Indian comity were dashed by the border dispute that erupted in armed battle in 1962. How antique the rallying cry *Hindi–Chini Bhai Bhai* now sounds. Nehru's land, whose secular standard he raised higher than all others, is still periodically disfigured by communal disputes such as the incident at Ayodhya in the early 1990s.[6] Hindus, Muslims, and Sikhs still do not live together in perfect tranquillity in the land of Gandhi, *ahimsa*, and Nehru. Nehru's belief in socialism, difficult as it is to pin down precisely what that belief was, would be painfully at odds with the bustling, hustling, deal-making India of today. Many of Nehru's aspirations for Indian leadership of the Third World have foundered on the shoals of post-Cold War realities.

This melancholy retrospective not infrequently attends contemporary assessments of Nehru's legacy. The passage of time emphasizes, perversely, the failures rather than the unheralded successes of a statesman: in Nehru's case much of what he accomplished lies interred with his bones.

I think it is good, therefore, to revisit in depth one facet of the Nehru legacy where we may speak largely in terms of praise without qualification so tedious that its accumulation eventually nullifies the praise. An Arjuna he may have been, hesitating between the lines of battle in the language wars of India's birth years, perplexed, raising questions and venturing doubts, suspicious of the ultimate issues at stake and of where pursuit of resolution of those issues would lead him and his country, for, by instinct, he sensed correctly that dark devices lay behind all the fine talk about language. But Arjuna fought through his vacillation and indecision, and led his brothers to victory as did Nehru in India's linguistic wars.

In Nehru's position as leader of independent India, nine men out of ten would, in my opinion, have rushed to settle the linguistic problems as quickly as possible and hoped to be done with them whatever the eventual harm to the country. Nehru was however the tenth man, and his way laid the foundation for an India that is far less language-plagued and language-divided than anyone could have predicted during the worst of the linguistic battles of the 1950s and 1960s.[7] He delayed when it was right to delay; he was wilfully obstinate when stubbornness was needed; he stood clear when it was time to let go. His instincts on language politics were perpendicular to those of his contemporaries, crossways; but those instincts were correct if not valued at the time, or later. The honour due to Nehru is therefore even greater. In Auden's verse:

Let us honour if we can
The vertical man,
Though we value none
But the horizontal one.

A wise leader knows by intuition when to push back and when to stand clear. Jawaharlal Nehru possessed that intuition where language was concerned, and like most intuitions in men of consequence it was gained through experience, observation, formal learning, and knowledge acquired from books and conversation. His deeper understanding of language and all its potential for good and bad was not least a gift — 'the unbought gift of providence', in Edmund Burke's phrase. India was extraordinarily fortunate to have had him as its leader during the language turmoil that followed Independence.

He led his country well through these treacherous shoals. I will go further. It is my considered opinion that if the first prime minister of India had been a linguistic naïf rather than a linguistic sophisticate like Nehru, then we should have today not a unified India with a strong government at the centre but an India weakly divided along linguistic and cultural lines into two or three semi-autonomous regions. The unity of India would be as a faded dream.

It is a dark scenario that does not reward contemplation. That this dark scenario did not materialize owes more to Jawaharlal Nehru than anyone else, and is perhaps his most enduring bequest to the Indian nation.

Notes and References

1. S. Kishore, *National Integration in India* (New Delhi: Sterling Publishers, 1987), p. 47.
2. *The Independent*, 20 May 1995.
3. *The New York Times*, 30 Oct. 1995; *The Wall Street Journal*, 26 Oct. 1995.
4. Winston Churchill called Britain's disengagement from India 'Operation Scuttle' in his speech of 6 March 1947 before the House of Commons.
5. P. Spear, *India: A Modern History* (Ann Arbor: The University of Michigan Press, 1961), p. 419.

6. S. Gopal (ed.), *Anatomy of a Confrontation* (New Delhi: Penguin Books India, 1991).
7. There was no shortage of gloomy assessments of India's prospects in the first years of its independence. Typical of the genre is Selig Harrison's bleak prognosis from the late 1950s, *India: The Most Dangerous Decades* (Princeton: Princeton University Press, 1960).

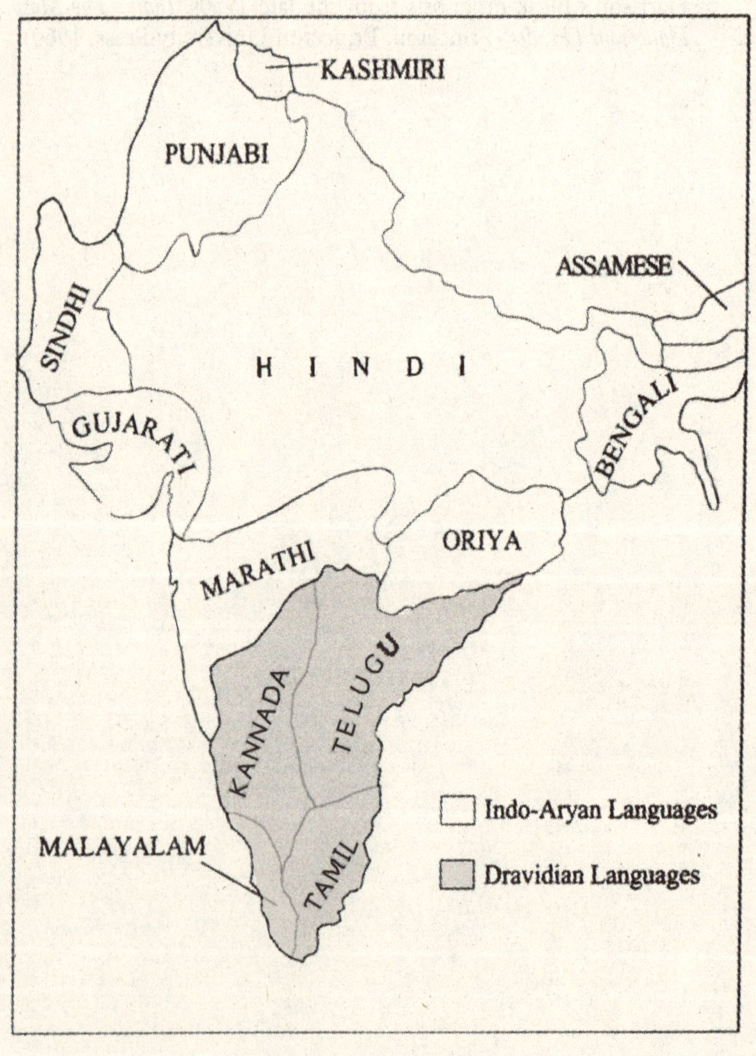

Map 1. Major Linguistic Regions (Schedule Eight Languages).

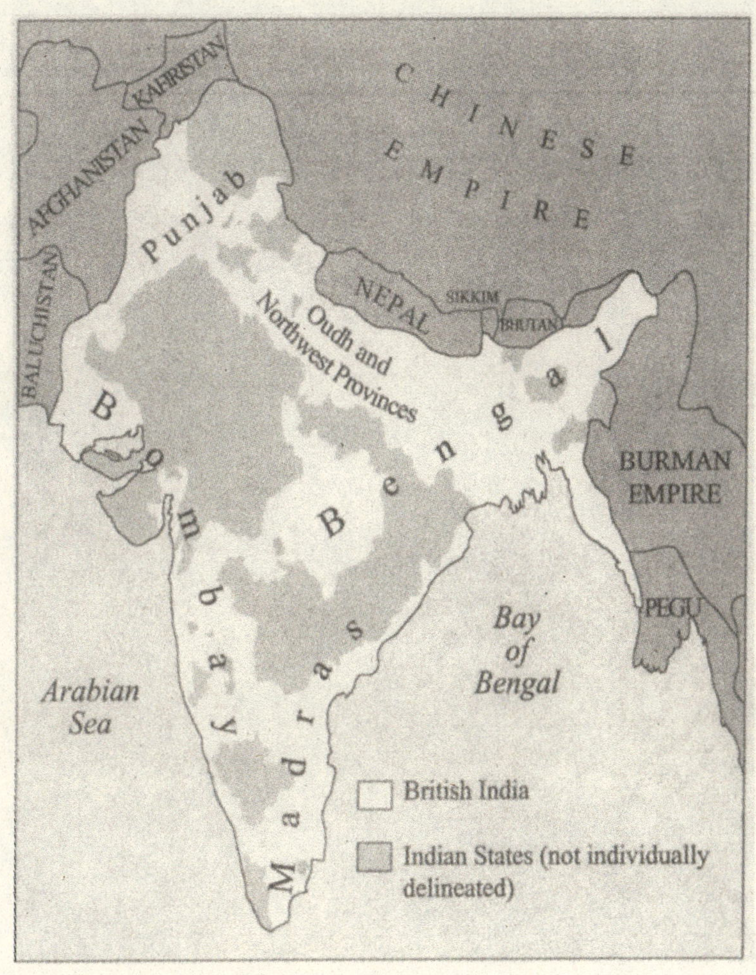

Map 2. Major Administrative Regions, 1857.

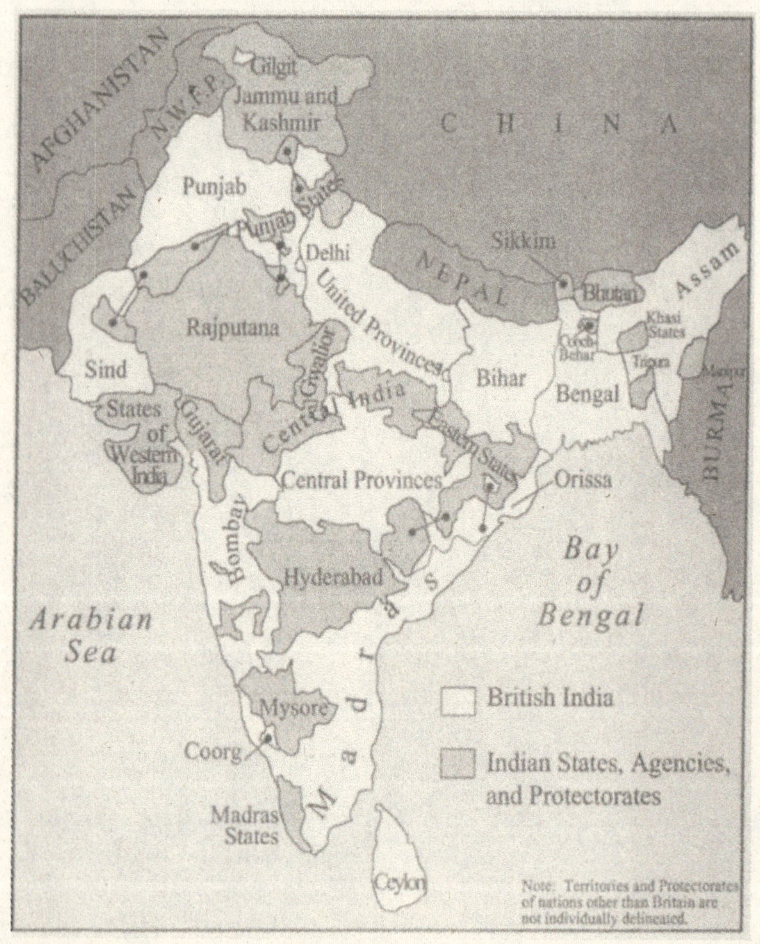

Map 3. Major Administrative Divisions at Independence.

Map 4. State Boundaries after Linguistic Reorganization.

Contents

Chapter 1

Introduction

When Jawaharlal Nehru became the first prime minister of India in 1947, he assumed the reins of government of one of the most linguistically complex countries in the world. Language has always been a subject of great consideration and concern in India: 'Hindus of reflective tendencies have always been much given to linguistic analysis and reflection.' [1] The ubiquity of language on the subcontinent seems to condition Indians from childhood to a heightened sensitivity to the uses and misuses of language, its mysteries and promises, its variety.

Visitors to India from earliest times have been drawn to comment on the country's astonishing linguistic diversity. Amir Khusrau observed on the occasion of his visit *c.* AD 1317:

> There is at this time in every province a language peculiar to itself, and not borrowed from any other — Sindi [Sindhi], Lahori [Punjabi], Kashmiri, the language of Dugar [Dogra of Jammu], Dhur Samundar [Kannada], Tilang [Telugu], Gujarati, Ma'bar [Tamil of the Coromandel Coast}, Gaur [Northern Bengali], Bengal Avadh [Eastern Hindi], Delhi and its environs [Western Hindi]. These are all languages of Hind [Hindustan, 'India'], which from ancient times have been applied in every way to the common purposes of life.[2]

The scholar–statesman Abu'l Fazl, famous for his support of the *Din Illahi* movement at the court of Akbar, in his *Ain-i-Akbari*, was even more inclusive and accurate than Khusrau in enumerating the 'dialects', as he called them, of 'Hindustan':

> Delhi [Western Hindi], Bengal [Bengali], Multan [Lahnda = Western Punjabi], Marwar [Western Rajasthani], Gujarata [Gujarati], Telingana [Telugu], Marhatta [Marathi], Karnatak [Kannada], Sind [Sindhi], Afghan of Shal [Pashto], Baluchistan [Balochi], and Kashmir [Kashmiri].[3]

Language manifests itself in cultures in many different ways. It matters more in some cultures than it does in others.[4] Publicly recited verse is a solemn, high event of Russian popular culture; it does not have this status in England or America. Certain cultures are more forgiving of the outsider's linguistic errors than others. Some cultures take it for granted that no one who is not 'of them' can ever speak their language very well. Japan and China tend in this direction. There are peoples among whom not just language but *words* are elevated to almost mystical ascendancy; the Jewish people traditionally has been one:

The midrash of the letters reveals an interesting dimension of the ancient Jewish love affair with words and language . . . G-d [the creator, whose name must not be written or pronounced] calls each aspect of existence into being by stating its name. This means that ultimate power, that by which all things come to be, resides in language.[5]

Some or all of these attitudes are found in India, though on the whole India must be counted among the most language-tolerant countries in the world. Nevertheless, the overriding reality is that language matters a great deal in India and always has. Language always mattered, in particular, a great deal to Nehru as a writer of books, as a former journalist, and as a letter writer of gargantuan proportions. However, as prime minister he would soon learn that what language meant to him and how language was important to him were one thing; what language meant to many of his countrymen and how it was important to them were something else altogether.

A share of the prodigious attention paid to language in India, both by Indians themselves and by outsiders, derives from the sheer number of languages spoken and from the very large numbers of people speaking them, both in absolute terms and especially in comparison with the numbers of speakers of European languages. Swedish, for example, is spoken today by some 9,000,000 people and Hungarian by 14,000,000.[6] Telugu, the state language of Andhra Pradesh and the language with the second largest number of native speakers in India, is spoken by 68,000,000 people,[7] which dwarfs the number of speakers of Swedish and Hungarian and exceeds by almost twenty million the number of speakers of French in France.[8] The combined number of speakers of Bengali in India and Bangladesh is estimated at between 145,000,000[9] and 184,000,000,[10] which exceeds the estimated 121,000,000 native speakers of French throughout the world.[11]

The numbers overwhelm the mind. They are too big, too beyond scale. The current population of India is estimated at around 850,000,000. If 'only', say, five per cent of the Indian population speak some language or other, we are nevertheless dealing with over 40,000,000 persons. English is thought to be spoken by two to three per cent of the Indian population, which is small as percentages go; but three per cent of the Indian population still represents some 25,000,000 people, which is almost half the English-speaking population of the United Kingdom.[12]

But it has always been the number of languages spoken rather than the numbers of people speaking them that has seemed to set India apart. What layman speaks of the 'many languages' of China, even though regional spoken variants of Chinese are routinely unintelligible? The monumental *Linguistic Survey of India* begun by George Grierson in the nineteenth century and completed twenty-five years into the twentieth enumerated 179 languages and 544 dialects.[13] While numbers as large as these can be defended by the measure of the scientific linguist, they include languages and dialects spoken by very few people, sometimes as few as a dozen or less. An enumeration of the languages, not to mention dialects of languages spoken in North America, would go into the hundreds because of the Native American languages, most of which have relatively few speakers, but only English, French (in Canada), and Spanish (in Mexico) are major languages with de facto and in some cases de jure official status.

Jawaharlal Nehru was always defensive on the point that India was said by many to 'have hundreds of languages':

> The notion that India has hundreds of languages is, like most other notions about her, entirely based on the lively imagination of some persons and has no basis in fact. India has a dozen languages, one of which — Hindustani — is spoken by about a third of her entire population and is understood by a great part of the rest.[14]

Writing a decade later, he alluded to the 'cry of the ignorant that India is a babel of languages with hundreds and hundreds of languages. India, as everyone who looks round him can see, has singularly few languages considering its vast size, and these are intimately allied to each other.'[15] And in *The Discovery of India*, written during his imprisonment during the war:

The oft-repeated story of India's having five hundred or more languages is a fiction of the philologist's and the census commissioner's mind, who note down every variation in dialect and every petty hill-tongue on the Assam–Bengal frontier with Burma as a separate language, although sometimes it is spoken only by a few hundred or a few thousand persons . . . According to the method adapted by census commissioners, Europe has hundreds of languages and Germany was, I think, listed as having about sixty.[16]

He never elaborated his misgivings on this score, but it is safe to assume that they belonged to the 'familiarity breeds contempt' category: a country with 'hundreds' of languages would be a country in which no language could be taken seriously; indeed would be a *country* that could not be taken seriously. 'How can you govern a country which has 246 varieties of cheese?', Charles de Gaulle asked of France. Nehru might well have put the same question to himself, replacing 'France' by 'India' and 'cheese' by 'language'. A point he returned to and dwelt on in his writings and speeches was that India had 'about a dozen' languages, which would be in line with the number of different languages in Europe; and India was larger in geographical area than Europe, hence the number of different — a dozen, more or less — languages in India was nothing much out of the ordinary and not freakish by any means.

The Eighth Schedule of the Indian Constitution of 1950 specified fourteen languages, thereby according them in some sense official status: Assamese, Bengali, Gujarati, Hindi, Kannada, Kashmiri, Malayalam, Marathi, Oriya, Punjabi, Sanskrit, Tamil, Telugu, and Urdu.[17] Sindhi was added by the Twenty-First Amendment Act of 1967 to the list of constitutionally recognized languages.[18] These then are the fifteen major languages of India which, taken with English, make up the sixteen languages that have some degree of statutory recognition. There are many other languages spoken by millions of people that lacked the political cachet to be included in Schedule VIII of the Constitution: Konkani (an Indo-Aryan language, and very close to Marathi), for example, and languages/dialects so close to Hindi that the decision not to call them Hindi is a matter decided by political semantics and emotion rather than by the austere calculus of linguistic academics — Rajasthani, Bihari, Magahi, Bhojpuri, and Maithili come to mind here. The numbers of speakers of languages not recognized in the Eighth Schedule are far from negligible. Santali, for example, a tribal language (Munda) spoken in Bihar, West Bengal, and Orissa, was estimated to have 3,000,000 speakers in 1986.[19]

In every way the most evocative account of the linguistic variety and richness of the subcontinent is that literary masterpiece of Anglo-India, the novel *Kim* by Rudyard Kipling. Hindustani — Hindi, Urdu — is the lingua franca of the novel, when Indian-accented and sahib-accented English is not the currency of suspect transaction. Mahbub Ali, the Pathan horse-dealer, normally uses Hindustani when talking to Kim, though his native language as an Afghan is Pashto. Pashto he would speak only 'for decency's sake', meaning when he did not want another to understand his cynical musings. Kim's lama has Tibetan as his native language, knows some Chinese, but speaks Hindustani ('"O Children, what is that big house?" he said in very fair Urdu') in his search throughout Hind for his river where the arrow fell. Kim is most comfortable in Hindustani, as one would expect of a boy who grew up in the streets of north India, though his English improves under the aegis of his British teachers at St Xavier's School; and from Lahore he has enough Punjabi to trump Sikh policemen and Jat farmers in the game of trading insults. Hurree Babu speaks everything — Bengali, Hindustani, 'Babu' English 'offeecially, by Jove' — and can read even 'Court Persian, which is the language of authorized and unauthorized diplomacy'. Creighton Sahib and Lurgan Sahib (of dubious antecedents) speak the Queen's English and 'fluent and inventive' Urdu — Hindustani — as that class of servant of the Raj would have done.

The Great Game was not a game for monolinguals or the language-shy. *Kim* conveys like nothing else the sprawling linguistic splendour of the Indian scene, and is described by Edward Said as 'a great document of its historical moment, as well as an aesthetic milestone along the way to midnight 15 August 1947'.[20]

Panini's Legacy

In view of the astounding variety of language on the subcontinent, it is little wonder that the seeds of a deeper understanding of linguistics lie thick upon Indian soil. Nehru was very acutely aware of this, as we shall see in Chapter 5 *(The Private Nehru)*. It is to the Indian past that linguists of all countries and all theoretical persuasions still look even today for one of the great glories of intellect in general, and linguistic science in particular — to Panini's grammar of the Sanskrit language, written we think some two and a half millennia ago.[21] The great grammarians of Sanskrit, Panini, and his followers Katyayana and Patañjali, created masterpieces of Sanskrit grammar; monuments of the mind as awe-inspiring in the linguistic cosmology as in other cultural spheres the Mona Lisa, the great pyramids of Giza, the Taj Mahal, or the magnificent temple of Konarak near Puri off the Bay of Bengal.

Pride of place among the Sanskrit grammarians and their grammars belongs to Panini's *Astadhyayi*, a description of Sanskrit so detailed, so shrewd, so comprehensive, so precise, that to this day it is unmatched in the annals of language description for completeness and subtlety:

> This grammar [Panini's *Astadhyayi*], which dates from somewhere round 350 to 250 BC, is one of the greatest monuments of human intelligence. It describes, with the minutest detail, every inflection, derivation, and composition, and every syntactic usage of its author's speech. No other language, to this day, has been so perfectly described.[22]

Ancient India conflated philosophy and linguistics to a degree unknown in the Occident and foreign to its antecedents. There is a Western linguistic tradition that joins hands with philosophy over part of the path though never to the scale that India achieved. Plato has Socrates devise gloriously wrong-headed etymologies of words in the *Cratylus*, for example. Mediaeval and post-Renaissance European linguistics were often as much a kind of religious exegesis as a prosaic language description, but little if any of what was produced in the West in those long centuries impinges on the concerns of contemporary theoretical linguistics. Indian linguistics was something entirely different.

Linguistics in ancient India was the core of the intellectual and scientific tradition. It possessed an intellectual centrality and scholarly hegemony that beggars belief today. Philosophy occupied centrestage in ancient Greece, as public administration in the broadest sense may fairly be said to have done in classical Rome. In classical India, however, from some half a millennium BC onward, it was language in the guise of Sanskrit grammar that was worshipped by the intellect.

The study of language in ancient India was a jewel in the crowns of both the Mauryan and the Gupta dynasties. Linguistics was suffused with the light of sanctity, endowed with religious purpose. This fusion of grammar and linguistics with religion is foreign to the Western mind; virtually impossible for Westerners to grasp, though it poses no difficulties for Indians familiar with this part of their tradition.

Patañjali, the author of the grammar *Mahabhasya*, has traditionally been identified with Patañjali the philosopher and yogi who wrote the *Yogasutra*. This celebrated treatise set out the eight 'limbs' from which all schools of yoga are derived. We do not know for certain whether Patañjali the grammarian was also Patañjali the philosopher, but we do know that the Patañjali — or the two Patañjalis — to whom the *Mahabhasya* and the *Yogasutra* are attributed is traditionally represented as a demigod; a coiled snake from the waist down and depicted sometimes with a cobra-like hood composed of five serpents over his head. There is at least one shrine in south India, the Anantisvara temple in Cidambaram, consecrated to the demi-deity linguist-cum-philosopher Patañjali.[23]

Linguistics in ancient India was the centre of the intellectual enterprise, religiously sanctioned, its practitioners philosopher–priests.[24] The Indian tradition was however exclusively concerned with what today is called descriptive or synchronic linguistics: how does one best, most efficiently, most simply, and most elegantly describe the way a language is composed? what formal theory best captures the knowledge that underlies the use of language? It is generally agreed that the Indian grammarians had one goal above all others, which was to preserve, down to the minutest detail, the ancient Sanskrit language, changing round them in the way all languages do, so that the rituals could be chanted past eternity the 'right way'; the way they had been chanted from time before knowing.

Upper-class education in ancient India began with the acquisition of the Sanskrit language in childhood. This was done by discussion and above all by memorizing Panini's grammar or one of the grammars based on it. Well after Sanskrit had ceased to be a widespread spoken language in India, classical Sanskrit literature was being written by men who had learnt their Sanskrit from grammars and dictionaries and teachers, as we might learn Latin or Greek today.

Descriptive linguistics today is predominantly formal linguistics. Linguistics qua formal linguistics says nothing about the social uses of language and the public effects of language, about 'language politics' or 'language planning' for example. Modern mainstream linguistics is thus squarely in the tradition of Indian grammar *(vyakarana)*, which focused resolutely on the *synchronic* ('same time') aspect of grammar: how to describe what the linguist hears spoken round him now, not how language got to be the way it is or indeed anything beyond the plain facts of how a language is spoken today. Nothing in the Indian tradition recognized language as a social or political force; indeed, as a 'force' of any kind. Language was; it simply was. The Indian grammatical tradition made language important. It did not make of language a political catalyst, or a means for unifying a country or for carving up a country into state units. It did not, in short, have anything to do with language as surrogate (one of the principal concepts of Chapter 2 — 'Linguistic Prolegomena'), with language as a 'proxy' that could be used to promote a political agenda or serve as an engine of social change.

There was nothing in the indigenous Indian linguistic tradition, therefore, which could direct the founding fathers of independent India in meeting the challenges posed to them by language. In particular, there was nothing in Panini or the ancillary classic Indian linguistic texts that might have conditioned Jawaharlal Nehru to think of language as anything other than an instrument of communication, the more polished the communication the better, even if Nehru had sat long years in the ashram of a pandit and steeped himself deeply in the study of Sanskrit. Nehru was in awe of Sanskrit; which is to put it far too mildly, as we shall see in Chapter 5 ('The Private Nehru'), and he was thoroughly familiar with the historical and cultural importance of Panini, if not with the details of his grammar.[25]

Nothing, however, in his intellectual background had prepared Nehru for the linguistic turmoil that would engulf him and his country between independence in 1947 and the year of his death, 1964, after which the intensity of India's linguistic disputes attenuated — more because the worst of the problems were essentially settled and the forces behind them spent than because of Nehru's death. Nothing in his experience, schooling, or sensibility had trained Nehru to grasp in 1947 that language was important in ways that went well beyond words or phrases, eloquence or style. Yet he learnt rapidly and, I shall argue, did far better than most would have done in negotiating his way through the minefields of the post-Independence linguistic battlegrounds.

A Brief Historical Account

There is need of a political history of language in India in which the strains of language, culture, history, and politics are woven together in a seamless narrative informed by a dispassionate though linguistically sophisticated point of view. That work has yet to be written. The history of language in India is a topic of such breadth, depth, and variety that it has almost by default been treated in the way of the three blind men and the elephant, and much of the literature on the subject is so crude and polemical or uninformed and outdated as to be useless.[26]

It is not my purpose to give here more than a thumbnail sketch of aspects of the linguistic history of India sufficient to acquaint the reader with some of the major 'fault lines' of Indian political–linguistic terrain. I should like to provide enough of the history of language in India that the general non-specialist reader unfamiliar with that history will gain some appreciation of the nature and the magnitude of the problems Nehru and the leaders of India had to face in 1947 when the country obtained its independence from the British.

Little as we know of the prehistory of the Indian subcontinent, it is unlikely that there was ever a time when only a single language was spoken over its expanse. Scholarly opinion now tends to agree that the Indus Valley civilization (*c.* 2500–2000 BC) that created the cities of Mohenjo-daro and Harappa in today's Pakistan was Dravidian, which in modern times is associated with the south, not the north, still less the north-west. We also know that

Austro–Asiatic peoples had come from the east into the subcontinent at some point, when we do not know for certain, but probably prior to the Indo–Aryan invasion from the north. Many of India's 'tribals' of today are Austro–Asiatic in origin (subfamily Munda), their languages related to the Mon–Khmer languages such as Vietnamese that stretch from Chotanagpur eastward to Indo–China.

Thus, when the Indo–European-speaking Aryans arrived, *c.* 1500 BC, from the north-west, they presumably found on their arrival an already vibrant linguistic scene of which, as conquerors, they need have taken as little notice as they wished. Of this early period we know, as far as languages are concerned, very little directly from texts and archaeological remains, from what is called 'hard' evidence. What we do know is that at least by Vedic times (roughly 1500–500 BC) Sanskrit, or at least some derivative of Sanskrit, was spoken over large parts of northern India.

By the time of Buddha's death in 487 BC Sanskrit had begun to evolve and become regionally differentiated as all languages do with the passage of time, and it is from this period that we date the emergence of the oldest forms of the Middle Indo–Aryan language varieties known as Prakrits, a cover term for 'vernaculars in contrast to the polished language' we call Sanskrit.[27] In a country as large as India it has always been necessary to have some one language to function, however imperfectly, as a lingua franca or, as it has usually been called in India, a 'link language' or a 'linking language'. The language that served that purpose prior to Muslim domination of the country was Sanskrit.

But Sanskrit was always more than a language; more than merely a voice for facilitating communication over the diverse regions of the country. It was the instrument of a way of life; a religion — Vedantism or Hinduism as purveyed by its Brahman priests; and the Sanskrit language carried that way of life far from its locus in the north of the country to the east and the south of the subcontinent. What the common man in the streets of the ancient cities of Tanjore and Conjeeveram on the Coromandel Coast spoke may have been Old Tamil or some other Dravidian language; but the language of his priests and the ashrams and the huts of pandits was Sanskrit. I shall discuss the concept of the 'unity of India' in Chapter 4 ('Nehru at the Helm'). This was a topic that deeply concerned Jawaharlal Nehru and had everything to do with his stance on the language disputes of his period. Suffice it to say here that the great unifier of India has always been 'Brahmanical ideology'; not only the familiar structures of Hinduism such as caste, cow worship, religious ceremonies, cremation, and so on, but the intellectual authority of the great classical texts, the *Vedas*, the *Upanishads*, the *Bhagavadgita*.[28] The instrument of penetration of Brahmanical ideology into the Deccan and the south was the Sanskrit language and the sacred texts written in Sanskrit.

Sanskrit has remained the language of cachet of Hindu India, even if few people have grown up with it as a cradle language since Panini's time. Throughout most of recorded Indian history it has been the language of learned treatises, of disputation between sages, and of the sacred words that must be spoken on holy occasions. It is far from uncommon even now for Indian intellectuals to devote a portion of each day to the study of Sanskrit, even as Indian captains of industry are given to meditation or the performance of yogic *asanas*. A few thousand people still give Sanskrit as their native language on the census returns (whatever that may mean), and at least as of 1995 All-India Radio in New Delhi was broadcasting the news in Sanskrit each morning at five minutes of seven.

We do not go seriously astray if we assume that the present-day linguistic configuration of India was in place by the third century BC or even earlier, meaning that Indo–Aryan languages (Sanskrit and its progeny, the Prakrits) were spoken from north India to well down in the Deccan, and Dravidian languages spoken in south India up into the lower reaches of the Deccan plateau. The vernacular ('spoken') languages of India have therefore for about two millennia been arranged over the subcontinent in something like the present distribution. The great divide has always been between an Indo–Aryan north India and a Dravidian south India, portentous even today (Map 1).

The vernacular languages, though always in the shadow of Sanskrit until the late nineteenth century, can lay claim to extremely old and distinguished literary pedigrees recorded in epigraphy and native literatures: in Dravidian India Tamil goes back to the second century BC; Kannada to the fourth century AD; Telugu dates from the seventh century AD; and Malayalam from at least the tenth century AD.[29] For comparison, the earliest written records of English and German, for example, date from about the fifth century AD. The Buddhist hymns called the *Caryapada* were composed in eastern India between AD 1000 and 1200. Their language was Old Bengali (though they are also claimed for Assamese and Oriya).[30]

How much Sanskrit to use in one of the vernacular languages is and always has been an aesthetic thing; a matter of balance, taste, and judgment. If a Tamil writer, for example, takes too much Sanskrit into his Tamil prose or poetry, it becomes bombastic, not genuine: he is not speaking in his own voice. It leads to a stilted, artificial language far removed from the actual rhythms of speech of the ordinary person, rather like Milton's use of Latin in English verse.

That the vernaculars lay in backwaters was not due solely to the prestige of Sanskrit. It had even more to do with the language used for administration throughout the country. Sanskrit had served that purpose along with the regional vernaculars in some cases in Hindu India, but with the coming of Islam to northern India the linguistic balance of power shifted. Persian was the language of love, culture, literature, poetry, diplomacy, music, and charm from Turkey eastwards. The Persian language was to the Islamic invaders of India, and to Babur and the Mughal dynasty he founded, what French was to the life of the spirit and to government in Europe from the sixteenth century onward. Persian was subtle and profound, highly developed, 'Islamic' to the core, even though, like Sanskrit, Indo-European in its genetic origin. Persian was perfectly suited for the administration of Mughal (and therefore Islamic) India.

Persian never altogether displaced Sanskrit, which continued to serve its ancient offices in the spiritual life of a predominantly Hindu country. But Persian was the official language of administration, and anyone — Muslim or Hindu — who was resolved to gain advantage in Mughal times perforce learnt Persian. There was no choice. Fluency in Bengali or Marathi or Tamil or Telugu could serve many purposes and fulfil many needs, emotional and ethnic; it could not advance one's career in the Mughal imperial hierarchy.

Persian remained the administrative language of the country long after the reins of the Mughal Empire had passed from strong to weak and then weaker imperial hands, eventually coming to rest in the more active and impatient hands of powerfully energized newcomers. Over the ruin and disorder of the Mughal Empire in decline came to rest the British presence. By the third quarter of the eighteenth century the British were effectively in control of most of the subcontinent, save hard-to-hold positions on the periphery, principally in the north-west and the north-east. The language of administration was increasingly English, naturally, but to a surprising extent Persian still functioned in an official capacity: language habits, even inconvenient and outmoded language habits, die hard. Sir William Jones, one of the first great 'Orientalists' of the British Empire, made his reputation by learning Persian when hardly another Englishman cared enough to do so. He secured his reputation by writing the *Grammar of the Persian Language*, published in 1771, which was used for many years after in training future stewards of the empire before sending them out to India. Warren Hastings, appointed governor of Bengal in 1772 ('stood forth as Dewan', as he put it), and far more interested in India and Indian ways than many who preceded him and came after him, learnt Persian from Jones' *Grammar*.[31]

But the days of Persian as a link language for the Indian subcontinent were numbered. Mughal emperors yielded to English governors-general, Persian gave way to English. By the first quarter of the nineteenth century the battle between 'Orientalists' who believed in educating 'the natives' in Sanskrit, Persian, and the vernacular languages, and the Utilitarians who believed otherwise — that English should henceforth be the language of schooling in India — had been fought out, and the Utilitarians had won. Their position is summed up in Thomas Babington Macaulay's famous 'Minute on Education' in 1835:

> I have no knowledge of either Sanscrit or Arabic. But I have done what I could to form a correct estimate of their value. I have read translations of the most celebrated Arabic and Sanscrit works. I have conversed both here and at home with men distinguished by their proficiency in the Eastern tongues. I am quite ready to take the Oriental learning at the valuation of the Orientalists themselves. I have never found one among them who could deny that a single shelf of a good European library was worth the whole native literature of India and Arabia.

The final curtain fell on the Persianization of India in the

1830s with the appointment of Lord William Bentinck to the governor-generalship. There followed a flurry of activity of the profoundest importance for the future not only of India but of the relationship between India and the English 'mother country'. Bentinck decreed that from 1835 the content of higher education should be Western learning and science and that the language of instruction should be English.

It will not do to leave the impression that the English simply ruled by diktat; that English would be the language for official purposes and for education. Macaulay's Minute has often been held responsible for the choice in favour of English, but a large part of the impetus came from middle- and upper-middle class Indians.[32] Macaulay's Minute did not rise, as so much else did, full-formed out of Macaulay's brain: Macaulay the 'book in breeches' he was called. Of course it had to be this way: English had become the path to power and riches; a vector towards the future. Indians of a certain class would want their children educated in English; of course they would, as upper-class Indians of a later generation such as Motilal Nehru, Jawaharlal's father, would want his son educated at Harrow and Cambridge.

Hand in hand with the growth of English domination in the language arena went paradoxically a renewal and rebirth of the Indian vernacular languages, long dormant under the weight of Sanskrit and Persian. Sir William Jones had first taught himself Sanskrit in the 1780s in order to learn legal precedents in native law, codified in Sanskrit for Hindus, in Persian and Arabic for Muslims; and this Orientalist bent in him and some of the British who followed him carried over into enthusiasm for many other things Indian such as the vernacular languages. British officers in the army used them, Hindustani (Hindi–Urdu) especially in the north, to order the Indian sepoys about, to listen to their problems and resolve their disputes, to carry out all the officer–man bonding associated with contented and successful armies.

British missionaries were considered a nuisance and a threat to the public order by the practical men who made up the leadership in India of the Honourable East India Company, and when the Baptists William Carey, Joshua Marshman, and William Ward arrived in India before the end of the eighteenth century they were banned from Calcutta by Wellesley and his officers and had to take refuge in the Danish enclave of Serampore.[33] Soon, however, the missionaries' zeal and talent for learning and teaching the native vernaculars (Bengali, Urdu, Telugu) outweighed the disadvantages of their tendency to foment trouble and meddle, and in 1801 Wellesley granted William Carey a professorship at Fort William College in Calcutta.

Whatever Carey's deficiencies as an observer of linguistic facts,[34] it was his and his fellow missionaries' enthusiasm for the vernaculars and their boyish eagerness to learn them that carried the day. They wrote grammars of Bengali and Telugu and Urdu and any Indian language that interested them, the purpose being of course to win converts to Christianity; but one cannot read far in the journals and reports of these men without soon appreciating that most of them were consumed by a love of God not greater than their love of languages. The languages they loved were not Latin, Greek, and Hebrew, or not only Latin, Greek, and Hebrew, but Tamil, Kannada, Marathi, and Bengali.

All the vernaculars had to come to grips with the problem of Sanskrit. Just as Sanskritization was the vehicle of Brahmanical ideology that had conquered the minds and hearts of the subcontinent, so too the Sanskrit language had 'conquered' portions of the vernacular languages, most commonly the lexicon (vocabulary). Sir William Jones in 1786 had been one of the first to point out the heavy influence of Sanskrit on the lexicon of Hindi: 'Five words in six, perhaps, of this language were derived from Sanskrit'; and Grierson had claimed that Bengali vocabulary in the early eighteenth century was composed of 88 per cent of such borrowings.[35]

In both cases it was the written and therefore the most artificial style of these languages that was so heavily Sanskritized. The spoken languages were quite different, as spoken languages are always more fluid, more 'real', than their written form. Sanskritization was by no means confined to Indo–Aryan languages like Hindi and Bengali that were themselves descended from Sanskrit. The Dravidian languages were equally susceptible, perhaps even more so; for Hinduism in the south lay just beyond the fingertips of Muslim rule from Delhi and so had remained 'purer', more faithful to its Sanskritic origins than Hinduism farther north. Malayalam had come under strong Brahmanical influence in the seventeenth century and had been heavily infused with words borrowed from Sanskrit.[36] Sanskrit — one must never forget it — has always captured the 'soul' of India, Hindu India at least, as no other language possibly could.

The nineteenth century witnessed the steady evolution of the vernacular languages as literary vehicles. Journalism played a role, as did in general the development of prose style. One of the greatest and most under-acknowledged gifts of the British Raj to India was English prose. Not simply narrative prose — after all *The Laws of Manu* was written in Sanskrit prose — but the prose style of the polished English essay, of a Macaulay, of Samuel Johnson's *Idler*, of Edmund Burke or John Stuart Mill. This kind of graceful, measured, disinterested prose was altogether different from the prose of indigenous traditions on the subcontinent. It was initially foreign to the 'cut' of any Indian language, from Sanskrit down to the meanest vernacular. But something about it struck fire in the Indian mind; its austerity, perhaps, its precision. By the end it would produce masters of the English language: Rabindranath Tagore, Sri Aurobindo, Sarvepalli Radhakrishnan and his historian son Sarvepalli Gopal, Raja Rao, and Nehru. But, from the vantage point of the 1830s, when the use of English became widespread, all this lay in the future. At the time, men like Macaulay and Bentinck fixed their gaze on planning for the education of Indians in English, and what came beyond was left to providence. English prose mastery carried with it the seeds of the perfection of prose style in the vernaculars, and as printing of newspapers and journals in these languages grew and spread in the nineteenth century, so did the use and suppleness of the vernaculars.

By the end of the nineteenth century English was as firmly entrenched as the English themselves in India, which is to say not as firmly entrenched as it appeared on the surface at the time. The first stirrings of a freedom movement had begun in 1885 with the creation of the Indian National Congress, if not earlier with the Sepoy Mutiny of 1857. Whenever the participants in this nascent struggle for independence came together from all the corners of India, they sorted out their plans and tactics in the English language. Of course: how else could a Maratha have communicated with a Bengali or a Tamil? But when the meetings were finished and the participants went back to their homes and their own kind, it was Marathi and Bengali and Tamil in which they greeted their families and friends at home. The vernaculars were there to stay. A Tilak who thundered against the English in their own language easily made the transition to the Tilak who thundered against the English in Marathi in the pages of his newspaper *Kesari* ('The Lion'). Sanskrit would always be in the picture somewhere; somewhere in the background in a place of honour along with English as a matter of practicality; but the century, the twentieth century, would belong to the vernacular languages of India.

Notes and References

1. F. Edgerton, 'Some Linguistic Notes on the Mimansa System', *Language*, 4 (1928), p. 171.
2. Ram Gopal, *Linguistic Affairs of India* (Bombay: Asia Publishing House, 1966), p. 11.
3. Ibid.
4. Cf. R.D. King, '"Triuwe" in Gottfried's *Tristan*', *Canadian Journal of Linguistics*, 17 (1972), pp. 159–66.
5. A. Green, 'The Aleph–Bet of Creation: Jewish Mysticism for Beginners', *Tikkun*, 7 (1992), p. 45.
6. V. Fromkin and R. Rodman, *An Introduction to Language*, 5th edn (Fort Worth: Harcourt Brace, 1993), p. 351; D. Abondolo, 'Hungarian', *in* B. Comrie (ed.), *The World's Major Languages* (New York: Oxford University Press, 1987), p. 577.
7. Fromkin and Rodman, *An Introduction to Language*, p. 354.
8. M. Harris, 'French', *in* B. Comrie (ed.), *The World's Major Languages* (New York: Oxford University Press, 1987), p. 211.
9. M.H. Klaiman, 'Bengali', *in* B. Comrie (ed.), *The World's Major Languages* (New York: Oxford University Press, 1987), p. 493.
10. Fromkin and Rodman, *An Introduction to Language*, p. 352.
11. Ibid., p. 351.
12. S. Gopal, 'The English Language in India since Independence, and its Future Role', *in* J. Grigg (ed.), *Nehru Memorial Lectures 1966–1991* (Delhi: Oxford University Press, 1992), p. 202; E. Finegan, 'English', *in* B. Comrie (ed.), *The World's Major Languages* (New York: Oxford University Press, 1987), p. 77.
13. G.A. Grierson, *Linguistic Survey of India*, 11 vols (Delhi: Motilal Banarsidass, 1967–8). This is a reprint of the first edition published between 1903 and 1928. See also the condensation of Grierson's linguistic classic by S. Varma, *G.A. Grierson's Linguistic Survey of India: A Summary*, 3 vols (Hoshiarpur: Vishveshvaranand Institute, Panjab University, 1972–6).

14. 'The Psychology of Indian Nationalism', *The Review of Nations*, 1 (1927). (Rptd in *Selected Works* I.2: 261.)
15. 'The Question of Language', *Unity*, p. 16.
16. *Discovery*, p. 161.
17. P. Diwan and P. Rajput, *Constitution of India* (New Delhi: Sterling Publishers, 1979), p. 471.
18. Ibid.
19. K. Katzner, *The Languages of the World* (London: Routledge & Kegan Paul, 1986), p. 23.
20. E. Said (ed.), *Kim*, by Rudyard Kipling (Harmondsworth: Penguin Books Ltd., 1987), p. 46.
21. 'Not later than early fourth century BC', G. Cardona, 'Sanskrit', *in* B. Comrie (ed.), *The World's Major Languages* (New York: Oxford University Press, 1987), p. 448.
22. L. Bloomfield, *Language* (New York: Holt, Rinehart & Winston, 1933), pp. 10–11. Bloomfield, one of the founders of modern structural linguistics, was himself a 'monument of the intellect'.
23. J.F. Staal, *A Reader on the Sanskrit Grammarians* (Cambridge: MIT Press, 1972), p. xvi.
24. 'All Indian [philosophical] systems deal more or less with problems of the nature of language, the relation of sound to sense, etc. When the time comes for a general History of Linguistic Theories, the Indian section will bulk large', Edgerton, 'Some Linguistic Notes on the Mimansa System', pp. 171–7.
25. *Discovery*, p. 106.
26. For broad orientation I refer the interested reader to K.S. Singh and S. Manoharan, *Languages and Scripts* (Delhi: Oxford University Press, 1993) and to the relevant portions of the standard histories of India such as *The Cambridge History of India* (Cambridge: Cambridge University Press, 1922–53) and J.A. Allan (ed.), *The Cambridge Shorter History of India* (Cambridge: Cambridge University Press, 1934); V.A. Smith, *Oxford History of India* (London: Oxford University Press, 1923); R.C. Majumdar (ed.), *The History and Culture of the Indian People* (Bombay: Bharatiya Vidya Bhavan, 1951). I also recommend the shorter histories H. Kulke and D. Rothermund, *A History of India* (London and Sidney: Croom Held, 1986); A.A. Macdonnell, *India's Past* (Oxford: The Clarendon Press, 1927); R.C. Majumdar, H.D. Raychaudhuri, and K. Datta, *An Advanced History of India* (London: Macmillan, 1961); K.M. Panikkar, *A Survey of Indian History* (Bombay: Asia Publishing House, 1956); Spear, *India*; S. Wolpert, *A New History of India* (New York: Oxford University Press, 1993); also the collections of primary sources in A.T. Embree and S. Hay, *Sources of Indian Tradition* (New York: Columbia University Press, 1988).

Ram Gopal, *Linguistic Affairs of India*, is particularly good. Grierson's *Linguistic Survey of India* (Grierson, *Linguistic Survey of India*, cf. also Varma, *G.A. Grierson's Linguistic Survey of India: A Summary*) is indispensable though now outdated in one or the other particular. Even more antique than Grierson is Beames' *Comparative Grammar of the Modern Aryan Languages of India*, first published in 1872–9 — J. Beames, *Comparative Grammar of the Modern Aryan Languages of India* (New Delhi: Munshiram Manoharlal, 1966); but what Beames lacks in up-to-date information and reliable opinion he more than compensates for by amusing observations and an entertaining style.

The following studies or collections of studies deal with specialized language topics. They are on the whole balanced, reliable, and reasonably accessible: E. Annamalai (ed.), *Language Movements in India* (Mysore: Central Institute of Indian Languages, 1979); M.L. Apte, 'Multilingualism in India and its Sociopolitical Implications: An Overview', *in* W.M. O'Barr and J.F. O'Barr (eds), *Language and Politics* (The Hague: Mouton, 1976), pp. 141–64; T. Burrow, *The Sanskrit Language* (London: Faber & Faber, 1973); P.H. Butter, *English in India* (Belfast: Queen's University, 1960); J. Das Gupta, *Language Conflict and National Development* (Berkeley: University of California Press, 1970); M. Deshpande, *Sanskrit and Prakrit, Sociolinguistic Issues* (Delhi: Motilal Banarsidass, 1993); M.B. Emeneau, *Language and Linguistic Area, Essays by Murray B. Emeneau*, edited by A.S. Dil (Stanford: Stanford University Press, 1980); C.A. Ferguson and J.J. Gumperz (eds), *Linguistic Diversity in South Asia* (Bloomington: Indiana University Research Center in Anthropology, Folklore, and Linguistics, 1960); B.B. Kachru, *The Indianization of English* (New York: Oxford University Press, 1983); B.I. Kluyev, *India: National and Language Problem* (New Delhi: Sterling Publishers, 1981); B.R. Nayar, *National Communication and Language Policy in India* (New York: Praeger, 1969). P. Brass, *Language, Religion, and Politics in North India* (Cambridge: Cambridge University Press, 1974) is a classic. S.K. Chatterji was one of the most outstanding historical linguists India has produced in modern times. See his *Languages and Literatures of Modern India* (Calcutta: Bengal Publishers, 1963); *Indo-Aryan and Hindi* (Calcutta: Mukhopadhyay, 1969); *India, A Polyglot Nation and its Linguistic Problems vis-à-vis National Integration* (Bombay: Mahatma Gandhi Memorial Research Centre, 1973).

27. G. Cardona, 'Indo-Aryan Languages', *in* B. Comrie (ed.), *The World's Major Languages* (New York: Oxford University Press, 1987), p. 441.

28. A.T. Embree, 'Indian Civilization and Regional Cultures: The Two Realities', *in* P. Wallace (ed.), *Region and Nation in India* (New Delhi: American Institute of Indian Studies, 1985).
29. S.B. Steever, 'Tamil and the Dravidian Languages', *in* B. Comrie (ed.), *The World's Major Languages* (New York: Oxford University Press, 1987), p. 726.
30. Klaiman, 'Bengali', p. 491.
31. R.D. King, 'West from India: The Odyssey of Sir William Jones', *The Library Chronicle*, 20 (1990), pp. 49–63.
32. Cf. R. Frykenberg, 'Modern Education in South India, 1784–1854: its Roots and its Role as a Vehicle of Integration Under Company Raj', *The American Historical Review*, 91 (1986), pp. 37–65; R. Frykenberg, 'The Myth of English as a "Colonialist" Imposition upon India: a Reappraisal with Special Reference to South India', *Journal of the Royal Asiatic Society*, 2 (1988), pp. 305–15; *pace* K. Ballhatchet, 'The Importance of Macaulay', *Journal of the Royal Asiatic Society*, 1 (1990), pp. 91–4.
33. Wolpert, *A New History of India*, p. 207.
34. Ram Gopal, *Linguistic Affairs of India*, p. 15.
35. Ibid., p. 8.
36. Ibid., p. 9.

Chapter 2

Linguistic Prolegomena

I attempt in this chapter to anticipate what will be useful in linguistic science and language history for a better understanding of Nehru's mind, thought, and actions in regard to language and to appreciate why I so highly value his prowess in linguistic politics as prime minister. Language was supremely important to Nehru from early childhood. As a grown man he enjoyed poetry and well-crafted prose, read voraciously, wrote extensively and gracefully. Few men of affairs in the English-speaking world of the twentieth century have used language as well or written as much as Jawaharlal Nehru.

If he was thoroughly conversant with 'language' as a means of expression, another use of 'language' — language as a political force, as a pawn in the tug of domestic politics — was initially foreign to him; uncongenial. Awareness of the potential of language for mischief and grief came slowly, and this slowness was chiefly responsible for his recalcitrance in reacting to the linguistic problems that inundated him as prime minister. It was this 'recalcitrance' that has so often drawn criticism.

Nehru was as gifted in his mastery of English prose as he was a prolific writer. I shall discuss in Chapter 5 the 'private' Nehru and how his knowledge of language and facility in its use grew from unpromising beginnings to maturity and sophistication. However, as important in his life as language was, Nehru had almost everything else on his mind except language when he became prime minister. There should be hesitation in faulting him for this; quite the contrary: language should not have been a top priority at free India's birth. It was not important enough. Forging the spirit of a new nation, creating a strong economy, dampening communal passions: all these, properly, had priority over language. Nehru was not therefore prepared for the intensity and bitterness of the language conflicts that very soon came crowding in on him as the leader of independent India. He did not initially recognize the non-linguistic uses to which language can be seduced for what they were. In this he continued the tradition of Panini for whom language was grammar, not a political jurisdiction; and in this he resembles, too, the archetypal modern academic linguist for whom language is first and foremost a neutral object of description rather than an emotional outlet or the essence of one's being.

For ordinary people language is a *means* of something, of expression, of communication, and for the linguist language is the *object* of something, of analysis, of study. Language-as-object: language as a thing to be analysed, pulled apart, understood historically and in its social effects, 'deconstructed'. Language-as-means: language as a tool to communicate with, to formulate thoughts as effectively as possible. Language is for most people language-as-means, not something to be thought about and torn apart as the linguist is wont to do, much as a watchmaker might take apart the mechanism of a watch to see what makes the thing work.

Linguists are 'clinicians of language'; we are not supposed to be sentimental about language; not at least in our 'official capacity'. We are schooled to be unemotional about it. We let others rhapsodize over the 'beauty' of French and cringe at the 'harsh gutturalness' of German. Not for us the arguments about which language lends itself best to opera or song. We are told that aesthetic insensitivity is an occupational hazard of certain menial professions: the man who mixes the paints is conventionally thought to lose his appreciation for the beauty of the painting.

Nehru and the linguist have in common at least a shared feeling that language — language-as-object as opposed to language-as-means — is nothing to become emotional about. Use it, yes, play with it if you like, probe it; but do not become overwrought about it. Nehru *used* language with emotion, but he did not *view* language with emotion. This lent him the shape of mind of the modern linguist; but it also put him profoundly at odds with those leaders of India in the post-Independence era to whom language was politics and at times more than politics; something more akin to religion.

Nothing had prepared Nehru to comprehend in 1947 that there were people in his country prepared to die for language;

that language was important to other people in ways that had nothing to do with words or phrases, eloquence or style. He perceived that language had material affect beyond its primary function as a mode of communication; he knew in his bones that too much fuss about the politics of language was a bad thing, but did not grasp the major implications of language as surrogate — of language and nationalism, and of language as icon.

Language and Nationalism

The 1990s dawned with the dissolution of the Soviet Union and the independence of countries that had formerly been part of the Soviet Empire. New flags and nations stood out. Latvia, Estonia, and Lithuania became independent, and Ukraine and Belarus became, if not totally independent, at least far more autonomous than before. Few years have gone by in the 1990s when some part of the world has not erupted in bitter and violent disputes over nationalism, almost always accompanied by ethnicity and religion — and language.

The twentieth century begins to look more and more like the pre-eminently nationalistic century. Serbian nationalism ushered in the beginning of the Great War as Serbian nationalism was on centrestage when the curtain descended on the final decade of the twentieth century. The end of the First World War in 1918 and the Treaty of Versailles unleashed powerful surges of nationalism among the former peoples of the Austro–Hungarian Empire, and the years following 1945 saw a wholesale dismantling of British, French, Belgian, and Dutch colonial empires. At the end of the twentieth century local nationalism asserted itself more urgently and more violently than most observers would have thought likely at mid-century when it was believed by the best thinkers that the Second World War and the creation of the United Nations had consigned nationalism to the dustbin of history. The events which stretch in time from 1914 through the end of the 1990s are as recurrent waves of a powerful nationalistic tide whose undercurrents will not be felt in their totality for a long time to come.

Language does not always play a role in nationalistic movements, but it frequently does. If one digs past the headlines of stories chronicling outbursts of nationalism, there usually lurk linguistic dissatisfactions which make up part of the charge-sheet of the aggrieved people.[1]

The linking of language and nationalism can be traced at least as far back as Rousseau, who had argued in his *Essay on the Origin of Languages* that language must develop before politics is possible and that language originally distinguished nations from one another.[2] It was only natural, given this intellectual provenance, that language lay in the intellectual background of the French Revolution. One of the lesser-known aims of the Revolution was to impose a standard national language on all the peoples of France, where regional languages such as Provençal, Breton, and Basque were still strong competitors of standard French; the French of the Ile de France.[3] As late as 1789, when the Revolution began, half the population of the south of France did not understand French (they spoke Provençal); earlier the playwright Racine said that he had had to resort to Spanish and Italian to make himself understood in the southern town of Uzès.[4] By the third quarter of the nineteenth century the association of language with nationalism was so taken for granted that we find assertions such as 'Mankind instinctively takes language as the badge of nationality' without any evident need for qualification or explication.[5] '[I]n the heyday of European nationalism from 1848 to 1919, language was more frequently invoked than any other criterion [to define nationality].'[6]

The Congress of Vienna (1813) imposed its boundaries upon Europe without regard to nationalisms, let alone languages; only Greece rose in opposition, in 1821.[7] In 1830 Belgium split from the Netherlands: French/Dutch (Flemish) language rivalries and loyalties, along with religious differences between Protestant and Catholic, were among the root causes. These outbreaks of ethnic nationalism increased in frequency and intensity, and reached a climax in the revolutionary events of 1848: Italy and Austria were at each other's throats; the Magyars threatened to bring down the Austro–Hungarian Empire, whose other subject peoples — Poles, Ukrainians, Czechs, Croats, Romanians — rapidly succumbed to the infectious passions so long held in check by Metternich's manipulations.

'Continental Europe at the end of the eighteenth century', wrote Hans Kohn, 'entered the Age of Nationalism.'[8] Nationalism, one of Barbara Ward's five ideas 'that change the world',[9] had come to stay, and language would always remain its handmaiden. The effects of the presence of these new conceptual dispensations out of Europe would wash up on the shores of the colonial empires only in the twentieth century.[10]

Let us look ahead to one of the linguistic questions that would bedevil India after Independence: the demand that the state boundaries should be redrawn to match language boundaries. The belief that political boundaries should coincide with linguistic boundaries is actually relatively recent on the world scene. It is ultimately a product of nineteenth-century nationalism.[11] People earlier thought nothing or very little of being ruled by other people in faraway places speaking a different language. This was so far from being unusual that it came close to the norm. Political boundaries were drawn to nature — rivers, mountain ranges — or for administrative convenience, or for no rational reason at all except usage and tradition, and not always even that reasonably. This was nowhere truer than in India, whether Mughal India or British India.

One need not look past central Europe to find an empire in which multitudes of languages were spoken, yet whose speakers found themselves ruled by other people in distant and alien capital cities speaking a language altogether different; and by later standards curiously indifferent to this state of affairs, unaware of the existence of any form of national insult. This was the Austro–Hungarian Empire, of course; the Dual Monarchy, its capital city Vienna, with effective control of subject peoples of the most varied and wildly discordant ethnicities throughout central Europe and most of eastern Europe. The official language of the Austro–Hungarian Empire was German, as was its lingua franca: 'From the Czech mountains to the Adriatic, from Innsbruck to Czernowitz [now in Ukraine], you could travel unhindered with the help of German. The German language was a veritable bridge which connected Slavs, Magyars, and Romanians with the Western culture.'[12]

But the conception that this was a tolerable arrangement — one language imposed for official purposes upon peoples who normally spoke other languages — changed rapidly with the ascendancy of nationalism. The imperative of the twentieth century became: one language, one nation; one nation, one language.[13] The great triumph of this desideratum was the Treaty of Versailles at the end of the First World War, when the allied victors redrew the map of central and eastern Europe according to ethnicity, which is virtually always identical with language, as best they could manage. By the first quarter of the twentieth century any other way of drawing national boundaries would have seemed queer, perverse, ahistorical. Arnold Toynbee observed in the post-First World War period that 'the growing consciousness of Nationality had attached itself neither to traditional frontiers nor to new geographical associations but almost exclusively to the mother-tongues';[14] and Toynbee did not like this; nor did Nehru, as we shall see.

The Soviet Union was the one great holdout against the equation of language and state, at least according to Stalinist doctrine. Stalin, who episodically had a greater than average interest in language, possibly because his native language was Georgian rather than Russian, enunciated the theory that 'A national community is impossible without a common language. . . . There is no nation which at once and the same time speaks several languages.'[15] The Russian language was hegemonic in Stalin's Soviet Union. Lenin's point of view was not Stalin's; indeed, was almost diametrically opposed, as I shall show in Chapter 5 ('The Private Nehru') when I discuss the impact of Nehru's visit to Soviet Russia in 1927 on his political education.

What then was one to make of India with its scores of millions of people speaking languages possessing important literatures and venerable histories, but where the British had drawn internal boundaries with almost no regard to language and as a matter of course used English as the 'link language' throughout? Before 1947 Nehru did not realize, except distantly and vaguely, that language had become one of the major defining criteria of nationalism; he did not perceive how strong the forces for regional linguistic nationalism in India had become. The battle to expel the British was a nationalistic struggle and had been from the beginning (*swaraj*, Bande Mataraṃ). If nationalism legitimized the fight against the British, then how in the name of logical consistency could regional nationalism be denied its seat at the table? Why should not the Andhras have their state in which Telugu would be the official language; and if the Andhras then why not the Marathas, a state demarcated by the limits of the Marathi language, and so on down the line like language–region dominoes?

Nehru, when he became prime minister, did not immediately grasp all the subterranean implications of the linking of language with regional loyalty or agree that it was a particularly pressing matter; and at first he could only contrive to delay. But the logic of linguistic provinces cannot be gainsaid so long as language and nationalism are so intimately entwined. And even if the full import of the feeding relationship between nationalism and language had been clear to Nehru in the 1950s when the language battles were most intense, there is no question that he would have agreed unreservedly with Arnold Toynbee, who scathingly dismissed 'the criterion of Nationality in the shibboleth of Language'.[16] Nehru wrote in the mid-1930s: '[T]he real reason why the Congress and other non-official organizations cannot do much for social reform goes deeper. We suffer from the disease of nationalism; that absorbs our attention, and it will continue to do so until we get freedom.'[17] One wishes, as Nehru so fervently did, that language loyalty, like other forms of tribal loyalty such as religion, caste, and class, could be placed in the museum of irrational beliefs and outmoded caprice, a casualty of progress and rising enlightenment; but that would be wishful thinking.

The fact is that ethnic unity and cultural identification are defined more by language than by geography or religion. This is notably and particularly true of Arabic and French: to be Arab is to speak Arabic; to speak French is to proclaim yourself part of French *gloire*. Arabs base identity on the use of a common tongue; culture without language is meaningless to the French.[18]

The locus of Bengali identity is found in language in spite of the division of the speakers of Bengali between two countries, India and Bangladesh, the number of speakers residing in Bangladesh being about half again as large as the number of those living in India. The name Bangladesh taken by the former East Pakistan when it seceded in 1971 is composed of *bangla* plus *desa* 'country'. The term *bangla* refers not to the Bengali people or to the territory of (East) Bengal but specifically to the Bengali language.[19]

There is much about nationalism and its connection with language and culture that we do not understand. For example, the Jews lost their Palestinian homeland to alien rule two thousand years ago. Julius Sextus Severus quelled Bar Kochba's revolt, and all but a handful of Jews were forced into exile. They were dispersed over the face of the earth, persecuted, massacred, subjected to intolerable pressures to assimilate. Yet they never lost their nationalism; their feeling of Otherness. Even in the darkest times devout Jews, and many not so devout, have each year finished the Passover meal with the cry 'Next Year in Jerusalem!'

The Celts once inhabited most of western Europe and could claim as their homeland even areas of central and eastern Europe. The Celts of Britain had their island isolation; with the natural defence of the Channel from the fevers of the Continent they had every possible excuse for remaining apart and different, yet they lost their national feeling save for pockets of Celticness in Ireland, Wales, and Scotland. On the Continent only the Bretons remain as a reduced remnant of a once great Celtic presence; and even the Bretons are Celts returned from the British isles.

The Jews lost their land but somehow managed to preserve their sense of nationality in the Diaspora. The Celts remained in their land, in their islands, yet lost their sense of nationality under foreign conquerors. Why such different outcomes? Why were these 'nationalisms', Jewish and Celtic, so different in their tenacity? Tentative and suggestive answers to these questions are easily formulated; compelling answers there are none. Modesty becomes the generalizations of students of national feeling.

Language as Icon

The joining of language and nationalism is subsumed under a more general category into which this 'non-linguistic' use of language fits, and this category I call 'language as icon' (or 'language as symbol'). The great social theorist Karl Mannheim referred to 'the meanings that make up our world'.[20] Language is precisely one such 'meaning'. As the British linguist J.R. Firth, whose acquaintance we shall again make when discussing the 'private Nehru' (Chapter 5), said: 'The bonds of family, neighbourhood, class, occupation, country, and religion are knit by speech and language. We take eagerly to the magic of language because only by apprenticeship to it can we be admitted to association, fellowship, and community in our social organization which ministers to our needs and gives us what we want or what we deserve . . .'[21]

Language, that is to say, can serve either as a badge of membership in the community or as a means of exclusion and exile. This is an iconic use of language: language as symbol to achieve non-linguistic goals. The notion that language could be an 'icon' that evokes murderous impulses in human beings, that even the written form of a language could goad people into murder and fury, was alien to a man of Nehru's sensibility and scorn of irrational mysticism. As prime minister Nehru gave few speeches touching on language problems in which he did not openly admit that he was baffled by the power of language to bring out what is base in men.

A typical iconic use of language, typical both because jejune, invisible to most passers-by, and harmless, can be seen in New Delhi on its street signs, which are normally written in four languages: Hindi in the Devanagari script, Urdu in its Persian-based script, Punjabi in the Gurmukhi script, and English. It really is not necessary in a practical sense to mark the streets in all these languages since Hindi and English would do quite well, but practicality is not the point. An iconic use of language is in play here. New Delhi, India's capital, is making, as it were, a 'statement': tolerance, receptivity to all cultures and ethnicities.

This is a commonplace example of language iconicity particularly appropriate for India, which has many languages and many different scripts for writing those languages. Both language and its script demand respect. It is not only the languages of India that can be used as symbol, as icon; it is the scripts the languages are written in that cause men to rampage and kill. This is all part of that hard lesson Nehru would learn at Independence: that language has an impact beyond words and literature; that language is an icon that possesses the power to alter history.

The Revival of the Hebrew Language in Israel

The rebirth of the Hebrew language in modern Israel is a now classic example of an iconic (and atypical) victory of language.[22] Hebrew as a spoken language became virtually extinct two thousand years ago. Jews living in the Holy Land spoke either Aramaic or Greek, though Hebrew continued in daily use as a liturgical language and as a language of disputation among rabbis. (The analogies with Sanskrit in Hinduism and Vedantism, or with

Latin in Roman Catholicism lie close at hand.) As Jews moved out from their ancestral homeland into Europe and the lands bordering the Mediterranean, they naturally began to speak the language of the countries in which they had settled during the early and mediaeval periods of the millennium. Jews in Spain spoke mediaeval Spanish; perhaps a Judaicized variant of Spanish in some cases but Spanish nevertheless (Ladino). Jews in France spoke Old French or, again, possibly a Jewish dialect of Old French (La'az). Jews living along the Rhine river in Germany spoke Middle High German, the German of AD 1050 to 1350, of one sort or another, probably always with a Jewish flavour and accent (Yiddish).

Hebrew remained dormant, its use confined to the rabbinate and the synagogue. In the late nineteenth century, however, there began a revival of the Hebrew language both in eastern Europe and in Palestine. The force behind the revival was more secular than religious: its purpose was to proclaim 'Jewishness'. To speak Hebrew was to assert membership in the worldwide community of Jews and as a proud member of that small but growing band of Zionist pioneers who had returned to the ancestral home. By the 1920s the majority of the Jews living in Palestine spoke Hebrew, though this represented only a tiny fraction of the world's Jewish population. The Hebrew language had become an icon for Jewishness.

After the Second World War had reduced the world's Jewish population from some 11,000,000 to around 5,000,000, Jews emigrated in large and growing numbers to Palestine, and in 1948 the reborn country of Israel gained its independence from the British. The question was: what should the language of the new country be? Other things being equal — as though other things could ever be equal — Yiddish would have been the leading candidate since most of the eastern European Jews who had managed to survive the Holocaust and get to Palestine spoke Yiddish. Yiddish, however, laboured under disabilities, one of which was that it was stigmatized as the 'language of the ghetto', a victim's language. It is difficult to imagine Ladino as the language of free post-1948 Israel, or German, for obvious reasons; English would have been a possibility since Israel (as Palestine) had been an English protectorate, and all leading Israelis knew English well.

Other things are never equal, however, when it comes to

language and its iconicity; practical considerations pale into insignificance alongside the power of the symbol. Hebrew it would have to be. Nothing else; no other language could possibly do for the new Israel, not English, not German, not Yiddish, not Ladino. Hebrew, as 'dead' a language as it had been over most of its recent history, linked the Jewish past and the Israeli future as no other language could. Hebrew was a sublime symbol of hope, of aspiration and rejuvenation — a symbol not only of Jewishness but of a particular muscular strain of Jewishness that would never allow another Holocaust to happen to its people: *Never Again!* was and is the rallying cry of modern Jewish pride and militancy. The Hebrew language is its symbol, its icon.

The moral then of the story of the revival of Hebrew is that sometimes, rarely, under very special circumstances, and usually not even then, the iconicity of language can create a miracle. In the normal scheme of things the attempted revival of Hebrew in the late nineteenth and early twentieth centuries would almost certainly have failed. Such is the fate of language revival. Languages, once dead, normally stay dead; unlike Lazarus they do not rise again. The fact that Hebrew was the language of the Bible, giving Hebrew a powerful iconic salience, was a necessary condition for the initial success in reviving the language, but that alone would have been far from a sufficient condition for the eventual wholesale rebirth and subsequent stabilization of the Hebrew language in Israel.

There were those who did not believe Hebrew could long remain the language of reborn Israel. The novelist and essayist Arthur Koestler was one of them.[23] Koestler felt that the archaic nature of the language, which he thought could not be brought up to the requirements of the twentieth century, foredoomed Hebrew to failure, as did the retention of the Hebrew script. Koestler was wrong. He underestimated the power of the Hebrew language as an icon of Jewish identity, and he did not understand that a part of the power of the Hebrew language as icon derives from its script — the script of the holy Bible.

The Failure of the Revival of the Irish Language

The case of the Irish language (Gaelic) is similarly instructive in the iconic aspect of language, though its outcome was in every way the opposite of Hebrew in Israel. Earlier, before the eighteenth century, most inhabitants of Ireland spoke Irish. Sometime between 1750 and 1850 a wholesale transfer to English, the language of the island's rulers, began. By 1851, when the first census to take language into account was held, only some 5 per cent of the population described themselves as monolingual Irish speakers; 23 per cent said they were bilingual in Irish and English.[24]

Although by the late nineteenth century the Irish language seemed destined for extinction, it secured standing as a badge of community by becoming transformed into an icon of Irish identification, hinting at a lost romantic Celtic past — wild, stormy, magical — in which anything could be dreamt of and all things were possible, even freedom from the British. The decline of the Irish language was noted with regret; people felt bad about it, and efforts were made to resurrect Irish and increase the numbers of its speakers. Clubs were formed, prizes for the best poems and essays offered. These are among the usual insignia that betoken a language in extremis; but nothing arrested the decline. It is almost impossible to reverse the decline of a language. Hebrew is the exception that proves the rule.

The Gaelic League was founded in 1893. One of its goals was to 'de-Anglicize Ireland; another was 'to foster Irish as the national language of Ireland and to spread its use as a spoken language'.[25] We note the now familiar fusion of nationalism and linguistics. The Gaelic League would probably have been one more well-intentioned effort to come to naught had it not been for the growth of revolutionary sentiment in favour of Home Rule culminating in the establishment of the Irish Free State in 1922. The leaders of the Home Rule movement were almost all prominent members of the Gaelic League.

When the Irish Revolution ended with independence from Britain in 1922, the whole situation changed almost overnight. Fresh problems faced the Irish government new to power; there were unanticipated challenges, unfamiliar accommodations to be made, reasons to reorder priorities, new hardships in place of the old ones. Understandably, perhaps, the creation of the Irish Free State brought with it a neglect of the Irish language revival. What was there that did not have priority over language as Ireland grappled with its independence? The energy that derived from the linguistic movement was absorbed by the success of the political movement, and even though nurture of the Irish language ranked high on the official agenda of the free Irish government, the life had gone out of the language movement in the cold dawn of 1922. The Commission on the Revival of Irish (Coimisiún um Athbheochan na Gaeilge, 1964) puts the case with an honesty unusual in such delicate matters, and there is no matter touched by the iconicity of language that is not delicate:

It stands to reason that people's enthusiasm would have waned as soon as the war with England was ended, and since the cultivation of the language [Irish] was seen as part of that war it was natural that their devotion should diminish . . . [M]any people felt that in an Irish state there would be no necessity for the [Gaelic] League to engage in work for the language . . . Due to the political divisions which resulted from the civil war, enmities arose within the language movement itself; some lost heart; others were disgusted by the bitter language and the cruelty of the great war, and others became indifferent and cynical. There was an end, to a great extent, to zeal for the language.[26]

The use of Irish has continued to decline; in the 1961 census less than 3 per cent of the school-going population gave Irish as the language of the home, and most of these were bilingual in English as well. Current estimates of the Irish-speaking population centre round 500,000.[27] The number of speakers of the Irish language has continued to decline, and this in spite of an array of expensive government-sponsored initiatives for encouraging the Irish to learn Irish. For the generation after 1920 at least, schools that taught all subjects in Irish received an additional 25 per cent on the capitation grants paid them by the government for each student. Students writing examination papers in Irish were given bonus points of five to ten per cent in various subjects.[28] There was every advantage to learning Irish. But ultimately all of this availed nothing. Nothing a well-motivated government attempted to do arrested the replacement of Irish by English. The inexorable historical process in train for some three hundred years continued. Nowadays people care about the Irish language, but not enough to make a difference. 'The prevailing attitude has been *pas trop de zèle*.'[29]

Politicians on the hustings invoke ritual introductory phrasings in Irish, the better to identify themselves with the history of the struggle; a struggle which now lies almost a century past and will never get closer. Once past the obligatory *A chairdhe ghael* ('my Irish friends') of the first sentence of the politician's speech, the speaker reverts to English, as of course he would have to unless in the *Gaeltachtaí* (Irish-speaking districts mostly in the west of Ireland).

The Irish example is instructive in a number of ways for the complex of language and nationalism and patriotism. The fighters for Home Rule honestly regarded the restoration of the Irish language as a vital part of their programme for independence. They were devoted to Irish, they loved its literature and poetry, they liked the sound of it; and Ireland's greatest poets such as William Butler Yeats were 'hurt into poetry' (as Auden's poem has it) by inspiration from the Gaelic past as well as by the pain of the British-ruled present. In his great poem of the Irish revolution, 'Easter 1916', Yeats calls the Irish language 'our wingèd horse'. The Irish language was an icon: it 'meant' independence from the British. To cherish Irish was to wear one's Irishness as a badge of honour and rebellion, similar to the use of Hebrew in Israel while Palestine was still a British protectorate.

The iconic use of the Irish language was one thing, the true restoration of Irish as the language of common currency something else altogether. As terrible and cruel as the Troubles were that led to the granting of Home Rule to the Irish Free State by the British in 1922, they paled alongside the destruction of 6,000,000 Jewish lives at the hands of the Nazis. It is not likely that the Hebrew language revival in Israel could have succeeded in the long run bar the Holocaust; and barring a dramatic and cruel event of such magnitude in Ireland it was preordained that the decline of Irish could not be arrested.

The lesson to be drawn from the Irish case is that language iconicity is not enough to prevail against historical determinism; iconicity is a necessary but insufficient condition for the rescue of a language in decline. It is hard to think of anything else the Irish government might have done to promote the Irish language.

It is of course always possible to argue the 'if only' position: if only the government had done this, if only the government had done that, if only the church had taken a greater interest, if only the educational establishment had had greater concern — it is not too late; no, not even now. Though of course it is. If only . . . It is pointless to speculate in this way, and one must resist the impulse. Nothing would have made the slightest difference. The Irish language served an iconic purpose: it symbolized Irish Otherness, it symbolized an Irish common front against the British. And it served that purpose well. It was a perfect icon for a freedom struggle. With the success of the political effort the language did not matter so much any longer. Most of the population spoke English anyway, and both the political will and the political energy to 'do something' about the decline of the Irish language ebbed away.

Critics who claim that Hindi would now be the true national language of India if only the government had done more on its behalf would do well to acquaint themselves with the Irish case. It is the most corrosive fallacy of them all among the language-sensitive: the belief that a language would flourish if only the government cared more and did more.

Language Reform in Turkey

Turkey went through a process of modernization in the earlier half of the twentieth century that is without parallel in the annals of social change. Many aspects of the Turkish case history apply directly to the Indian linguistic scene. But this is not the only reason I choose to discuss it. The Turkish case shows how heavy-handed a government must be to accomplish genuinely radical linguistic reforms. No country can obey the demands of its language fanatics and yet remain free.[30]

A modern Turk cannot read anything written before the First World War without special instruction. The problems are two-fold: there is the vocabulary of the language, and there is the script in which the language is written. The language of the Ottoman Empire was Turkish, but it was a peculiarly artificial kind of Turkish anointed with sanctity. It had absorbed massive infusions of Arabic and Persian and was unintelligible to the Turkish peasantry and inaccessible without lengthy study. It was the language of the Islamic religion in the Caliphate and, as such, highly developed, overly refined, and artificial.[31]

This mandarin language, Osmanlica, was written in the Arabic script, and this caused serious problems. Arabic is a Semitic language, as is Hebrew. Turkish is not a Semitic language; it belongs to a language family known as Altaic to which also belong such languages as Tatar, spoken in south-western Russia, and Uzbek, the language of Uzbekistan. For traditional and religious reasons most languages spoken in Muslim countries adopted versions of the Arabic writing systems when those countries got round to developing a writing system in which to write their languages. This was done whether or not the Semitic-based script suited the language in question. Thus, Persian and Urdu, both Indo–European languages not Semitic, are written in Arabic-derived scripts, as the Turkish of the Ottoman Empire was, as Swahili, a Bantu language, was written in an Arabic-derived script when under Arab/Islamic hegemony, though nowadays Swahili is written in romanized script.

But the script was only one of the problems with the language. It was not less of a problem that Osmanlica had so many borrowings of words and phrases from Arabic and Persian that it was felt to be not real Turkish. Already in the nineteenth century questions had arisen about how best to take into Turkish the new administrative, legal, educational, and military terms that adapting to the modern world required.[32] Some of these could be borrowed from Arabic or Persian, but these languages had their own set of problems with absorbing words such as *liberty, justice, nation, nationalism*.[33] Language movements sprang up in the latter half of the nineteenth century with the aim of 'purifying' the Turkish language of unnecessary borrowings from Arabic and Persian. Turkish nationalism during this period took the form of discovering the 'true' Turkish language that lay hidden under centuries of accretion of Arabic and Persian coats of language paint. These first faltering steps were not greeted enthusiastically by Islamic clerics and Ottoman traditionalists, but by the turn of the century change was in the air. Little did anyone know how rapidly it was to come.

The Young Turk Revolution of 1908, and of even greater importance the First World War, had far-reaching consequences for language reform. Turkey allied itself with the losing side of the Great War as it so frequently had in the little Balkan wars leading up to 1914. When the First World War ground to an end the Osmanlica language was on its death-bed, unmourned, orphaned by events outside its ken. A more realistic Turkish language was arising from the speech of educated urban Turks. The language was still written in an alien and complicated script and was weighted down with an excess of borrowings from Arabic and Persian, but the new language was on the march and had been since the middle of the nineteenth century. Osmanlica was dying along with the multilingual Ottoman Empire.[34]

Then came Atatürk, Mustafa Kemal, the strong-willed leader whose gaunt and ascetic visage, as unsmiling as a wolf's, stares down from countless Turkish office and schoolroom walls onto the people of the country whose father he is still reckoned to be. Atatürk is perhaps best known in linguistic quarters as the man who decreed in 1927 that henceforth Turkish would be written in roman letters rather than in the Arabic script of the Ottoman Empire. Such was the will of the man and such his ruthlessness that the changeover was accomplished in a remarkably short time. One must never forget that ruthlessness: Atatürk let nothing stand in his way. The new roman letters were first taught in November 1928, Arabic writing abolished in 1929, and the Arabic and Persian languages dropped from school curricula in September 1929. Nothing Atatürk did had greater effect in turning Turkey away from the Arab countries of the Middle East and facing it towards the West.[35]

The success of Atatürk's drive was aided enormously by the fact that in 1927 only about ten per cent of the Turkish population was literate. Also, whatever romantic attachment to the Ottoman past there might have been had worn very thin. Hence, for the majority of the population, the Arabic script had no iconic value. Not so for the Muslim clerics, however. They bitterly opposed this and Atatürk's other reforms, as well they might, for one of his clearest purposes was to sever what he considered the dead hand of the Islamic past from the renewed Turkey he had willed into existence.[36] For the clerics, and indeed for orthodox Muslims in general, the Arabic script, the language of the *Qur'an (Koran)*, is a symbol of everything they hold sacred and one that may on no account be violated, altered, changed, or tampered with. Atatürk had no patience with resistance from this quarter, and his Turkey was, we recall, a one-party dictatorship and remained so after his death in 1938 until November 1945.[37]

The reform of the Turkish language that reached its apogee in Atatürk's draconian decrees illustrates handsomely the complex interplay of nationalism, patriotism, language purism, and language-as-icon that the late twentieth century has come to confront as inevitable (if unfortunate). Language reform and social modernization often go hand in hand, but rarely are they as ambitious and as successful as Atatürk's programme. Language resists change. No one willingly gives up the comfortable linguistic habits of childhood. A state cannot ordinarily effect such changes.

Turkey is the exception. But why? What made Turkey unique in the annals of linguistics? The answer is Atatürk. Time has dimmed memories of how authoritarian a leader he was, but the historical record is there for all to see. 'Kemalism', as Atatürk's ideology is called, was much more than a benevolent dictatorship. His one-party regime built schools and hospitals, closed mosques, stifled dissent, and banned traditional dress. He brought religion under the control of the state, limiting the number of mosques, clerics, and Islamic schools, and regulating what they could teach. 'It is not our fault if 80 per cent of the nation is illiterate', said Atatürk in a 1929 speech. 'It is the fault of those who bound the head of the Turk in chains . . . It is time for us to eradicate, root and branch, the errors of the past.'[38]

The kind of radical, 'root and branch' language reform that Turkish was subjected to is possible only when a state has a ruler who is not reluctant to use extreme force to accomplish his purposes; who is calmly resolved to imprison and torture or even shoot people who resist change and do not go along. The thing cannot be done in a democracy. That is the lesson of the Turkish case. Massive linguistic change can be compelled by a ruthless dictatorship. Democratic governments are close to powerless to effect radical changes in language behaviour: so sad, so true. In anticipation of later chapters of this book, I am content to observe at this point only that India is a democracy, and it would be inconvenient to imprison people who do not want to learn Hindi.

Nehru was intimately familiar with what Atatürk had accomplished in Turkey. In 1948, about a year after he had become prime minister and before the storms of linguistic controversy had broken over him, he said in a speech:

I do not know how many of you remember that when Kemal Pasha wanted to develop Turkish — he did not like the use of Arabic words in Turkish. He appointed a commission to tour villages and collect good village words and see that these were incorporated and popularized in schools and colleges. This strengthened Turkish tremendously and brought literary Turkish in common touch with the people. That shows that if a language is cut off from the people it will not grow. It might be used in courts among courtiers but it cannot grow in these days of democracy, popular assemblies and parliaments.[39]

The Linguistic 'Free Market'

According to the Irish Constitution, 'The Irish language as the national language is the first official language. The English language is recognized as the second official language.'[40] That is what the Irish Constitution says, but this legalism is the reverse of Irish reality.

It is futile what the constitution of a free country such as Ireland proclaims in regard to 'official' and 'national' languages. That decision, in a free or even more or less free country, is never made by words written on a piece of paper and ratified by parliaments but by people doing what they want to do and refusing to do what they do not want to do. They will continue to speak the language or languages they feel comfortable with and have grown up using and are motivated to speak or learn to speak, and they will refuse to speak a language that is not theirs by birth and which they see no compelling reason to acquire. This should be a principle secured by common sense. It is not. Indeed, most people have difficulty accepting it, and language fanatics flatly reject it. Nehru, as we shall see, knew as by instinct how impotent government wishes are in the linguistic domain.

There is a 'free-market' principle at work in regard to language. People will speak and use the language that they feel will be of the greatest advantage to themselves and their children. 'Advantage' is to be understood in the widest possible sense: I should not like my invocation of the phrase 'free-market' to suggest that only economic motives play a role in decisions about which language to use. So reductionist a position is abhorrent. The choice of language is of course often economically determined: English speakers in Ireland will have more opportunities than monolingual Irish speakers, as Indians who speak English will have more opportunities than monolingual Hindi or Tamil speakers. It is usually a practical question: which language will help me the most? Ideally it would be better if the matter were thought of as 'both–and' rather than 'either–or': to be bilingual both in Irish and English or both Hindi and English is better than speaking and writing only one of these languages. But bilingualism is hard to achieve and almost impossible to legislate. Moreover, it is usually ephemeral. If one generation of speakers is bilingual, the next generation may continue to be bilingual; but more commonly the next generation favours one language over the other, and the next generation after has given up all but one language. Bilingualism fades, and bilingual parents and grandparents have monolingual sons and daughters. The language that survives will always be the language that offers the greatest number of opportunities for learning, culture, and economic advancement. The choice will have been made by the 'linguistic free-market'.

This 'free-market' of language choice goes well beyond nation and region. There are global aspects too. English has willy-nilly become the de facto working language of most of the world. For politicians, businessmen, academics, and sports heroes alike, English is far more often than not their working language as soon as they leave the linguistic comfort of their home countries. This is not a decision compelled by a world government, by the United Nations, by any government; it is a decision 'made' by the linguistic free-market of which I have spoken. A world as compressed as ours by modern technology works best with a common medium of communication. While it would be diverting if some international artificial language like Esperanto or Volapük filled this need, this will never happen. English works not because it is intrinsically better for this purpose than any other language; it works only because so many people in the world already speak it.

In the big things, such as making a language a true national language, governments are largely irrelevant. Few better examples than that of Irish in Ireland can be found. As I pointed out earlier in this chapter, the government of the Irish Republic attached the greatest importance to the resurrection of the Irish language. The government offered enticements for pupils, students, and civil servants who learn Irish. But it has been a finger in the dike against the decline in the percentage of the population competent in the Irish language; a historical decline now in train for some three centuries. This is a sad thing if you love the Irish language; this is a sad thing if you are a professional linguist, for we as a profession want languages to thrive and prosper, and not simply for the selfish reason that scientific linguists need living languages to 'work on'. As Samuel Johnson told Boswell: 'I am always sorry when any language is lost, because languages are the pedigree of nations.' Sad it is for many reasons to see a language go down (for it means the extinction of a culture), but feelings have less than nothing to do with the stark linguistic facts.

It is widely felt that social engineering is possible for language, that bilingual education programmes actually do work dramatically on the large scale if enough money is put behind them, that a government can, with proper advice from people who actually know something about language — that is, from linguists or sociologists of language — bring about radical changes in the language usage of its people. Under the precisely right circumstances, progress along these lines is sometimes possible, which is why I have presented the examples of Hebrew, Irish, and Turkish. It was possible to bring the Hebrew language back to life — because Israel had come back to life. It was possible to achieve radical reforms of script, vocabulary, and phrasing in the Turkish language — with an Atatürk running the show. It was not possible to transform the political success of a free and independent Ireland into a new life for the Irish language. The story of every national language is *sui generis*.

The plain fact is that almost nothing can be done in a free society ('free' underscored) to force unwilling people in multi-language countries to adopt, except on paper, one regional language as the national language even when that regional language has more native speakers and a stronger political power base than the others. It is one thing to mandate a national standard language in a society prepared to use bullets and bayonets and canings to enforce its decisions; it is quite another to try to do so in a free country — in a society as diverse and democratic, let us say, as that of India, whose regional languages have such rich literary and intellectual pedigrees and where the English language simply will not go away.

Language is conservative; the most conservative form of cultural behaviour that there is, arguably more conservative than religion in its resistance to enforced change. East and West Pakistan had a shared religion; they had also joined in the same freedom struggle and the same struggle for partition. But a shared religion and national history were not enough in the end to prevent the secession of East Pakistan and its rebirth as Bangladesh: 'land of Bengali-speakers'. Language is highly resistant to government intervention. It rebels against legislative and bureaucratic injunctions. Wise governments keep their hands off language to the extent it is politically possible to do so.

This point — that language resists government meddling — is axiomatic among most linguists, but ordinary people for some reason are rarely prepared to accept it. Something makes one want to believe that governmental action can always make a difference *if only* the will were there. Politicians and many other people like to believe that to pass a law is to change behaviour; but passing laws about language in a free society almost never changes behaviour. The Irish language we know about. The Welsh language is alive today in Wales in spite of heavy discrimination. The Yiddish language, which never even had a territory or a government to call its own, prevailed against massive bigotry and repression in eastern Europe for centuries and succumbed only when most of its speakers had been murdered by the Nazis. Romani, the language of the Gypsies, survives in the face of centuries-long discrimination of the cruelest and more unspeakable kinds against it and its speakers. Governmental actions can induce major changes in many kinds of group behaviour and attitudes; policies of the federal government of the United States led to a long overdue revolution in race relations in the American south in the latter half of the twentieth century. But there is not much that governments, other than harsh dictatorships, can do to change linguistic behaviour very dramatically.

Can the government of a free country do anything at all about linguistic usage and behaviour? Yes — but in the little things at the margins, not in the big things; not, for example, in ramming through as the national language of a country one of the regional languages when too many of the country's citizens are opposed.[41] If the question of a national language has been resolved, then schooling and literacy projects can be put in place and made to work. If, for example, one of the regional languages of India (say Telugu, Kannada, or Bengali) is destined for official purposes, then that language can be modernized to make it more useful for coping with the contemporary world.[42]

However, the question of the 'national language' has been fraught with difficulty for those countries that have emerged from the dissolution of empires since the end of the Second World War. Once the English had departed, what would the language be of countries such as India, Kenya (a Crown Colony), Uganda (a Protectorate), and Tanganyika (a Mandated Territory)? After the Dutch had left, what would be the language of Indonesia? After Belgium, with two official languages (French and Flemish) gave up the Congo with its four vernaculars and 200 dialects, what linguistic picture would come into focus through the smoke and ashes of the withdrawal?[43] No two situations are ever the same. India is by no means unique in its groping towards consensus on the issue of the 'national language', and it is instructive to see what decisions other newly independent countries reached.

Tanzania and Kenya were part of the British Empire until 1961. The linguistic configurations in these neighbouring countries were superficially similar yet strikingly different under the surface. These differences led to completely different resolutions of the question of national language.

Tanzania had probably the easiest way of the African countries formerly ruled by the British. Given Tanzania's language arrangements and complex linguistic make-up,[44] it is completely understandable that when Tanzania gained its independence in 1961 Swahili was proclaimed the national language by Julius Nyerere. The only possible choices could have been English or Swahili. Swahili was spoken and understood by far more people than English, competing tribalisms favoured it, and English laboured under the familiar liability of having been the language of the colonial rulers.

The decision to make Swahili the national language of Tanzania was natural, it was organic, it had history behind it. It made sense. It reinforced national unity rather than undermined it. 'Language planning' in Tanzania amounted therefore to systematic implementation of Swahili in the educational system, modernizing the language, increasing literacy, and extending the use of Swahili to domains where English had hitherto been the language of normal usage such as governmental institutions and the legal system.[45]

The lay of the land in Kenya was a good deal less suitable for so easy a resolution of the language problem.[46] When independence was granted the chief sound that was heard in Kenya concerning language was the sound of silence. The Republic of Kenya proclaimed no national language. English was sullied by its colonial past, Swahili would have had support primarily only on the coast with its Islamic leanings, and the choice of a leading but non-Bantu vernacular such as Kikuyu or Luo would have been fought tooth and nail by the proponents of English, Swahili, and other vernaculars. 'Language planning' in Kenya — if one can call a goalless meander 'planning' — was a good deal more muddled than in Tanzania. English, Swahili, and the major vernaculars have subsequently sorted themselves out in a complicated way over the regions and classes of the country. English is used for this purpose or that depending on region and class; likewise Swahili, likewise one or another of the vernaculars.[47]

Indonesia has been a republic since 1949. Formerly, as the Netherlands East Indies, it had been an overseas territory of the Dutch Empire. The language of administration during the colonial period was Dutch, which was also the language of instruction from grammar school through university. Malay had been the lingua franca of the Malay archipelago for a thousand years as the only practical means of communication in an area of intense trading activity with some 250 separate but related languages.[48] Javanese, the variety of Malay that had evolved in the Dutch East Indies, was structurally more complicated than the lingua franca; lexically it was indebted to languages as various as Sanskrit, Arabic, English, and of course Dutch.

During the Second World War, when the Japanese occupied most of south-east Asia, they banned the use of Dutch in the East Indies and attempted to compel the use of Japanese as the official language; a policy as much a failure in this case as any other, in spite of Japanese bayonets. Wartime exigencies left no time for such trifling linguistic disputes more suited for common-room debate and, unwilling for patriotic reasons to give way on Dutch, the Japanese fell back on the use of Javanese (Indonesian, which is the modern designation). All legal proclamations intended for the Indonesian population were published in the Indonesian language, and all instruction in the school system was conducted through the medium of Indonesian. Unwittingly, the Japanese had helped the Indonesian freedom movement — freedom from the Dutch is meant — achieve one of its most fervently sought goals: in 1928 the Oath of the Indonesian Youth had called for one fatherland, one nation, and the Indonesian language as national language of free Indonesia.[49] The Japanese even went so far as to create an Indonesian Language Committee charged with the task of standardizing and modernizing the language.

For Indonesia it requires little in the way of guesswork to predict the linguistic outcome of independence. The national and official language would be Indonesian, and the only problem would be to adjust the language to the speed and rhythm of the post-War world and implement it throughout the schools, universities, courts, and bureaucracies. The Indonesian case simply called for language planning as language modernization.

Once a national language or a regional official language has been agreed upon, certain kinds of language planning become possible. Terminology can be modernized, bilingualism encouraged. Spelling and writing systems can be rationalized. Much along these lines can be done, but these are all matters of detail. They are the little things. On the really big questions, however, such as the choice of a national language from among competitors, language planning fails. Language planning *sensu stricto* is possible; language planning *sensu lato* is not.

A many-languaged nation such as India cannot make people adopt a single national language — Hindi or English — if there is widespread resistance. It is socially destabilizing for governments to intrude very rudely into language matters. In countries with as many languages as India has, a wise national leader keeps a very light hand on the linguistic reins. All of which, as we shall see in the chapters that follow, anticipates Nehru's position, whose preference it was to cast the reins aside altogether rather than holding them in his hands, however lightly.

Notes and References

1. The research literature on language and nationalism is very extensive. In addition to those works I shall cite in the present section and those general and specialized works on language to which I made

reference in Chapter 1 ('Introduction', A Brief Historical Account) I should like to recommend the following: H.L. Bretton, 'Political Science, Language, and Politics', *in* W.M. O'Barr and J.F. O'Barr (eds), *Language and Politics* (The Hague: Mouton, 1976), pp. 431–48; L.F. Brosnahan, 'Some Historical Cases of Language Imposition', *in* J. Spencer (ed.), *Language in Africa* (Cambridge: Cambridge University Press, 1963), pp. 7–24; J. Das Gupta, 'Religion, Language, and Political Mobilization', *in* J. Rubin and B.H. Jernudd (eds), *Can Language Be Planned?* (Honolulu: The University Press of Hawaii, 1971), pp. 53–62; J. Das Gupta, 'Practice and Theory of Language Planning: The Indian Policy Process', *in* W.M. O'Barr and J.F. O'Barr (eds), *Language and Politics* (The Hague: Mouton, 1976), pp. 195–212; K. Deutsch, 'The Trend of European Nationalism — The Language Aspect', *American Political Science Review*, 36 (1942), pp. 533–41; K. Deutsch, *Nationalism and Social Communication* (Cambridge: MIT Press, 1953); C.A. Ferguson, 'The Language Factor in National Development', *Anthropological Linguistics*, 4 (1962), pp. 23–7; J.A. Fishman, 'Nationality–Nationalism and Nation–Nationism', *in* J.A. Fishman, C.A. Ferguson, and J. Das Gupta (eds), *Language Problems of Developing Nations* (New York: John Wiley & Sons, 1968), pp. 39–51; J.A. Fishman, *Language and Nationalism: Two Integrative Essays* (Rowley: Newbury House, 1972); S.S. Harrison, 'An Overview: Region and Nation in India', *in* P. Wallace (ed.), *Region and Nation in India* (New Delhi: American Institute of Indian Studies, 1985), pp. 300–8; E. Haugen, *Language Conflict and Language Planning* (Cambridge: Harvard University Press, 1966); E. Haugen, 'Instrumentalism in Language Planning', *in* J. Rubin and B.H. Jernudd (eds), *Can Language Be Planned?* (Honolulu: The University Press of Hawaii, 1971), pp. 281–9; H.C. Kelman, 'Language as an Aid and Barrier to Involvement in the National System', *in* J. Rubin and B.H. Jernudd (eds), *Can Language Be Planned?* (Honolulu: The University Press of Hawaii, 1971), pp. 21–51; H. Kloss, 'Notes Concerning a Language–Nation Typology', *in* J.A. Fishman, C.A. Ferguson, and J. Das Gupta (eds), *Language Problems of Developing Nations* (New York: John Wiley & Sons, 1968), pp. 69–85; H.L. Koppelmann, *Nation, Sprache und Nationalismus* (Leiden: Sijthoff, 1956); S. Lieberson, *Language and Ethnic Relations in Canada* (New York: John Wiley & Sons, 1970); R. Roy, 'Nation and Region: A Heretical View', *in* P. Wallace (ed.), *Region and Nation in India* (New Delhi: American Institute of Indian Studies, 1985), pp. 269–86; L.I. Rudolph and S.H. Rudolph, 'The Subcontinental Empire and the Regional Kingdom in Indian State Formation', *in* P. Wallace (ed.), *Region and Nation in India* (New

Delhi: American Institute of Indian Studies, 1985), pp. 40–59; D.A. Rustow, 'Language, Modernization, and Nationhood — An Attempt at Typology', *in* J.A. Fishman, C.A. Ferguson, and J. Das Gupta (eds), *Language Problems of Developing Nations* (New York: John Wiley & Sons, 1968), pp. 87–105; P.L. Van den Berghe, 'Language and "Nationalism" in South Africa', *in* J.A. Fishman, C.A. Ferguson, and J. Das Gupta (eds), *Language Problems of Developing Nations* (New York: John Wiley & Sons, 1968), pp. 215–24.

The following collections in which many of the above-cited essays appeared offer useful elaboration on the basic themes of this chapter: E.C. Dimock, Jr., B.B. Kachru and Bh. Krishnamurti (eds), *Dimensions of Sociolinguistics in South Asia* (New Delhi: Oxford & IBH Publishing Co., 1992); J.A. Fishman, C.A. Ferguson, and J. Das Gupta (eds), *Language Problems of Developing Nations* (New York: John Wiley & Sons, 1968); W.M. O'Barr and J.F. O'Barr (eds), *Language and Politics* (The Hague: Mouton, 1976); E.C. Polomé and C.P. Hill (eds), *Language in Tanzania* (London: Oxford University Press, 1980); J. Rubin and B.H. Jernudd (eds), *Can Language Be Planned?* (Honolulu: The University Press of Hawaii, 1971); J. Rubin, B.H. Jernudd, J. Das Gupta, J.A. Fishman, and C.A. Ferguson (eds), *Language Planning Processes* (The Hague: Mouton, 1977); P. Wallace (ed.), *Region and Nation in India* (New Delhi: American Institute of Indian Studies, 1985); W.H. Whiteley (ed.), *Language Use and Social Change* (London: Oxford University Press, 1971). Brass, *Language, Religion and Politics in North India* and Harrison, *India: The Most Dangerous Decades* go well beyond language issues per se but are particularly valuable for that reason among others.

2. A.M. Cohler, *Rousseau and Nationalism* (New York: Basic Books, 1970).
3. R. Emerson, *From Empire to Nation* (Cambridge: Harvard University Press, 1960), p. 134.
4. J.A. Fishman, 'The Impact of Nationalism on Language Planning', *in* J. Rubin and B.H. Jernudd (eds), *Can Language Be Planned?* (Honolulu: The University Press of Hawaii, 1971), p. 9.
5. E.A. Freeman, 'Race and Language', in *Historical Essays*, 3rd srs (London: Macmillan, 1879), p. 203.
6. D.A. Rustow, *A World of Nations* (Washington: The Brookings Institution, 1967), p. 47.
7. Emerson, *From Empire to Nation*, p. 190.
8. H. Kohn, *Prelude to Nation-States* (New York: D. Van Nostrand, 1967), p. 7.
9. *Five Ideas That Change the World* (New York: W.W. Norton, 1959).

10. J. Kennedy, *Asian Nationalism in the Twentieth Century* (London: Macmillan, 1968).
11. H. Kohn, *The Idea of Nationalism* (New York: Macmillan, 1944), pp. 6–16, 346–50 *et passim*; Kohn, *Prelude to Nation-States*; F. Hertz, *Nationality in History and Politics* (New York: Oxford University Press, 1944), pp. 78–97; F. Znaniecki, *Modern Nationalities* (Urbana: University of Illinois Press, 1952).
12. O. Jászi, *The Dissolution of the Habsburg Monarchy* (Chicago: The University of Chicago Press, 1929), p. 138.
13. There is a theoretical distinction between 'nation' and 'state' that is important in certain kinds of discussion and analysis, though not especially so here. These distinctions are clarified in R. Frykenberg, 'State, Empire and Nation in South India: Demythologizing as a Scholar's Enterprise', *in* P. Wallace (ed.), *Region and Nation in India* (New Delhi: American Institute of Indian Studies, 1985), pp. 60–84.
14. A.J. Toynbee, *Survey of International Affairs 1925* (London: Oxford University Press, 1927), vol. 1, p. 18.
15. J. Stalin, *Marxism and the National and Colonial Questions* (Moscow: Foreign Languages Publishing House, 1940), p. 138.
16. A.J. Toynbee, *A Study of History* (London: Oxford University Press, 1934–61), vol. 8, p. 536.
17. *Autobiography*, p. 245.
18. C.F. Gallagher, 'North African Problems and Prospects: Language and Identity', *in* J.A. Fishman, C.A. Ferguson, and J. Das Gupta (eds), *Language Problems of Developing Nations* (New York: John Wiley & Sons, 1968), p. 129.
19. Klaiman, 'Bengali', p. 492.
20. *Ideology and Utopia* (New York: Harcourt Brace, 1936), p. 21 *et passim*.
21. *Papers in Linguistics 1934–1951* (London: Oxford University Press, 1957), p. 185.
22. A. Bar-Adon, *The Rise and Decline of a Dialect: A Study in the Revival of Modern Hebrew* (The Hague: Mouton, 1975); H. Blanc, 'The Israeli Koine as an Emergent National Standard', *in* J.A. Fishman, C.A. Ferguson, and J. Das Gupta (eds), *Language Problems of Developing Nations* (New York: John Wiley & Sons, 1968), pp. 237–51; W. Chomsky, *Hebrew — The Eternal Language* (Philadelphia: Jewish Publication Society of America, 1957); J. Fellman, *The Revival of a Classical Tongue: Eliezer Ben Yehuda and the Modern Hebrew Language* (The Hague: Mouton, 1974).
23. *Promise and Fulfillment* (New York: Macmillan, 1949), pp. 311–15.
24. Many of the data in the discussion of Irish are taken from

J. Macnamara, 'Successes and Failures in the Movement for the Restoration of Irish', *in* J. Rubin and B.H. Jernudd (eds), *Can Language Be Planned?* (Honolulu: The University Press of Hawaii, 1971), pp. 65–94. C.C. O'Brien (ed.), *The Shaping of Modern Ireland* (London: Routledge & Kegan Paul, 1960) is useful for background on many Irish issues including the fate of the movement to restore the Irish language, as is J.G. Beckett, *The Making of Modern Ireland 1603–1923* (London: Faber & Faber, 1966). Specifically on the language issue the following are useful: R.A. Breathnach, 'Revival or Survival? An Examination of the Irish Language Policy of the State', *Studies*, 45 (1956), pp. 129–45; R.A. Breathnach, 'Irish Revival Reconsidered', *Society*, 53 (1964), pp. 18–30; T. Corcoran, 'The Irish Language in the Irish Schools, *Studies*, 14 (1925), pp. 377–88; D. Gwynn, *The Irish Free State, 1922–1927* (London: Macmillan, 1928); *The Restoration of the Irish Language* (Dublin: Stationery Office, 1965); B.O Cuív, 'The Changing Form of the Irish Language', *in* B.O Cuív (ed.), *A View of the Irish Language* (Dublin: Stationery Office, 1969), pp. 23–34; T.O Flaich, 'The Language and Political History', *in* B.O Cuív (ed.), *A View of the Irish Language* (Dublin: Stationery Office, 1969), pp. 101–11; E.O Neíll, 'The Language Revival in Ireland', *in* F.G. Thompson (ed.), *Maintaining a National Identity* (Dublin: The Celtic League, 1968), pp. 54–63; M. Wall, 'The Decline of the Irish Language', *in* B.O Cuív (ed.), *A View of the Irish Language* (Dublin: Stationery Office, 1969), pp. 81–90.

25. Macnamara, 'Successes and Failures in the Movement for the Restoration of Irish', p. 67.
26. Ibid., pp. 68–9.
27. Fromkin and Rodman, *An Introduction to Language*, p. 351.
28. Macnamara, 'Successes and Failures in the Movement for the Restoration of Irish', p. 75.
29. Ibid., p. 69.
30. My account relies upon C.F. Gallagher, 'Language Reform and Social Modernization in Turkey', *in* J. Rubin and B.H. Jernudd (eds), *Can Language Be Planned?* (Honolulu: The University Press of Hawaii, 1971), pp. 157–78 and U. Heyd, *Language Reform in Modern Turkey* (Jerusalem: Israel Oriental Society, 1954), both of which deal primarily with linguistic issues. For the more general political and intellectual background of Turkey's modernization, *see* N. Berkes, *The Development of Secularism in Turkey* (Montreal: McGill University Press, 1964); B. Lewis, *The Emergence of Modern Turkey* (London: Oxford University Press, 1968); D.A. Rustow, 'Turkey: The Modernity of Tradition', *in* L.W. Pye and S. Verba

(eds), *Political Culture and Political Development* (Princeton: Princeton University Press, 1965), pp. 237–86.

31. Gallagher, 'Language Reform and Social Modernization in Turkey', p. 161.
32. Ibid.
33. F. Rosenthal, *The Muslim Concept of Freedom* (Leiden: E.J. Brill, 1960); C.F. Gallagher, 'Language, Culture, and Ideology: The Arab World', *in* K.H. Silvert (ed.), *Expectant Peoples: Nationalism and Development* (New York: Random House, 1963), pp. 199–231.
34. Gallagher, 'Language Reform and Social Modernization in Turkey', p. 163.
35. Ibid., pp. 164–5.
36. Ibid., p. 164.
37. Heyd, *Language Reform in Modern Turkey*, p. 44.
38. *The Wall Street Journal*, 1 March 1995.
39. Speech at a convocation at Osmania University, Hyderabad, on the occasion of his receiving an honorary degree Doctor of Laws, 26 Dec. 1948, *Selected Works* II.9: 115–17.
40. *Constitution of Ireland* (Dublin: Stationery Office, 1937).
41. My premise here is a free or more or less free country where the popular will cannot be thwarted forever. Dictatorships, especially brutal dictatorships, are a different matter, as Turkey under Atatürk was a different matter.
42. The research literature on this aspect of language planning is extensive. Representative of the major trends are E. Annamalai, *Language Movements in India*; R.L. Cooper (ed.), *Language Planning and Social Change* (Cambridge: Cambridge University Press, 1989); J. Das Gupta, *Language Conflict and National Development*; H.R. Dua, *Language Planning in India* (New Delhi: Harnam Publications, 1985); C.M. Eastman, *Language Planning: An Introduction* (San Francisco: Chandler & Sharp, 1983); Fishman, Ferguson, and Das Gupta, *Language Problems of Developing Nations*; Haugen, *Language Conflict and Language Planning*; Nayar, *National Communication and Language Policy in India*; O'Barr and O'Barr, *Language and Politics*; Rubin and Jernudd, *Can Language Be Planned?*.
43. E.C. Polomé, 'The Choice of Official Languages in the Democratic Republic of the Congo', *in* J.A. Fishman, C.A. Ferguson, and J. Das Gupta (eds), *Language Problems of Developing Nations* (New York: John Wiley & Sons, 1968), pp. 295–311.
44. M.H. Abdulaziz, 'Tanzania's National Language Policy and the Rise of Swahili Political Culture', *in* W.H. Whiteley (ed.), *Language Use and Social Change* (London: Oxford University Press, 1971), pp. 160–78; W.M. O'Barr, 'Language Use and Language Policy in

Tanzania: An Overview', *in* W.M. O'Barr and J.F. O'Barr (eds), *Language and Politics* (The Hague: Mouton, 1976), pp. 35–48; Polomé and Hill, *Language in Tanzania*; W.H. Whiteley, 'Ideal and Reality in National Language Policy: A Case Study from Tanzania', *in* J.A. Fishman, C.A. Ferguson, and J. Das Gupta (eds), *Language Problems of Developing Nations* (New York: John Wiley & Sons, 1968), pp. 327–44; W.H. Whiteley, 'Some Factors Influencing Language Policies in Eastern Africa', *in* J. Rubin and B.H. Jernudd (eds), *Can Language Be Planned?* (Honolulu: The University Press of Hawaii, 1971), pp. 141–58.

45. J.F. O'Barr, 'Language and Politics in Tanzanian Governmental Institutions', *in* W.M. O'Barr and J.F. O'Barr (eds), *Language and Politics* (The Hague: Mouton, 1976), pp. 69–84; F. Dubow, 'Language, Law, and Change: Problems in the Development of a National Legal System in Tanzania', *in* W.M. O'Barr and J.F. O'Barr (eds), *Language and Politics* (The Hague: Mouton, 1976), pp. 85–99.
46. Whiteley, 'Some Factors Influencing Language Policies in Eastern Africa'.
47. Ibid., pp. 152–5.
48. S.T. Alisjahbana, 'Some Planning Processes in the Development of the Indonesian–Malay Language', *in* J. Rubin and B.H. Jernudd (eds), *Can Language Be Planned?* (Honolulu: The University Press of Hawaii, 1971), pp. 179–87.
49. Ibid., pp. 180–1.

Chapter 3

Linguistic States and the National Language

Two great issues of language politics confronted the new nation when India gained its independence in 1947. One was the problem of linguistic states ('linguistic provinces'), the other the problem of the national language. Conceptually and in substance these were altogether different things. The former was a matter of division and category — how best to define the local governing units of the new country. The latter was more a matter of national prestige: what language best captured the character and unity, the essence, of the newly independent country? Though different, the two language problems shared a common core which was of course 'language'; but more than that they went to the heart of the greatest question which independent India had to face: was India a unity, or was it a geographical amalgam of entities so disparate that only the distorting simplifications of colonialism could for a time make these units appear to be one? The rubric of 'language politics' subsumes both the issue of linguistic states and the issue of the national language, but the former was the more exigent of the two, and it is the problem of linguistic states with which we shall deal first.

Linguistic States

As we saw in the preceding chapter, there is nothing intrinsic to universal history and human nature for national boundaries to be drawn along lines of language difference. The idea that nations or states should correspond to boundaries of language dates from the nineteenth century and is therefore, as such things go, a relatively recent truism of geopolitics. Nonetheless, it has become difficult to imagine drawing national boundary lines in any other way. By the early twentieth century, received opinion had settled upon a one-to-one relationship between nation and language as virtually the only natural or rational relationship between the two. It was a principle elevated to the status of a 'natural law'. Its political equivalent was the principle of 'self-determination' associated with the Treaty of Versailles and Woodrow Wilson at the end of the First World War, when the boundaries of the former states created out of the Austro–Hungarian Empire were drawn more nearly according to language (qua ethnicity) than any other single consideration.

Certainly one can see why 'nation as language area' has its appeal. Countries with, for all intents and purposes, but a single national language — Japan, Germany, France, England, the United States — transparently have advantages of ease of communication if little else. Countries united by one language do of course have their problems. The fact that it is possible to communicate with someone else in a common language does not guarantee that problems will disappear or be easily resolvable. People disagree and even come to blows within the same family, and countries with only one language do have civil wars. However, it is an empirically observable fact that countries with only a single national language do tend to have greater political stability than multilingual countries. When even two languages are spoken by large percentages of a country's population, as in Belgium, eastern Canada, Sri Lanka, in many of the countries that were formerly part of the Soviet Empire, or in any number of African nations that gained independence following the Second World War, political stability appears harder to achieve and to sustain in the long run. Switzerland, with German, French, Italian, and the increasingly marginal Romansch, is of course an exception to this socio–political generalization; but it is recognized that Switzerland is an anomaly in all 'social-science' theorizing, whether about politics, language, culture, economics, or stability.

It is in many ways something of a political miracle that India has remained a single country throughout its long history, and a free country at that. Many have predicted its break-up for one or another of many reasons; but there it stands a single country still, immovable as a rock, deaf to the voices of the prophets of doom. 'Gloom and doom' have always figured prominently in speculations about the fragility of India's unity. Harold A. Gould has provided an instructive and amusing account of the history of pessimism about India, and about Indian unity in particular.[1] The pessimists have never won.

The 'unity' of India is a problematic concept. It was one of Nehru's major preoccupations throughout his life and, as we shall see in Chapter 4 ('Nehru at the Helm'), a major factor in his attitude towards language politics; but it is plain to see that India is and remains a single 'nation' whatever its unity is grounded in and whatever the clever bodies say, all doomsaying to the contrary. India, that is to say, is the exception to the general rule that the relationship between country and language should be what mathematicians call 'isomorphic': one language, one nation; one nation, one language. The peculiarity that India is and remains a single nation, yet divided linguistically and culturally, is the core of the 'paradox' of which the novelist Salman Rushdie wrote in the wake of the tragic assassination of prime minister Indira Gandhi on 31 October 1984.[2] 'Italy is a geographical expression', Prince Metternich said. A Metternich might have said the same of India, but he would have been wrong.

The map of India prior to Independence was a porridge of irregular and improbable jigsaw puzzle shapes composed of British India, native states and territories, and territories permanently administered by the Government of India.[3] The native states ranged in size from tiny to huge; they were hereditary demi-empires in which language had played little if any role in the drawing of boundaries. Their boundaries bespeak chance and force of arms. Rulers spoke this, the ruled spoke that. There was the familiar example of Hyderabad, with a largely Telugu-speaking Hindu populace ruled by an Urdu-speaking Muslim aristocracy under the Nizam-ul-Mulk. It is not recorded that any of the Nizams spoke a word of Telugu, though a favourite diversion among them was writing poetry in elegant Persian. Mysore State was largely Kannada-speaking, but in 1951, prior to the creation of linguistically delineated states, 34 per cent of the inhabitants of Mysore State spoke other languages.[4]

Perhaps this is as good a place as any to observe that 'perfect' linguistic states are never possible in the real world. A state or province would have to be some kind of ethnically homogeneous island like Iceland or Japan to contain all and only the speakers of a single language. Modern India has done an extraordinary job of drawing its state boundaries in such a way as to bring down the percentage of speakers of minority languages in its component states to an irreducible minimum.[5] Even so, there will always remain linguistic minorities, in India or anywhere else, however the lines are drawn.

If the boundaries of the native states had arisen out of historical disorder with little specific attentiveness to language, the internal boundaries of British India were drawn with an indifference to language that approaches the sublime (Maps 2 and 3). The officials of the British East India Company had carved up the map of those parts of India under British control not according to logical principles of any kind but by an historical process, if something so haphazard and disjointed deserves the name of process, of consolidations and treaties, treachery, bribery, and force. For administrative convenience British India was divided up into an assortment of units: the Bombay, Bengal, and Madras Presidencies, the United Provinces, Punjab, the Central Provinces, Sind, and so on. Of these only Bengal, Punjab, and Sind had arguably any claim to historical organicity based on culture, language, land use, and ethnography.

The Madras Presidency is representative. It had been formed at the end of the eighteenth century as the final resolution of skirmishes between Tipu Sultan of Mysore and the Company Bahadur against a tedious background of bewildering confrontations and negotiations and betrayals involving, among others, the Marathas, Warren Hastings, the Nizam of Hyderabad, the Nizam's devious brother, Tipu's father Haidar Ali, Cornwallis, and Sir John Shore.[6] Language and religion were the last and least important ingredients to be tossed into the cauldron. Greed and avarice surpassed all other ingredients. The Madras Presidency stretched from Cape Comorin on the south-eastern decline of the southern tip of India north to Jagannath's temple at Puri, now located in Orissa. It touched the Bay of Bengal in the east and the Arabian Sea along the Malabar coast in the west. It encircled Mysore State and impinged on the princely states of Cochin and Travancore on the Coast of Coromandel. The major languages spoken in the Madras Presidency were Tamil, Telugu, Oriya, Malayalam, and Kannada. In 1931, 60.3 per cent of the population of the Madras Presidency spoke a language other than Tamil, the language of the majority of Indians living in the city of Madras. In the same year 57.2 per cent of the population of the Bombay Presidency spoke a language other than Marathi, notably Gujarati, Sindhi, and Kannada.[7]

When the British did make adjustments to the boundaries of its administrative subdivisions, language played a puny role in the decision, if any at all. A celebrated chapter in the history of British bungling illustrates the case. In 1905 the then viceroy Lord Curzon announced the partition of Bengal into two provinces. The reason he gave for the partition was administrative convenience. The Presidency of Bengal had grown so much with the expansion of British rule that by 1803 it had reached the river Sutlej in the Punjab in the north-west. Various pieces of the Bengal Presidency — the United Provinces, Oudh, Assam — had been progressively shed or merged into other administrative units, but even so, by the turn of the twentieth century the Bengal Presidency encompassed not only Bengal proper, as commonly understood, but also Bihar and Orissa. It had a population of 70,000,000 people. It lends perspective to observe that the population of France in 1911 was 39,600,000.[8] Curzon proposed to divide the Bengal Presidency roughly in half, creating a province of eastern Bengal and Assam with a population of 31,000,000 and two major languages, Bengali and Assamese, and a province consisting of western Bengal, Bihar, and Orissa with three major languages, Bengali, Hindi (in its Bihari variant of eastern Hindi), and Oriya.

It is no doubt true that Lord Curzon had administrative decentralization as his primary consideration. Partition for administrative reasons had been talked of for years. It is impossible however to overlook that an effect, almost casual as it were, of the partition of Bengal was to create a largely Muslim eastern Bengal and a largely Hindu western Bengal, thus foreshadowing the later division of Bengal between East Pakistan (Bangladesh) and India. Whatever Curzon's innermost intentions, the politics of the thing were catastrophic for the British. The partition of Bengal was a spur to Indian nationalism as great as the tragedy of Jallianwala Bagh. Out of the uproar that greeted Curzon's announcement came the Swadeshi movement, Tilak's coining of the magical word *swaraj* (self-rule), the *hartal* (general strike), the smoothing of the way for Gandhi, and in general the political hypersensitization of the Indian middle class.[9] It was one of the stupidest blunders the British Government of India ever made — of a sameness with the issue in 1856 of the greased cartridges for the new Enfield rifle — and its nullification in 1911 could not begin to undo its corrosive damage to the underpinnings of the British Raj. The partition of Bengal had shaken the confidence of the Indian middle class and the intellectual class in British intentions, and nothing the British could have subsequently done would have restored that precious trust without which a small country cannot rule a large country on another continent.

For present purposes it is sufficient to observe that the idea of linguistic boundaries was very nearly the last thing on Curzon's mind when he proposed the partition of Bengal. Whether his motive was that of a thoughtless bureaucrat simply trying to move pieces around on a geographical chessboard to ease administration, or whether it was one more instance of *divide et impera*, language played a trifling role in his considerations. This is not to say that it played no role at all, for one argument given in favour of partition was that it would unify the Oriyas under one rule and, so said Sir Herbert Risley, Home Secretary, Government of India, and a man linguistically knowledgeable, in a letter to the Government of Bengal, 'would solve the question of [the Oriya] language once and for all'.[10] The statement is curiously disingenuous, for any benefits procured from uniting speakers of the Oriya language under a common government were nullified a hundred times over by the splitting of the vastly larger number of vastly more labile Bengali speakers into two groups under separate governments.

In general, during British rule in India linguistic arguments were advanced, if at all, as a posteriori justification for decisions the British government wanted to make anyway. Language was mentioned in the partition resolution of 1905 as well as in a dispatch of Lord Hardinge to the Secretary of State, 25 August 1911, proposing to annul the partition of Bengal. But, as the *Report of the States Reorganization Commission 1955* says:

> The linguistic principle was, however, pressed into service on these occasions only as a measure of administrative convenience, and to the extent it fitted into a general pattern which was determined by political exigencies. In actual effect, the partition of Bengal involved a flagrant violation of linguistic affinities. The settlement of 1912 also showed little respect for the linguistic principle, in that it drew a clear line of distinction between the Bengali Muslims and Bengali

Hindus. Both these partitions thus ran counter to the assumption that different linguistic groups constituted distinct units of social feeling with common political and economic interests.[11]

These examples are instructive of the muddleheadedness of the British about Indian language sensitivities. But the muddleheadedness must be understood in a larger context of world indifference to language sensitivities, that is, indifference to language iconicity. It is altogether typical not only of British thinking about India in 1905 but of European thinking about political boundaries in general at the time. The received view can be summed up in the question: what is so special about the equation one language = one nation? The *Report of the States Reorganization Commission of 1955* states the matter with an objectivity and lack of rancour infrequently encountered in the chronicles of politico–linguistic public statement:

> The existing structure of the States of the Indian Union is partly the result of accident and the circumstances attending the growth of the British power in India and partly a by-product of the historic process of integration of former Indian States. The division of India during the British period into British provinces and Indian States was itself fortuitous and had no basis in Indian history. It was a mere accident that, as a result of the abandonment, after the upheaval of 1857, of the objective of extending the British dominion by absorbing princely territories, the surviving States escaped annexation. The map of the territories annexed and directly administered by the British was also not shaped by any rational or scientific planning.[12]

History of the Movement[13]

The attempt by Lord Curzon to partition Bengal was not the first instance of a government initiative to adjust administrative boundaries. Assam had been acquired by the Crown in 1826 and made part of the Bengal Presidency. This created a very large, sprawling Bengal Presidency that included not only the Bengali-speaking area but the United Provinces (today Uttar Pradesh) and beyond, far into the north-west. The Charter Act of 1833 provided for the creation of the North-West Provinces, which improved matters slightly, but the Bengal Presidency was still fantastically large for a single governor to administer sensibly. Assam was plucked out in 1874, and though this happened to amount to a division along a linguistic boundary (since Assamese is the language of Assam), linguistic considerations were nowhere to be seen. It was simply a matter of reducing the size of the Bengal Presidency in the least noxious way. Likewise, in 1901 the North-West Frontier Province was separated from the Punjab of which it had been a part since 1849. This created a linguistically homogeneous Punjabi-speaking Punjab, but Curzon 'was actuated purely by political exigency: while Punjab had accepted British rule as a settled fact, many people in the Frontier nurtured a temper of revolt and often actively manifested it. Curzon felt that the latter needed a wholly different kind of administrative setup'.[14]

The earliest intimation of an Indian sentiment in favour of redrawing administrative boundaries to reflect linguistic differences came from B.G. Tilak, the leader of the left wing in Congress politics. In the Marathi-language newspaper *Kesari* ('The Lion') which he edited, Tilak wrote on 17 November 1891:

> The present administrative division of India is the result of a certain historical process and in some cases is exclusively the result of chance circumstances . . . If it is replaced by a system of administrative units created on a linguistic basis, each of them will be to some degree homogeneous and will facilitate the development of the people and the languages of the respective peoples.[15]

It is not surprising to find these sentiments being expressed at this particular time, for the end of the nineteenth century was accompanied by major strides forward in the development of the vernacular languages and their rise in estimation among the English-knowing élites, as we saw in Chapter 1 ('Introduction', A Brief Historical Account). And it is hardly surprising that it was a Maratha who expressed the sentiment, for the Marathas since the days of their great national hero Shivaji were habitually outspoken and constitutionally disposed towards going their own way on most things. The growing strength of the vernacular languages was of a piece with the growing tide of nationalistic feeling.

In the wake of the uproar over the Bengal partition we find the Indian National Congress beginning to rethink its organizational structure in terms of vernacular units. In 1908 a separate 'Congress province' of Bihar was created, followed by the formation of similar Sind and Andhra units in 1917. However, these were nothing more than subdivisions within the structure of the Indian National Congress. So far as the Government of India were concerned, Bihar belonged to the Bengal Presidency, Sind to the Bombay Presidency, and Andhra to the Madras Presidency.

The first official notice of any consequence of the growing strength of the vernacular movement appears in §246 of the *Montagu–Chelmsford Report* of 1918,[16] which was an attempt to respond more constructively than before to the demands of the Indian National Congress and of Gandhi and his associates for greater Indian involvement in the business of running the country:

> We cannot doubt that the business of government would be simplified if administrative units were both smaller and more homogeneous; and when we bear in mind the prospect of the immense burdens of government in India being transferred to comparatively inexperienced hands, such considerations acquire additional weight. It is also a strong argument in favour of linguistic or racial units of government that, by making it possible to conduct the business of legislation in the vernacular, they would contribute to drawing into the arena of public affairs men who were not acquainted with English.[17]

But for all the fine words, which summon memories of the language and sentiments of Macaulay's Minute, very little changed in the attitude of the Government of India towards the vernaculars and the redrafting of the map according to language. Things went on as before; the Government of India Act, 1919, for example, made no provision for promoting the regional languages. In the Congress movement, however, events had been decisively launched on a different course.

In 1920 Gandhi had come out in favour of linguistic provinces, though only three years earlier he had agreed with Mrs Besant in wishing to defer action on the question. At that time Andhra, meaning the community of Telugu-speakers in the broadest sense, had made a strong case for separate status, arguing that inclusion in the Tamil-dominated Madras Presidency was a great disadvantage. There was a receptive impulse within Congress for the Andhra position, but soon the contagion for separate linguistic provincial status spread to supporters of Sind

(Sindhi language) and Karnataka (Kannada language). Tilak, always keen on language, supported the movement.[18]

But Gandhi and Mrs Besant in 1917, with the Congress meeting in Lucknow, were of one mind that there were more important items on the Indian National Congress agenda than linguistic provinces. They also feared, perhaps without knowing exactly why, the potentially divisive effects of the politics of language. We must recall that this was the beginning of the Khilafat movement, and the Congress leaders — Gandhi, really the others falling in line behind him — had made common cause with Muslim unease about the abolition of the Caliphate. Apart from eastern Bengal, largely Muslim and Bengali-speaking, the language of most Muslims throughout India was Urdu, but it was nowhere spoken in so solid a geographical mass as to make the drawing of an Urdu provincial boundary possible for any given region: it would have been to raise the spectre of an unborn Pakistan. Even to ask the question, let alone table a resolution regarding it, would have been to ask for trouble. This, more than anything else, lay behind Gandhi's and Mrs Besant's coolness to linguistic provinces in 1917. An additional reason for Gandhi's reluctance to endorse linguistic provinces was his fear, expressed in an article of 21 January 1920 in *Young India*, that encouraging use of the regional language would detract from his mission to make Hindustani (Hindi) the national language.[19]

However, with Gandhi having reversed field on the issue, the Congress at its meeting in Nagpur in 1920 accepted the general principle that provincial boundaries should be drawn on language lines and that the political machinery of the Indian National Congress should be organized according to language. The Congress constitution was drafted to make provision for the vernacular units, which took the form of Provincial Congress Committees (PCC), of which twenty-one were created. From this time onward in the accounts of the proceedings of meetings and motions of the Indian National Congress we find references to the Andhra PCC, the Tamil Nadu PCC, the Karnataka PCC, and so on.[20]

Gandhi's volte-face was tactical: it arose less out of intellectual conviction or emotional fervour than his desire to ease Muslim reservations about *swaraj* in provinces such as Sind. The plain fact is that the Congress position on linguistic provinces was never carefully thought through. The inherent contradiction between the idea of linguistic provinces and the unity of India as a single nation hovered dimly in the recesses of percipient minds but was never allowed to circulate in public for long. All reservations were submerged in the common aspiration for *swaraj*. The Congress support for linguistic boundaries was almost always a consequence of other considerations, usually communal in nature. Even the very first glimmering of a Congress position on linguistic and political boundaries, in 1905 when a newly galvanized Congress demanded reunification of Bengal, was motivated as much by communal considerations as any others, 'communal' in the sense that the Congress was at the time trying to find the middle ground between extremist Hindu and Muslim opinion.

In 1927 the Indian National Congress passed a resolution stating that 'the time has come for the redistribution of provinces on a linguistic basis' and arguing for the creation of separate provinces of 'Andhra, Utkal [Orissa], Sind, and Karnataka'.[21] By 1936 there was a general consensus, the accumulation of much realpolitik and very little sequential thinking about the practical consequences of implementation, in favour of linguistic states. Nehru himself explicitly accepted linguistic provinces in 1937: 'I might add that my frequent references to linguistic areas and the language of the province necessitate that provincial units should correspond with such language areas.'[22] It is noteworthy that this is the most unequivocal statement Nehru ever made in favour of linguistic provinces; and I observe too that his formulation is very subdued, very *piano*, and made a decade prior to his assuming power in independent India. It is a tedious commonplace that political leaders say things when out of power, that they do not endorse with enthusiasm when in power.

It is the accepted view that since 1920 a great deal of the organizing energy and success of the Indian National Congress derived from the principle of linguistic units. Certainly Nehru believed this. As Selig Harrison wrote: 'There can be no disputing Nehru when he cites [*Autobiography*, p. 66] the demarcation of Congress provincial machinery on a linguistic basis in 1920 as the turning-point which saw the Congress transformed from a middle-class assembly of leaders to a mass movement able to speak to the people in their own language.'[23] Harrison's opinion is probably correct, but the historical force behind the freedom movement was such that the final result, namely independence after the Second World War, would in all likelihood have been the same no matter what the organizational arrangements of the Congress were. It is obvious that the Congress message could not have been communicated directly to the masses except in the vernaculars,[24] but one can accept the truth of that assertion while rejecting the proposition that states should be established along linguistic lines as opposed to lines drawn, say, along natural boundaries or in order to aggregate economically cohesive units. There are two quite different issues here: how to communicate to the masses, and whether to draw state lines according to linguistic boundaries. Indeed, Nehru says precisely this in his reply to debate on the President's Address, Lok Sabha:

Some hon. members are perhaps not well-acquainted with the development of the Congress outlook on the subject of linguistic provinces. Undoubtedly, in the 'twenties we were strongly in favour of all work being done in the language of the area in order to enable the local people to play their part. In so far as the importance of the language in doing work is concerned, we hold to the same principle. But let us not mix up two things, namely, the importance of the development of a language and linguistic boundaries. The two are not the same thing. If you see the Congress resolutions of the last three or four years, you will find that all of them have stated quite clearly that language is an important factor but that there are other economic, geographical and developmental factors which are equally important. Finally, the most important factor, the overriding factor, is the unity of India.[25]

Some of this conceptual confusion can be seen in the Report of the Nehru Committee of the All-Parties Conference, 1928. The All-Parties Conference had been established to devise solutions to the most serious constitutional and political problems dividing the major parties lodged together within the Indian National Congress. The Nehru Committee Report came out with a strong endorsement of the linguistic principle:

If a province has to educate itself and do its daily work through the medium of its own language, it must necessarily be a linguistic area. If it happens to be a polyglot area difficulties will continually arise and the media of instruction and work will be two or even more languages. Hence it becomes most desirable for provinces to be regrouped on a linguistic basis. Language as a rule corresponds with a special variety of culture, of traditions and literature. In a linguistic area all these factors will help in the general progress of the province.[26]

One cannot disagree with the general drift of this statement, but fundamental contradictions are concealed within it. Many areas of India are 'monoglot' areas, to continue the language of the report, but many and most of the urban areas, in India in particular, are 'polyglot' areas. In a great city such as Bombay, Marathi and Gujarati jostle against one another on every street, as Tamil and Telugu do in Madras. The 'media of instruction and work' will indeed be those two languages. But this does not automatically make it 'most desirable for provinces to be regrouped on a linguistic basis'. In the town of Jeypore in Orissa, District of Koraput, Oriya and Telugu are both spoken, with Oriya being dominant but Telugu very much in evidence: something on the order of 60 per cent Oriya to 40 per cent Telugu speakers.[27] This then is a 'polyglot' area, and it is impossible to see how it will help things and make people get on with each other better to designate the Koraput area as a part of Orissa rather than as a part of Andhra Pradesh, or vice versa for that matter. Difficulties will indeed 'continually arise', and no decision about which linguistic state to locate Jeypore in is going to change this. The States Reorganization Commission of 1955 awarded the District of Koraput to Orissa over Andhra objections,[28] on the basis of arguments that one wishes not to take issue with, but there is always an element of arbitrariness in such decisions and necessarily so. It is unavoidable in the real world of a country of many languages such as India that linguistic islands are going to remain no matter how the lines are drawn, and it is not obvious that redrawing lines on a map 'will help in the general progress of the province'.

But it would have been judged churlish, perhaps even unpatriotic, to raise such tedious academic objections at the time. Linguistic nationalism was in the ascendancy in India, as it had been a decade earlier in Europe at Versailles. It had become a juggernaut, smashing and crushing other conceptions of how to draw political boundaries. The idea of linguistic provinces had the aura of freedom about it. The rallying cry of 'linguistic provinces' had become an icon in the language of Chapter 2; an icon standing for *swaraj* and *swadeshi* and every conceivable kind of '*swa-*': freedom to run our country the way *we* want to, not the way the British would have us run it, freedom to draw the boundaries of *our* destiny. The words in support of the linguistic principle of the Nehru Committee Report were fine words, noble words, chosen to stir a people to action, but much more appealing when the British Raj was still intact and freedom an uncertain eventuality than when the British had departed and the rulers of independent India, that is to say, Jawaharlal Nehru and others, had then to contemplate the consequences of implementing their earlier wishes. 'Hoist with one's own petard' is the phrase that one struggles, unsuccessfully, to avoid dredging up.

The English never on the whole grasped the intricacies of the language problems lurking below the Indian surface of things. Few of them actually had to learn a vernacular to do their jobs; fewer still were scholars of language. Language did not, as it were, show up on the radar screen of most English observers. For example, in an otherwise well-written book, of which Nehru himself spoke with praise, Alan Campbell-Johnson's *Mission with Mountbatten*, there is one diminutive paragraph that touches on language, and even there the facts are commonplace, predictable, and mostly wrong.[29] Campbell-Johnson, like his chief, Lord Mountbatten, knew little about languages. Language as icon was out of the line of sight of almost all the English.

The linguistic stirrings in the Indian National Congress began to be perceived by British official opinion in the 1930s, though there was nothing remotely approaching a wholesale acceptance of the idea of reforming the map of India according to language divisions. The greatest step in this direction appears in 1930 in the *Report of the Indian Statutory Commission*, better known as the *Simon Commission Report* after its chairman, Sir John Simon. Only a small part of the voluminous *Simon Commission Report* deals with language, but the heart of the relevant section deserves to be quoted at length, in part because it shows the dawning perception among the more sympathetic and well-meaning of British officialdom that the boundary lines on the map of British India had arisen helter-skelter and had no sense behind them; also because the reservations expressed are so similar to those we shall encounter in Nehru in Chapter 4 ('Nehru at the Helm'). Some of Nehru's arguments for delay in implementing linguistic provinces after he became prime minister could easily have been lifted verbatim from the Simon Report, and probably were:

> These boundaries, as a rule, have none of the characteristics of a natural frontier; the lines they follow are largely due to the way in which British authority happened to spread over the subcontinent and to the order of time in which different accretions became joined to what was already organized as an administrative unit. As long as the Government of India was entirely centralized, and both the administration and the finance of any area were provided and directed from the Centre, the line taken by a provincial boundary was of less importance. But now that the provinces have a real political existence of their own, the situation is changing, and if, as we hope, the time is coming when each province will not only have its own provincial Government and its own provincial resources, but will form a unit in a federated whole, it is extremely important that the adjustment of provincial boundaries and the creation of proper provincial areas should take place before the new process has gone too far. Once the mould has set, any maldistribution will be still more difficult to correct . . . The shifting of landmarks is proverbially an operation which may bring down anything but blessings on the head of the reformer; it can be prudently undertaken only after taking full account of the interests and even the prejudices concerned.[30]

True, we have here recognition that all was not right in the way political boundaries were drawn, and this was at the time a considerable concession on the part of the British rulers. But nowhere in the Simon Report is language privileged as the basis for reorganizing provinces. This was Nehru's position precisely, as we shall see in Chapter 4. The unstated criterion of provincial boundaries seems to be 'administration' in some sense; 'efficiency' in the way of British reformers of India since Hastings and Cornwallis through the Benthamites. However, the adjoining section of the *Simon Commission Report* is explicit in citing the Nehru Committee Report of 1928 as its source for the notion of 'linguistic areas':

> There is a considerable body of opinion in India which calls for some readjustment of boundaries and redistribution of areas, and we entirely share the views of those who think that the present

arrangement is not altogether satisfactory. The existing provincial boundaries in more than one case embrace areas and peoples of no natural affinity, and sometimes separate those who might under a different scheme be more naturally united. There are, however, very great difficulties in the way of redistribution, and the history of the partition of Bengal stands as a warning of the caution needed before undertaking any operation so likely to run counter to old associations or to inflame suspicion and resentment. Moreover, the consequential administrative and financial adjustments are bound to be of an extremely complex character. The Nehru Report contains an interesting chapter on redistribution of provinces and discusses the difficult subject of 'linguistic areas' with a good deal of detail, though without coming to final conclusions. If those who speak the same language form a compact and self-contained area, so situated and endowed as to be able to support its existence as a separate province, there is no doubt that the use of a common speech is a strong and natural basis for provincial individuality. But it is not the only test — race, religion, economic interest, geographical contiguity, a due balance between country and town and between coast line and interior, may all be relevant factors. Most important of all perhaps, for practical purposes, is the largest possible measure of general agreement on the changes proposed, both on the side of the area that is gaining, and on the side of the area that is losing, territory. It is manifestly impossible for us to recommend a redrawing of the map of India according to some new pattern.[31]

Something of the large-minded sentiment of this part of the *Simon Commission Report* informs the *Report of the States Reorganization Commission 1955*, which effectively drew the linguistic state boundaries that would eventually be adopted and are in place today. Indeed, many of Nehru's pronouncements in the post-Independence debate over linguistic states are almost certainly influenced at a distance of almost three decades from the reservations about the sole use of language as criterion for provincial boundaries that are found in this section of the *Simon Commission Report*. The language of Nehru's pronouncements in the later 1940s and early 1950s is often word-for-word identical to the language of the Simon Commission. Lord Erskine, Governor of Madras, said in 1935 that 'One certainly cannot have a united India if he is going to have a government conducted in many languages. I do not believe that the two things [Indian unity and linguistic provinces] are possible nor do they coincide.'[32] Lord Lothian said much the same thing in a letter to Nehru,[33] and one must believe that these suspicions planted a seed that grew into Nehru's position on linguistic states as prime minister, when as we shall see in Chapter 4, he expressed many of the same reservations as Lords Erskine and Lothian.

Unlike most earlier pronouncements of the British, the *Simon Commission Report* had actual though piecemeal consequences in regard to the linguistic–state movement: the creation of separate provinces of Orissa and Sind in April 1936. Linguistic and cultural considerations overtly played the major role in the creation of Orissa:

An urgent case for consideration and treatment is that of Oriya-speaking people, most, but not all, of whom are now included in Orissa, because we consider that so close a union as now exists between Orissa and Bihar is a glaring example of the artificial connection of areas which are not naturally related [the language of Bihar was eastern Hindi]. We were so much impressed with this instance that we arranged, in cooperation with the Indian Central Committee and the Bihar and Orissa Provincial Committee, for the appointment of a Sub-Committee to investigate it more in detail.[34]

The Joint Parliamentary Committee (session 1932–3) had noted that the 'demand of the Oriyas for separation has been long and insistent'.[35] It was, as the subtitle of one book has it, the 'success of the first linguistic movement in India'.[36]

The creation of the province of Sind, now in Pakistan, might appear at first glance to parallel the creation of Orissa for linguistic and cultural reasons. The language of Sind was Sindhi, its population predominantly though not exclusively Muslim. However, the real reason for the creation of Sind had less to do with language and culture than with the wish to allay Muslim unrest:

Sind came into existence, along with Orissa, in April 1936, but the demand for this province was conceded mainly to placate Muslim opinion. The Indian Statutory Commission [Simon Commission], while expressing sympathy with the claim for the separation of Sind, had taken the view that there were grave administrative objections to isolating Sind and depriving it of the powerful backing of Bombay . . . However, the Joint Committee on Indian Constitutional Reforms, 1933–4, took note of the fact that separation of Sind had been pressed not merely by the Sindhi Muslims but also by Muhammadan leaders elsewhere in India and recommended it on the ground that 'apart from other considerations, the communal difficulties that would arise from attempting to administer Sind from Bombay would be no less great than those which may face a separate Sind administration.'[37]

Sir Reginald Craddock was very blunt:

> Whatever may have been the motives of those who framed the constitution of the White Paper the whole of India considers that the proposal to create a new Province of Sind is intended to placate Moslem sentiment and similarly the creation of a new Province of Orissa is intended as a counterpoise to gratify Hindu sentiment.[38]

The creation of Sind and Orissa was the last action under British rule to alter internal organization of the map of India. The Congress, meeting at Calcutta in October 1937, reiterated its support of the principle of linguistic provinces but demanded only two more in addition to Orissa and Sind, Andhra and Karnataka. Almost a year later spokesmen for Kerala announced their wishes for an autonomous linguistic province that would be Malayalam-speaking, and in 1938 the Congress Working Committee, meeting in Wardha, assured all the interested parties that changes would be made as soon as they had the power to effect such changes; that is, when the British were out of the way.

With this we have arrived at the outbreak of the Second World War and language slips below the political horizon. The battle for linguistic provinces faded in sound and significance as the battles of an altogether more tumultuous kind of war gained the upper hand of historical events. The bustle and excesses and sacrifices of a country waging war leave no room for refinement, for engagements of the intellect as vaporous as language, linguistic provinces, and the proper place of the vernacular languages. The resignation of the Congress ministries, troops here, troops there, food shortages, the great Bengal famine of 1943 — everything is in movement, in flux. Words and phrases, most of them devised by Gandhi, that word magician with a wicked gift for creating language which, like a surgeon's scalpel, went straight to the soft underbelly of British guilt about India, assume control: 'individual civil disobedience', 'blank cheque on a failing bank', and 'Quit India'. Most of the leaders of the Congress movement ended up in jail (Nehru for the ninth and final time) as world events on a momentous scale swamped mundane concerns such as demands for reorganization of India's internal boundaries along linguistic lines. The war became, for Jawaharlal Nehru at least, an enforced period of reflection, reading, and writing, as always before for him when imprisoned, a not altogether unwelcome refuge from the rage and passion of public life and the trials of private life (cf. Ch. 5, 'The Private Nehru', Jail Time).

There is a hiatus of almost five years' duration in Indian political development. The India of the Second World War is a heavily 'British' India in a way it never was before because of the enforced cessation of political activity, and the accumulated issues of a half century's march towards independence go figuratively into a kind of hibernation. By the war's end, in its election manifesto of 1945–6, the Congress again repeats the view that 'administrative units should be constituted as far as possible on a linguistic and cultural basis'.[39] But by then it somehow no longer really matters, and these resolutions have about them the tired predictability of routine. Events have come crowding in upon events, all too rapid and pell-mell to be absorbed whole, and a partitioned India would soon awaken to take control of its own destiny. Desires long banked would now be consummated by an Indian government in Indian hands, Nehru's chief among them. What had seemed so clearly right through those long years of Congress resolutions since 1920 — the reorganization of the country according to linguistic provinces — would now appear no longer quite so right, quite so timely, quite so urgent, in an independent India as it had in a colonial India.

Ulterior Motives

And something else would gradually begin to emerge from the shadows, namely the dawning realization that behind the drive for linguistic states or provinces lay aspirations grounded not so much in language as in caste and communal rivalries, in grappling for privilege. The Andhras had been among the first to agitate for a state of their own in which Telugu would be the official state language, a 'Land of the Andhras', Andhra Pradesh. Left unstated in this innocent formulation of the claim are the deep-rooted caste and class resentments of the Andhras. The leadership of the Andhra movement had attached itself to resentment of the putative Brahman monopoly on education, wealth, opportunity, and power in Tamil-dominated Madras. The Kammas and the Reddis, their puissance diluted in Madras caste politics, became among the strongest advocates of an Andhra State whose creation could only strengthen their position of power.[40]

It is soon noticeable how curiously absent from most of the history of the Andhra movement the Telugu language is. The vying of Brahmans, Kammas, and Reddis for power in Madras, the slipping of control of Congress from the hands of Brahmans, educational jealousy, all dwarfed in actuality everything else that played a role in the Andhra movement, and language most particularly.[41]

The caste–language nexus has often led to political coalitions that could not be predicted on the basis of language alone. The Andhra movement was ostensibly a language-and-culture movement, but not all speakers of Telugu wanted an Andhra Pradesh: 'Telugu-speaking cultivating castes in predominantly Tamil districts of Madras opposed the establishment of Andhra as did both Tamil- and Telugu-speaking Brahmans in Telugu majority districts, the former because of concerns about Tamil chauvinism, the latter because of fear in regard to mounting anti-Brahmanism.'[42]

The mistake should not be made of assuming that the caste background of the agitation for linguistic provinces was somehow a monopoly of the Andhras. Indeed, caste figured in every single demand for a linguistic state, such as those for a Kannada-speaking Karnataka and a Marathi-speaking Maharashtra. One aspect, indeed the leading publicly announced reason given for the demand behind a Kannada-speaking Karnataka province, was competition not between Brahmans and non-Brahmans but between two powerful peasant–proprietor subcastes within non-Brahman ranks, the Lingayats and the Vakkaligas.[43]

B.R. Ambedkar, Law Minister and father of the Constitution, a Mahar untouchable, had the deepest forebodings regarding the creation of linguistic states, in particular Maharashtra:

> Take Andhra. There are two major communities spread over the linguistic area. They are either the Reddis or the Kammas. They hold all the land, all the offices, all the business. The untouchables

live in subordinate dependence on them. Take Maharashtra. The Marathas are a huge majority in every village in Maharashtra. In a linguistic state what would remain for the smaller communities to look to?[44]

Linguistic States qua Caste Privilege is the equation. Seen in this light the caste and communal aspects slither to the surface and the linguistic aspect assumes an altogether different hue, indeed sinks out of sight. A so secular and reason-loving individual as Jawaharlal Nehru began to notice this. It is akin to picking up a rock, perhaps even an appealing rock, attractively contoured, only to find that slimy, nasty things crawl out from under it. Language is a good thing. As icon language has even a certain chaste nobility about it; but language as instrument of oppression is repellent, however often the case occurs. And it was not only caste that entered the equation of the linguistic states: a state of Kerala equals ostensibly a Malayalam-speaking state; however, a state of Kerala also equates with a sense of discrimination at the hands of the Tamils.[45] Demands for a separate Marathi-speaking Maharashtra were coupled with economic resentments directed against the Marwaris.[46] How much more uplifting it is to say 'Language Freedom — Now!' than to say 'Give Us More — Now!' It is a familiar ploy, this camouflaging of political motives; politics, Henry Adams reminds us in *The Education of Henry Adams*, has often been the 'systematic organization of hatreds'.

The point is that language is often a stalking horse for other claims altogether non-linguistic in nature and often awkward to articulate openly, for they basically reduce to greed, to a demand for 'more': more political power, more economic power, more latitude to kick the people around who used to kick us around. What the proponents of 'Khalistan' want is surely a great deal more than respect for the Gurmukhi script, in which the holy scriptures of the Sikh religion, in the Punjabi language, are written.

One notices how easily the discussion has shifted from the high plane of language and culture to the lower regions of caste and religious grasping, to communalism in so many words:

Let us be frank and accept the Dal–Roti ['Dal' is spiced lentils, 'roti' bread; both are staples of the folk diet] basis of this enthusiasm. It is the middle class job hunter and place hunter and the mostly middle class politician who are benefited by the establishment of a linguistic state, which creates for them an exclusive preserve of jobs, offices and places by shutting out, in the name of the promotion of culture, all outside competitors.[47]

After Independence Nehru, though with few of the other leaders of India alongside him, was quickly to become attuned to the subtleties of caste–class–communalism in the frantic drive to put in place the linguistic provinces. It gave him pause and more than pause, as we shall see in Chapter 4 ('Nehru at the Helm'). Within three months of Independence the dark side of the linguistic states movement quelled altogether whatever enthusiasm he may have once had to redraw the boundaries of India.

THE NATIONAL LANGUAGE

The other great linguistic battle, besides linguistic provinces, was what the 'national language' should be — Hindi or English. Or should there even be a designated national language? However conceptually different the two issues were — linguistic states and the national language — when brought into the political arena they had everything to do with one another and fused together into a single something called 'language politics':

> The drive to make Hindi the national language offended the non-Hindi-speaking areas, and opposition to it tended to strengthen the demand for local units of administration where a local language could be used for state business. If you will force Hindi on us for national purposes, ran the argument, then you should let us use our own language in our own state.[48]

The Constitution of 1950 designated Hindi 'the official language of the union', though English was after Independence and is today the only language understood and spoken by élites from all parts of India. English was and is, practically speaking, the lingua franca of India. English is the working language of government and academics and middle-class businessmen. But English had been the language of the colonial rulers and was scorned for the memories it evoked of ruler and ruled. Hindi was opposed by most of Dravidian India, by the Tamils especially so, and, with less overt fervour, by most of the non-Hindi-speaking states of northern India and the Deccan. If Hindi in fact became the true national and official language, then where would that leave the speaker of a different vernacular in the competition for employment?

There was at Independence and there is now realistically no alternative to English as an all-Indian language for official working purposes. In the original Constitution English was allowed to coexist alongside Hindi for 'official purposes of the union' for fifteen years, after which — 1965 — it was supposed to give way altogether to Hindi. This wish, born in the idealism and high-mindedness of the earliest days of Independence, foundered on the opposition to Hindi outside the Hindi-speaking heartland of northern India as 1965 drew near.

Before Independence, and indeed afterwards, Nehru was as insistent as any other leader of India that Hindi and not English would eventually have to become the national language. But, unlike many of his comrades in the struggle for freedom, Nehru was never an extremist on the issue. He himself was far more comfortable in English than ever in Hindi, and no one knew better than he that official India could not function without English. The designation of Hindi as the national language or 'language of the union' was for Nehru of symbolic ('iconic') value, but he was, on this issue if not certain others, extremely pragmatic, and he was appalled by the passions brought into politics by Hindi zealots. In order to understand the positions that Nehru took on this issue throughout his adult life, we must look into the relationships among the three languages — Hindi, Urdu, and Hindustani.

The Hindi–Urdu–Hindustani Nexus

This topic — Hindi–Urdu–Hindustani — though now slightly musty and antiquarian, occupies an important place in Indian political and intellectual history of the twentieth century. It has to do with the issue of the national language. It has to do with Hindu–Muslim antagonisms and ultimately with the unity of India. It is the issue that, because of the communal aspect, drew Mahatma Gandhi into the linguistic fray and for him overshadowed in importance all other language problems of his linguistically divided country. And partly because Gandhi devoted so much attention to this question Nehru did too. We shall see, however, that the two men could march to a common drummer only part of the way together when it came to language as a political issue.

Hindi and Urdu are variants of the same language which, in its common spoken form, used to be — and on occasion still is, more by laymen, however, than by linguists — called Hindustani, a linguistic designation which fell into limbo with the partition of what had been north-western India into India, predominantly Hindu, and Pakistan, predominantly Muslim. Pakistan has too few Hindus for the Hindi language to be much of an issue in Pakistan. In India, on the other hand, Urdu, as an icon of Muslim identification, struggles to maintain its place, as Muslims themselves do. Indian Muslims constitute approximately 10 per cent of the population, or almost 100,000,000 persons. The language of a great many of them, especially in northern India and in Hyderabad in Andhra Pradesh, is Urdu. In contemporary India communal resentments of Muslims and what is perceived as political favouritism on their behalf has occasionally led to discrimination against Urdu in schools or discrimination against Urdu when used for official purposes. Urdu is the national language of Pakistan, even though natively spoken by fewer Pakistanis than speak other regional languages such as Punjabi and Sindhi. Hindi has 'Hindu' overtones; Urdu has 'Muslim' associations. Hindi is written in the Devanagari script, derived from one of the scripts used to write Sanskrit. Urdu is written in a modified version of the Persian script, itself originally derived from the Arabic script. The essential iconic proportion that must always be borne in mind is this: Hindi : Hindu : Hinduism = Urdu : Muslim : Islam.

Hindi and Urdu belong to the Indo–European language family. The other major languages of northern and central India are Indo–European, as we saw in Chapter 1 ('Introduction'): Bengali, Marathi, Gujarati, Oriya. These languages are, like Hindi, written in Devanagari-derived scripts. Hindi written in the Devanagari script 'looks' Indian — or at least north Indian: south Indian language scripts look different, as does for that matter the script of Oriya, an Indo–European language spoken down into the eastern Deccan but written in a script that was almost certainly influenced by Dravidian script styles. Urdu written in its Perso–Arabic script 'looks' Middle Eastern, 'Islamic'. Visually — iconically — its written form stands quite apart from any of the other Indian languages of the north or south. Learned variants of Hindi look to Sanskrit for inspiration and enrichment of vocabulary and metrics, learned variants of Urdu to Persian and Arabic. Urdu has a few sounds (phonemes) that Hindi does not have, though this causes no problems in mutual comprehension. Hindi and Urdu diverge from each other cumulatively, mostly in vocabulary,[49] as one moves from the bazaar to the academy, and in the highest and therefore most artificial literary forms the two languages are mutually incomprehensible. The iconic associations of Hindi are with Hindu revivalism and Sanskritization — the spread of Brahmanical culture.[50] The iconic associations of Urdu are with Muslim renaissance and the Mughal courts.[51]

Both Hindi and Urdu evolved from Khari Boli, a branch of Western Hindi *(Madhyadeshi)* spoken in regions and cities such as Haryana, Delhi, and Meerut, which is derived from Sanskrit via one of the Prakrits. Urdu arose as the everyday language of the Mughal Empire, whose official and administrative language was Persian, as noted in Chapter 1 ('Introduction'). Urdu was the language of the princely courts such as Delhi and Lucknow. The designation 'Urdu' is not found until 1752, when the poet Mir gave it the name *Urdu-e-Mu'alla*, 'courtly language'.[52] The word 'Urdu' is of Turkish origin *(ordu)* and originally meant the language of the army or camp. Because of its Islamic provenance Urdu had by AD 1600 diverged from its Hindi origins by extensive absorption of Persian and Arabic linguistic material: loan words, syntactic turns of phrase, borrowed sounds such as *q, z*, and *gh* (phonetically the voiced velar fricative), a certain precious 'courtly style', a Persianized cast to poetry and song. The *ghazal*, for example, is Persian, and of course it was only natural that Urdu would have been written from its earliest days onward in a variant of the Arabic script, unsuited as such a script is to any Indo–European language.[53]

Hindi has a relatively young literary tradition within India, being customarily dated to around 1800.[54] Compared with the literature of Bengali, Tamil, Kannada, Telugu, or indeed almost any Indian language, Hindi literature is not very old. But it was never on the cards that Bengali or Tamil or any of the other regional languages with longer literary pedigrees should have become a pan-Indian language. There is a 'localness' about them, a proud 'regional' Otherness, that precludes them from candidacy for the national language.

I have mentioned that the difference in script between Hindi and Urdu is not only visually striking but laden with iconic portent. There is also the matter of borrowed words, especially from the higher regions of vocabulary. For enrichment of its vocabulary Hindi reaches back to Sanskrit and other north Indian languages, especially Bengali, and Urdu looks to Arabic and Persian. An Indian linguist has illustrated the problems this causes by asking how the abstract expression 'salvation's true path' would be translated into Hindi and Urdu at different style levels and among different ethnic–social groups.[55] Simple village people would render this as *mukti-ki sacci sarak* (bazaar Hindustani). Pandits or educated Hindus would say *mukti-ki satya upay* (highbrow Hindi). Cultured Muslims would translate the phrase as *nájat-ki haqq rah* (highbrow Urdu). Indians comfortable in the English language and not shy about showing it might say *salweshan-ki tru path*. The only indication that these four 'languages' are in some sense variants of the same language is the possessive (genitive) marker-*ki*. One sees how dramatically the character of a language is changed when the sources of borrowed words for new concepts are as far apart as they are in Hindi and Urdu: we might as well be dealing with different languages.

Standard (highbrow) Hindi and standard (highbrow) Urdu diverged even more startlingly after Partition, and with the spread of radio and now television.[56] Under the new, increasingly Sanskritized Hindi that became fashionable among some élites after Partition, the distance between the official rendering of a phrase and its rendering in colloquial educated style increased. The following illustrations are taken from one of the classic scholarly studies of the subject.[57] Items 1 and 2 are from signboards intended for the general public. In both cases *a* gives the official text, *b* gives the English translation, and *c* an approximate equivalent in the colloquial educated style:

Item 1

a. dhuumrpaan varjint hai
b. smoking prohibited
c. sigret piinaa manaa hai

Item 2

a. binaa aagyãã praveesh nisheedh

b. entrance prohibited without permission

c. binaa aagyãã andar jaanaa manaa hai

Hindi-speaking Indians frequently say that they simply cannot understand the Urdu of Radio Pakistan; Urdu-speaking Pakistanis say the same of the Hindi heard on All-India Radio.[58] Nehru himself complained that he could not understand the increasingly Sanskritized Hindi language promulgated by All-India Radio. He frequently commented on this in his letters, and on at least one occasion he rose in the Lok Sabha to complain that he could not understand Hindi broadcasts of his own speeches.[59]

The difference between Hindi and Urdu may be illustrated by a different sort of example involving Indian journalistic English. Consider the following account of a musical evening in New Delhi:

> He set the pace for the recital with a briskly rendered Pranamamayakam in Gowlai a composition of Mysore Vasudevachar. One liked the manner in which he and his accompanying vidwan built up the kriti embelling it with little flourishes here and there . . . Then came Kamboji alapana for Pallavi . . . With Vedanayagam Pillai's Nane Unnie Nambinane in Hamsanandi the recital came to a glorious end.[60]

Those versed in Carnatic music can make sense out of this newspaper report, but it is Greek to the average educated speaker of English. So it is when a Hindi speaker hears a kind of Urdu steeped in Persian and Arabic expressions, or an Urdu speaker hears Hindi loaded with Sanskrit or borrowings from other Indo–Aryan languages.

Until communal strife between Muslims and Hindus overwhelmed Indian public life in the last generation of the British Raj, the juxtaposition Hindi : Urdu did not evoke the immediate communal response that it does today and has since the turn of the century. Motilal Nehru, Jawaharlal's father, spoke Urdu as his native language. 'Motilal himself was, like his ancestors, more fluent in Arabic and Persian, and in Urdu than in any other Indian language.'[61] Jawaharlal Nehru wrote of his father:

> Meanwhile my father was going through school and college in

Cawnpore and Allahabad. His early education was confined entirely to Persian and Arabic, and he only began learning English in his early teens. But at that age he was considered to be a good Persian scholar, and knew some Arabic also, and because of this knowledge was treated with respect by much older people.[62]

Nehru himself wrote with admiration of the Persian heritage: 'Persia was the France of the East, sending its language and culture to all its neighbours. That is a common and precious heritage for all of us in India.'[63] The Nehru family were of course 'Hindu' to the core. They were progressive, 'liberal', cosmopolitan, religiously tolerant — but Hindu. As Kashmiri Brahmans they had, like many leading Hindu families, joined the bureaucratic service of the Mughal Empire, or what was left of it by the end of the eighteenth century. Indeed, the last Nehru to be born in Kashmir had come down in 1716 '[t]o seek fame and fortune in the rich plains below. Those were the days of the decline of the Mughal Empire. Raj Kaul was the name of that ancestor of ours, and he had gained eminence as a Sanskrit and Persian scholar.'[64]

There is a memorable portrait of Jawaharlal Nehru's grandfather, Pandit Ganga Dhar Nehru, in Mughal court dress, carrying the symbol of office, a curved sword.[65] The portrait remains a rich stimulant to the associations of memory. The language of the Mughal civil service was Urdu and, for higher purpose and greater authority, Persian. Jawaharlal Nehru ordinarily stated that Urdu was his native language, though on the few occasions that he wrote it he almost always used the Devanagari script rather than the more traditional Urdu Perso-Arabic script. He also admired the Urdu of Muhammad Iqbal, sometimes regarded as the 'spiritual father' of Pakistan, who for that reason should have been anathema to Nehru but was not, perhaps because 'he came from Kashmiri Brahman stock'.[66] Nehru's cradle language in Allahabad was Urdu–Hindi, but by any unbiased evaluation his 'native' language was English: 'Nehru took trouble to attain sufficient proficiency in Hindi so as to be able to communicate with large numbers of his people; but it was primarily in English that his thoughts were formulated and expressed.'[67]

Growing communal tensions in the post-Mutiny period sharpened the edges of the Hindu–Urdu controversy. The British introduced Urdu in the Perso–Arabic script as the language of the courts and administration in the North-Western Provinces, and Urdu was mandated as the language of the army in 1864. British officials were in agreement that Urdu, or as they had begun to call it, Hindustani, should become the lingua franca of all India, certainly of north India. However, Hindi written in Devanagari script enjoyed greater popularity among the common people than Urdu in the Perso–Arabic script;[68] and so matters stood — muddled — at the turn of the nineteenth century.

As the First World War ended, several superficially unrelated strains of potential danger drew together and joined in propelling Hindi–Urdu linguistic differences qua Hindu–Muslim communal differences to centrestage of Indian public life. There was the growing importance of the Congress movement, which was as effective in bringing Hindu and Muslim together as it was in sowing seeds of suspicion between them. The great Muslim underclass was in bad shape economically, and the traditional religious-based Islamic education system was widely held responsible for at least part of Muslim economic stagnation by forward-looking Muslims such as Sir Syed Ahmad Khan, who had founded the Anglo–Oriental College in 1875 (renamed Aligarh Muslim University in 1920), and whom Nehru admired, albeit with reservations because of Syed's fondness for British ways.[69] Above all there was a feeling of anomie engendered by the loss of the 'Caliphate'. The Ottoman Empire was finished and dismembered; and it remained uncertain what would take its place as protector of Islam and the holy places. 'The Muslim masses were uneasy but inarticulate; their traditionalist leaders were both alarmed and determined.'[70]

Such anxieties worked themselves out in every direction. There was a great fear for the Urdu language and for its place in India's future. It is a universal law that fear of loss of national identity translates itself wherever possible into anxiety for language preservation. From 1920 onwards language always played an important role in the agenda of the Congress Movement, and it is from this period, with *swaraj* a more thinkable possibility than ever before, that the question of the 'national language' became acute. Hindi, Urdu, and now, increasingly, 'Hindustani' were the alternatives. Gandhi pleaded for the latter — Hindustani — as the national language.

'Hindustani' as the name of a language had been popularized by the British as the 'lowbrow' bazaar language of the larger cities of India and the 'middlebrow' style of the daily language of northern India. However, 'Hindustani' was also in use as a designation for the literary style of Urdu. The Hindustani Academy, which had been created by the government of the United Provinces, meant by 'Hindustani' the coexistence of 'highbrow' styles of both Hindi and Urdu. Gandhi's definition of Hindustani, which he backed as the national language, was the 'middlebrow' style of north India. His definition extended equal rights to both Hindi and Urdu and to their scripts; in this way he hoped to evidence his recognition of Muslim culture as an important constituent of all-Indian culture and thereby assure the Muslim minority of its rights in (a Hindu-majority) India. Gandhi's notion of Hindustani consciously and specifically represented a turning away from both Persian and Sanskrit, the historical languages of the élites. The spoken language was the language of the people, and *this* is what Gandhi meant, quite intentionally, by 'national language'.[71]

Gandhi's Position, and Nehru's

Whatever may have been the precise alignment of Hindi, Urdu, and Hindustani, by the end of the nineteenth century, it was widely felt and widely recognized that, in north India at least, Hindi–Urdu–Hindustani did in fact function as a lingua franca. Observers as diverse as the Bengali political leader Rajendra Lal Mitra in 1864 and the American missionary S.H. Kellogg in 1875 agreed at least on that point, whatever else lay between them.[72]

One of the first major political leaders to take up the cause of Hindi as national language was B.G. Tilak who, we recall, had been the first Indian leader to espouse the cause of the linguistic provinces. At a meeting of the Nagari Pracharini Sabha at Benares in December 1905, he told the assembled: 'If you want to draw a nation together, there is no force more powerful than a common language for all.'[73] He went on to plead the case for a common script for all Indian languages, both Indo–Aryan and Dravidian. Devanagari was not surprisingly his nominee for the pan-Indian common script, 'not surprisingly' because Tilak's native language was Marathi, which is written in Devanagari.

There was so great an accumulation of argument and tradition behind the Hindi movement that independent India would have declared itself for Hindi — or Hindustani — as the national language in any case, but the movement took on a strong aura of historical inevitability when Mahatma Gandhi made the cause his own. Gandhi himself was a native speaker of Gujarati, and by all accounts he knew little of the literary or linguistic heritage of either Hindi or Urdu. He was never completely at home in Hindi and still less Urdu. In a speech at the All-India Script and Common Language Conference in Lucknow, 29 December 1916, he said, haltingly: 'I hail from Gujarat. My Hindi is broken. I speak to you, brothers, in that broken Hindi of mine, because even if I speak a little of English, I have the feeling that I am committing a sin.'[74]

As early as 1909 Gandhi wrote in *Hind Swaraj*: 'A universal language for India should be Hindi.'[75] By 1917 the argument for Hindustani — the term he normally favoured in preference to either Hindi or Urdu — had become an invariant in Gandhi's thinking and his political and educational programmes, and while he was never against tactical accommodation on other issues, on this one he never wavered. Gandhi defined Hindustani incidentally as 'a resultant of Hindi and Urdu, neither highly Sanskritized nor highly Persianized or Arabianized'.[76]

In speech after speech, editorial after editorial, from 1917 onwards Gandhi relentlessly hammered on the theme of Hindustani as national language, dismissing as trivial or unworthy the difficulties that enforcing Hindustani on the country as a whole might entail, riding roughshod over every iconic, emotional, or patriotic association speakers of a language might have: 'Let no Dravidian think that learning Hindi is at all difficult . . . Dravidian children take to Hindi in a remarkably easy manner';[77] 'An average Bengali can learn Hindustani in two months if he gave it three hours per day and a Dravidian in six months at the same rate.'[78] And in an outburst shocking in its linguistic *naïveté*: 'A spirit that is so exclusive and narrow as to want every form of speech to be perpetuated and developed, is anti-national and anti-universal. All underdeveloped and unwritten dialects should . . . be sacrificed and merged in the great Hindustani stream. It would be a sacrifice . . . , not a suicide.'[79]

As for the script in which the national language should be written, he wavered between Devanagari and no choice at all:

A common script for all India is a distant ideal. A common script for all those who speak the Indo–Sanskrit [Indo–Aryan] languages, including the Southern stock [Dravidian], is a practical ideal, if we but shed our provincialism, as the latter is good to the extent that it serves the still larger end of the universe . . . That the Devanagari script should be the common script, I suppose, does not need any demonstration — the deciding factor being that it is the script known to the largest part of India.[80]

Earlier, and later too, however, he contemptuously dismissed the script question. In his presidential address to the Hindi Sahitya Sammelan, Allahabad, in 1918, he had moved much further into the realm of 'utopian' linguistics:

Hind[ustani] is that language which is spoken in the north by both Hindus and Muslims and which is written either in the Nagari or the Persian script. [It] is neither too Sanskritized nor too Persianized . . . The distinction made between Hindus and Muslims is unreal. The same unreality is found in the distinction between Hindi and Urdu . . . A harmonious blend of the two will be as beautiful as the confluence of Ganga and Yamuna and last forever . . . There is no doubt or difficulty in regard to script. As things are, Muslims will patronize the Arabic script while Hindus will mostly use the Nagari script. Both scripts will therefore have to be accorded their due place. Officials must know both scripts.[81]

A beautiful ideal; but the world is not yet prepared for so much insult to the iconicity of language. It is an easy error to make — to underestimate the emotive power of language and the way that language is written. The fundamental flaw in Gandhi's espousal of a Hindustani neutral between Hindi and Urdu was its failure to take the symbolism — the iconicity, in the phrasing of Chapter 2 — of language into account.

Nehru accepted Gandhi's espousal of Hindustani as national language and fleshed it out in novel and interesting ways, including the idea of a 'Basic Hindustani' along the lines of the 'Basic English' proposed as an international auxiliary language by C.K. Ogden and I.A. Richards in such books as Ogden's *Basic English* and *Debabelization*, and Ogden and Richards' *The Meaning of Meaning*, all of which Nehru read in prison in 1934.[82] In the

1930s, as we shall see in Chapter 5 ('The Private Nehru') and Chapter 6 ('Essays on Language'), Nehru was much engaged in language. He wrote an essay, 'The Question of Language', in 1937 in which he brought together a number of his ideas on the national language, linguistic provinces, and related matters such as the possibility of partially unifying the diverse scripts of the Indian languages.[83] This all goes back to the notions of Gandhi, and before him Tilak and others who had occupied themselves with the question of a common script.[84] Nehru wrote his essay 'The Question of Language' specifically at Gandhi's request and for a specific purpose. I shall discuss this essay and its origins in Chapter 6 ('Nehru's Essays on Language'), where I shall also frame more precisely the differences between Gandhi and Nehru with regard to language.

The question of the script in which Hindustani was to be written was left completely open by both Gandhi and Nehru, and one understands why: to commit to one over the other was to take sides in the communal struggle between Hindu and Muslim, and that above all is what both Gandhi and Nehru were determined not to do. Those who favoured the traditional Urdu Perso-Arabic script were free to write in that; those who preferred the traditional Hindi Devanagari script were free to use that. Better yet — this is the impression one forms — speak Hindustani, just don't write it.

But this will not do; not in the real world of human imperfection. Communal hatreds between Muslims and Hindus cannot be simply wished away by pretending that the scripts used to write their language are devoid of evoked meaning. The power of language as icon must never be underestimated. Like it or not, the Urdu script *means* Muslim, the Devanagari script *means* Hindu. The Urdu script as seen by an angry, inflamed Hindu mob summons up talismanic images from the present and the past: cow-slaughter, temple-bashing, iconoclasm, crescent and star, Aurangzeb, green. When Hindus bent on doing violence to Muslims see a shop sign in Urdu, they want to smash it and burn that shop down. And vice versa. The Hindi script conveys to an enraged Muslim mob Vishnu and Shiva and a score of many-handed, many-headed gods and goddesses, cowdung, music before the mosque, dead pigs flung into mosques, Shivaji. Old sins cast long shadows. Nowhere is this truer than in India's burning sun.

The Report of the Official Language Commission of 1956 put it that language is 'of no intrinsic importance'.[85] Would that that were so, for then we could all communicate in any language we liked or in mathematical symbols or in some artificial and culturally neutered language like Esperanto or Volapük, or the child-speak Basic English of Ogden and Richards, and the millennium would have arrived. But, alas, language is symbol, sublime; an icon for a hundred emotions beyond the dour calculus of communication. Language is, like it or not, of most definite intrinsic importance; and it is necessary to look no further than its power to cause mischief in the India of the 1950s and 1960s to appreciate the point.

There are all sorts of reasons why Hindi could never have been accepted in south India as the national language. There were fears that Hindi speakers would gain advantages in competition for government jobs; and they would have. If the national, official language really were Hindi and no other, what chance in the competition for jobs against a native Hindi speaker would an Indian have whose native language was not Hindi? There were resentments of an 'upstart' language, a language without pedigree as Hindi was widely thought to be, awarded priority over languages of much greater antiquity and accumulated literary merit such as Tamil, Telugu, and Bengali. Who among Hindi writers had the standing of a Rabindranath Tagore, a Bengali Nobel laureate? There was pride in having worked so hard to acquire a good command of English, especially among the Tamil élite.

More deeply, more primordially, there was also resentment of the symbolism of Hindi; a symbolism that is in part iconographic. The image of Hindi, the icon of Hindi — not just the words and sentences that are the Hindi language, not just the idea of Hindi, but the Hindi Devanagari script with its horizontal overhead line and angular shapes — summons racial memories of Aryan (and Brahman) domination over Dravidian India.[86]

Nehru tells a charming little story having to do with Hindustani and the script used to write it.[87] In 1933 his younger sister, Krishna, had become engaged to be married. There was a problem, in that she was engaged to a non-Brahman, and under then-existing British law no religious ceremony had validity for an inter-caste marriage. A recently passed Civil Marriage Act came to the rescue, however, and the marriage could proceed.

Since Motilal Nehru was dead, the task of making the wedding arrangements fell to Jawaharlal, who decided to issue the wedding invitation in Hindustani in the roman script. There does not seem to have been any great outcry over the invitation, but Nehru notes laconically that 'Gandhiji did not approve of this'.[88] Nehru was perhaps exaggerating slightly here, however, for Gandhi's letters to Nehru or Krishna herself from the period around her engagement — in which Gandhi himself had played something of the role of matchmaker — are warm and amiable.[89] Indeed, the only reference in the published correspondence to anything about Hindustani in the roman script is in a letter to Jawaharlal of 15 October 1933 in which Gandhi asks: 'Have you introduced the Roman character for writing Hindi?'[90]

However much or little Gandhi actually disapproved of this, Nehru goes on to say:

> I did not use the Latin script because I had become a convert to it, although it had long attracted me. Its success in Turkey and Central Asia had impressed me, and the obvious arguments in its favour were weighty. But even so I . . . knew well that it did not stand the faintest chance of being adopted in present-day India. There would be the most violent opposition to it from all groups, nationalist, religious, Hindu, Muslim, old and new. And I feel that the opposition would not be merely based on emotion. A change of script is a very vital change for any language with a rich past, for a script is a most intimate part of its literature.
>
> I have no doubt whatever that Hindustani is going to be the common language of India . . . Its progress has been hampered by foolish controversies about the script. An effort must be made to discourage the extreme tendencies and develop a middle literary language, on the lines of the spoken language in common use. With mass education this will inevitably take place.[91]

There is linguistic subtlety here, but there is an equal amount of wishful thinking; indeed, a certain muddleheadedness is in evidence here. Nehru acknowledges the emotional (iconic) importance of the script in which a language is written — 'an intimate part of its literature' — but proceeds to act as if that does not matter. Did he not realize that there would be 'the most violent opposition' to *any* script mandated for Hindustani? Muslims would hate a Devanagari script, Hindus would hate a Perso–Arabic script; everybody would hate a roman script.

People have died in India for lesser causes. Or is there rather, as I surmise, simply an unwillingness on Nehru's part to come to grips with the fact that a language and its script are conjoined iconically as intimately in the linguistic sphere as dharma and karma are in Hindu philosophy?

There was in Congress thinking of the time a realization of the iconic importance of script and its emotional evocations. The 'Karachi Resolution of 1931' of the All-India Congress Committee meeting, 6–8 August 1931 in Bombay, includes as its third point under Fundamental Rights and Duties: 'The culture, language and script of the minorities and of the different linguistic areas shall be protected.'[92] The principal 'minority', indeed likely the only minority, targeted here would have been the Muslims and the script in question the Urdu Perso-Arabic script.

Whatever the finer points of the debates over Hindi, Urdu, and Hindustani, the Congress movement was at least on the surface in robust agreement with Gandhi that this north Indian language, spoken as a first language by never more than about a third of the Indian population even in pre-Partition times, should be the national and official language of India once the British had departed. I say 'robust agreement', but that is a pitiful understatement. Few Congress sessions ever were held that resolutions were not tabled to the effect that Hindi (or Hindustani or Hindi–Urdu: call it what you will) should be the national language of a free India. South Indians, Bengalis, and Muslim members of Congress each outdid the other in announcing their support for the notion, even if almost all of them outside north India had perforce to express their ardour in English since they would not have been understood in their home vernacular, and few of them would have had an adequate command of Hindustani for effective public speaking. In 1925, at Gandhi's insistence, the Indian National Congress amended its constitution to read: 'The proceedings of the Congress shall be conducted as far as possible in Hindustani. The English language or any provincial language may be used if the speaker is unable to speak Hindustani.'[93]

The great Tamil leader C. Rajagopalachari, known after Independence for his bitter opposition to the imposition of Hindi on the south, was no different to any other Congress potentate during the 1930s in contriving novel ways of expressing his commitment to a language he cared for little if at all. Rajagopalachari, while premier of Madras in 1937–9, introduced Hindustani as a school subject at considerable political cost to himself,[94] and his biographer and grandson, Rajmohan Gandhi, would no doubt have had at least one different set of grandparents if his father, Gandhi's son, had not been 'sent south' to teach Hindi in Dravidian India as part of Gandhi's drive for the propagation of Hindi there under the aegis of the Dakshina Bharat Hindi Prachar Sabha.[95] Rajagopalachari, C.R. as everyone called him, had his differences with Nehru, though they had marched a long way together, but the bald truth is that Rajagopalachari was exactly as lukewarm about language politics — linguistic states and Hindi as the national language — as Nehru was after 1947, and for much the same reasons, as we shall see in the next chapter.

We are dealing here, quite simply, with Hindustani as icon; as icon of Independence, home rule, of anti-British feeling. The drive for Hindustani (Hindi) as national language is much the same as the drive for Irish as national language in independent Ireland (Chapter 2 — 'Linguistic Prolegomena', Language as Icon, The Failure of the Revival of the Irish Language). The need for the icon is understandable and evokes sympathy. Hindi was a rallying point for the freedom movement, and as a language Hindi was laden with iconic value: *Swaraj!*, British Out!, Quit India!, Freedom Now! But the essential need for the national language movement receded into the background — NB 'receded into the background', not 'disappeared' — once Independence had been secured, though that is a home truth that disturbs sensibilities even today in India, or at least in the Hindi heartland among Hindi patriots. What had unified the freedom movement before Independence threatened to divide the nation thereafter. That, in a nutshell, is why Nehru's enthusiasm for imposing Hindi as the national language waned.

Hindi enthusiasts wanted Hindi to be the national and official language in 1947 without delay and without tiresome exceptions. It was largely at Nehru's insistence that the fifteen-year interim arrangement regarding the use of English was included in the Constitution.[96] It was also Nehru who put his personal prestige on the line by insisting on permissive legislation allowing the official use of English past 1965.[97] We shall look into these matters in greater detail in Chapter 4 ('Nehru at the Helm'), but I allude to them now in order to foreground the complexity of dealing with the problem of 'national language' after 1947: what appeared so clear under alien rule grew difficult and indistinct around the edges when the alien rule was no longer there to draw opposition as lightning to a lightning rod and to unify at least on the surface otherwise warring parties. An open question is what would have happened if Nehru had not been around in 1963 to bring the great weight of his authority to bear on the question of English versus Hindi.

English

The title of this section of the present chapter is The National Language, by which I mean the issue of Hindi, the term I shall ordinarily use in the remainder of this book in order to avoid the awkwardness of either choosing among the words Hindi, Urdu, Hindustani, or Hindi–Urdu.[98]

Hindi remains today, as it has been for centuries, the lingua franca of northern India. Hindi is more widely spoken outside of its north Indian homeland than ever before; more studied abroad than ever when the British controlled India. The Hindi language has been modernized, has accumulated greater literary merit, has been a force for Indian unity. Hindi *is* the 'national language' of India in some recondite sense of the phrase; in other words, symbolically, emotionally. Hindi, outside India, serves as an icon for India, for example as part of the lettering on Air India airplanes.

However, the exact phrasing of the enabling language of the Indian Constitution, Article 343, *Official Language of the Union*, is: (1) 'The official language of the Union shall be Hindi in Devanagari script.' This is followed by a second clause: (2) 'Notwithstanding anything in clause (1), for a period of fifteen years from the commencement of this Constitution, the English language shall continue to be used for all the official purposes of the Union for which it was being used immediately before such commencement.'[99] In Chapter 4 ('Nehru at the Helm') we shall see what delicate political considerations called for such sedulously contrived phrasing and what political events led to postponement of the date ('fifteen years from the commencement of this

Constitution', that is, 1965) at which time the English language was to go out of use for official purposes. In Chapter 4 we shall get a better grip on what lies behind the use of circumlocutions such as 'union language' and 'linking language' or 'link language' when referring to Hindi or English.

To return to the theme of this section, 'The National Language', and to bring it to conclusion, it simply remains to be said that English could never have been chosen by legislative vote as the national language of India. That may seem so obvious as to appear almost a simple-minded observation rather than a merely stupid one. However, we must recall that other city–states and nations that emerged from the British Empire — Singapore, South Africa, Hong Kong — have in fact kept English as a national language without overmuch agonizing and apology.

It is not in other words a foregone historical conclusion that a country emerging from colonial status will reject the language of the colonizer. However, it was never a real possibility that English should be officially recognized as the national language of India. Such an outcome was possible in former British colonies like Singapore, but not in India; never. One will seek in vain through the voluminous minutes of the All-India Congress Committee meetings for resolutions affirming English as a 'national' or 'official' language. Hindustani yes, English never. But this of course goes back to the notion of the 'iconicity' of language. Hindustani, for all the problems associated with it, symbolized freedom and independence, *swaraj*. English symbolized precisely the opposite: servility, meekness, bowed heads before the sahib and the memsahib, the topi. The English language was an icon for all that was wrong in the colonial relationship.

Indian intellectuals have always had something of a love–hate relationship with the English language.[100] They recognize that India cannot get along without it, but rather than gladly and happily accepting that fact they tend to resent it and wish things were different. Nehru was typical of the case when he wrote in 1935:

> Some people imagine that English is likely to become the lingua franca of India. That seems to me a fantastic conception, except in respect of upper-class intelligentsia . . . It may be, as it is partly today, that English will become increasingly a language used for technical, scientific, and business communications, and especially

for international contacts . . . I should like our universities to encourage the learning of other languages besides English — French, German, Russian, Spanish, Italian. This does not mean that English should be neglected, but . . . [101]

Naturally one understands and sympathizes with resentment of the colonial language, as of the colonizers. It seems to be necessary, even today, for some Indian intellectuals to decry their dependence on English. It all comes down in the end to the matter of iconicity. English 'stands for' a part of the nation's history some people wish to forget; it 'stands for' élitism, class, and distance from village India and Gandhi's ideals and a score of other things better not thought about.

Nehru eventually perceived the iconic strength of language, though he would not of course have called it that. It is that understanding or impulse towards understanding that lies behind such of his writings on language as the passage quoted above. He recognized the symbolism of language and over time would come to terms with it, but he was ill-prepared for the political consequences of language — the mischief it could cause — upon taking the reins of power into his hands.

Notes and References

1. 'On the Apperception of Doom in Indian Political Analysis', *in* P. Wallace (ed.), *Region and Nation in India* (New Delhi: American Institute of Indian Studies, 1985), pp. 287–99. *Fatalismus der Geschichte* — Gould's 'apperception of doom' — has a venerable if not honourable pedigree among observers of events on the subcontinent. An apogee of sorts was reached by Karl Marx in his dispatches in the 1850s to the *New York Daily Tribune* as its 'European correspondent'..It is almost impossible to find anything positive in Marx's articles on India about the country, its inhabitants, its history or its hopes for the future. Cf. S. Avineri (ed.), *Karl Marx on Colonialism and Modernization: His Despatches and Other Writings on China, India, Mexico, the Middle East and North Africa* (New York: Anchor Books, 1969), pp. 88–95, 132–9.
2. *The New Republic*, 26 Nov. 1984.
3. Spear, *India*, pp. 378–9.
4. J.E. Schwartzberg, 'Factors in the Linguistic Reorganization of

Indian States', *in* P. Wallace (ed.), *Region and Nation in India* (New Delhi: American Institute of Indian Studies, 1985), Fig. 6.

5. Ibid., pp. 155–82. Schwartzberg's maps tell a lively tale of the fitting of state lines to language 'isoglosses', which are lines dividing one language area from another.
6. Spear, *India*, pp. 217–20.
7. Schwartzberg, 'Factors in the Linguistic Reorganization of Indian States', p. 158.
8. *Encyclopaedia Britannica* (1946), vol. 9, p. 596.
9. Spear, *India*, pp. 318–19.
10. Govt of India letter No. 3678 of 3 Dec. 1903 to the Govt of Bengal, *SRC*, p. 10.
11. *SRC*, pp. 10–11.
12. Ibid., p. 1.
13. In this account of the origins of the movement for linguistic states and the events leading up to Independence I have drawn heavily from the essential government *Report of the States Reorganization Commission 1955 (SRC)*, which is instructive and even-handed both in its exposition of the history of the movement towards linguistic provinces and in explaining its recommendations on where to draw the state boundaries, whether one agrees with either the logic and reasoning of the Commission or its recommendations (*pace* Gopal, *Biography* 2: 261 and Ram Gopal, *Linguistic Affairs of India*, p. 77). Chapter 5 ('The Principle of Linguistic Homogeneity') and Chapter 6 ('Linguistic States') of Ram Gopal, *Linguistic Affairs of India* have been especially useful, as are Schwartzberg, 'Factors in the Linguistic Reorganization of Indian States', and Kluyev, *India: National and Language Problem.* Schwartzberg's maps showing the evolution of the match between provincial boundaries and linguistic boundaries speak more eloquently than a volume of essays on the linguistic history of vernacular India. Kluyev is a useful study from a Marxist perspective, a pre-glasnost and pre-perestroika Marxist perspective, useful not only because of the different viewpoint but because Kluyev uncovered archival and bibliographical facts about the political history of language in India gone unseen by other researchers.

    The volume of publication spawned by the issue of linguistic states is gargantuan, much of it partisan, tendentious, badly argued, and intellectually provincial — of dubious value in a scholarly discussion of the subject. I judge the sources from which I have drawn most of my discussion to be among the most balanced and sober accounts available. I have tried to blend information in such a way as to provide a narrative flow uninterrupted by overly frequent citation of a specific source. However, direct quotations are acknowledged in the usual way.

14. Ram Gopal, *Linguistic Affairs of India*, p. 64.
15. This reference was unearthed by a Russian scholar, V.I. Kazakov, *see* Kluyev, *India: National and Language Problem*, pp. 120–1.
16. Of which the official title is *Report on Indian Constitutional Reforms*, 1918.
17. Ram Gopal, *Linguistic Affairs of India*, pp. 65–6.
18. K. Dittmer, *Die indischen Muslims und die Hindi–Urdu Kontroverse in den United Provinces* (Wiesbaden: Otto Harrassowitz, 1972).
19. *Collected Works of Mahatma Gandhi*, vol. 16, pp. 492–4. There were serious differences between Gandhi and Mrs Besant on the issue of the 'national language'. Mrs Besant knew Sanskrit but was not comfortable in Hindi, and Gandhi observed 'that Mrs. Besant was disappointed that the proceedings of the Congress were conducted [now] mainly in Hindustani', *Young India*, 21 Jan. 1920.
20. Kulke and Rothermund, *A History of India*, p. 320.
21. *SRC*, p. 13.
22. 'The Question of Language', *Unity*, p. 258.
23. *India: The Most Dangerous Decades*, p. 276.
24. Cf. Nehru, 'The Question of Language', *Unity*, p. 243.
25. 'Growth of Violence', 23 Feb. 1956, *Speeches* 3: 193.
26. *SRC*, p. 13.
27. C.J. Bennett, 'The Morphology of Language Boundaries: Indo-Aryan and Dravidian in Peninsular India', *in* D.E. Sopher (ed.), *An Exploration of India: Geographical Perspectives on Society and Culture* (Ithaca: Cornell University Press, 1980), p. 243.
28. *SRC*, pp. 199–200.
29. *Mission with Mountbatten* (New York: Atheneum, 1986), p. 320.
30. *Simon Commission*, vol. 2, p. 26.
31. Ibid., vol. 2, pp. 24–5.
32. *The Indian Express*, 2 Dec. 1935.
33. Lothian to Nehru, 31 Dec. 1935, *A Bunch of Old Letters*, pp. 133–40. There is considerable correspondence between Nehru and Lord Lothian on the unity of India and the constitutional provisions proposed to secure this unity. The tenor and gravity of the very closely argued correspondence, and indeed its warmth not to mention its very existence, speak well of both men. Other contributions to this correspondence are the letters from Lothian to Nehru of 8 Nov. 1935 and 6 Dec. 1935 (*A Bunch of Old Letters*, pp. 128–30); Nehru to Lothian, 9 Dec. 1935 and 17 Jan. 1936 (*A Bunch of Old Letters*, pp. 130–2, 140–54).
34. *Simon Commission*, vol. 2, p. 24.

35. Ram Gopal, *Linguistic Affairs of India*, p. 68.
36. S.C. Patra, *Formation of the Province of Orissa: The Success of the First Linguistic Movement in India* (Calcutta: Punthi Pustak, 1979).
37. *SRC*, p. 12.
38. *Joint Committee on Indian Constitutional Reform*, Session 1933–4, vol. I, pt II, p. 444; cf. K.V. Narayana Rao, *The Emergence of Andhra Pradesh* (Bombay: Popular Prakashan, 1973), p. 123.
39. *SRC*, p. 14.
40. Harrison, *India: The Most Dangerous Decades*, p. 110.
41. Narayana Rao, *The Emergence of Andhra Pradesh*, p. 205.
42. Schwartzberg, 'Factors in the Linguistic Reorganization of Indian States', p. 170.
43. *India: The Most Dangerous Decades*, p. 111.
44. *Hindustan Times*, 3 Sept. 1953. *See also* B.R. Ambedkar, *Thoughts on Linguistic States* (Bombay: Ramkrishna Press, 1955).
45. *India: The Most Dangerous Decades*, p. 47.
46. Ibid., pp. 118–19.
47. K. Mukerji, *Reorganization of Indian States* (Bombay: Popular Book Depot, 1955), p. 31.
48. Spear, *India*, pp. 440–1.
49. Hindi uses Sanskrit and Urdu uses Persian and Arabic for learned vocabulary and above all 'great tradition' words in the sense of the anthropologist Robert Redfield, *The Little Community and Peasant Society and Culture* (Chicago: University of Chicago Press, 1967).
50. Embree, 'Indian Civilization and Regional Cultures: The Two Realities'.
51. A.R. Kelkar, *Studies in Hindi–Urdu* (Poona: Deccan College Post-graduate and Research Institute, 1968), pp. 6–7.
52. Dittmer, *Die indischen Muslims und die Hindi–Urdu Kontroverse in den United Provinces*, p. 48.
53. Cf. Ch. 2 — 'Linguistic Prolegomena', Language as Icon, *Language Reform in Turkey*.
54. Kelkar, *Studies in Hindi–Urdu*, p. 16 [foldout]; Chatterji, *Indo-Aryan and Hindi*, especially pt II, lectures II and III; also Y. Kachru, 'Hindi–Urdu', *in* B. Comrie (ed.), *The World's Major Languages* (New York: Oxford University Press, 1987), pp. 470–89.
55. J. Ornstein and W.E. Gage, *The ABC's of Languages and Linguistics* (Philadelphia: Chilton Books, 1964), p. 123.
56. Kelkar, *Studies in Hindi–Urdu*, p. 17n; J. Das Gupta and J.J. Gumperz, 'Language, Communication and Control in North India', *in* J.A. Fishman, C.A. Ferguson, and J. Das Gupta (eds), *Language Problems of Developing Nations* (New York: John Wiley & Sons, 1968), pp. 151–66.

57. Das Gupta and Gumperz, 'Language, Communication and Control in North India', p. 161.
58. Kelkar, *Studies in Hindi–Urdu*, p. 17n.
59. *National Herald*, 5 April 1958; G.C. Awasthy, *Broadcasting in India* (Bombay: Allied Publishers, 1965), p. 132.
60. *The Statesman*, 14 Dec. 1969; B.B. Kachru, 'Lexical Innovations in South Asian English', *in* R. Mohan (ed.), *Indian Writing in English* (New Delhi: Orient Longman, 1978), p. 86.
61. Gopal, *Biography* 1: 17.
62. *Autobiography*, p. 18.
63. Ibid., p. 292.
64. Ibid., p. 16.
65. Ibid., p. 34; Gopal, *Biography* 1: 48.
66. *Discovery*, p. 352.
67. Gopal, 'The English Language in India since Independence, and its Future Role', p. 198.
68. Dittmer, *Die indischen Muslims und die Hindi–Urdu Kontroverse in den United Provinces*, pp. 86–7.
69. *Autobiography*, pp. 289–90.
70. Spear, *India*, p. 342.
71. Dittmer, *Die indischen Muslims und die Hindi–Urdu Kontroverse in den United Provinces*, pp. 141–2.
72. Ram Gopal, *Linguistic Affairs of India*, p. 169.
73. Ibid., p. 175.
74. *Collected Works of Mahatma Gandhi*, vol. 13, p. 321.
75. Ram Gopal, *Linguistic Affairs of India*, p. 180.
76. *Young India*, 27 Aug. 1925.
77. Ibid., 16 June 1920.
78. Ibid., 2 Feb. 1921.
79. Ibid., 27 Aug. 1925.
80. Ibid.
81. Ram Gopal, *Linguistic Affairs of India*, pp. 186–7.
82. *Selected Works* I.6: 421–4.
83. *Unity*, pp. 241–61.
84. Ram Gopal, *Linguistic Affairs of India*, pp. 175–6.
85. *Official Language Commission Report*, p. 9.
86. R. Gandhi, *The Rajaji Story 1937–1972* (Bombay: Bharatiya Vidya Bhavan, 1984), vol. 2, p. 19.
87. *Autobiography*, pp. 286–7.
88. Ibid., p. 286.
89. See the letters dated 23, 24 Sept. 1933 and 7 Oct. 1933 in *The Collected Works of Mahatma Gandhi*, vol. 56, pp. 19–20, 23–4, 63.
90. *The Collected Works of Mahatma Gandhi*, vol. 56, p. 98.

91. *Autobiography*, pp. 286–7.
92. *Unity*, App. A, p. 406.
93. Ram Gopal, *Linguistic Affairs of India*, p. 187.
94. R. Gandhi, *The Rajaji Story 1937–1972*, vol. 2, p. 18f.
95. Rajmohan Gandhi is the paternal grandson of Mahatma Gandhi and the maternal grandson of C. Rajagopalachari.
96. M. Brecher, *Nehru* (London: Oxford University Press, 1959), pp. 424–5.
97. Intervention in the Lok Sabha debate on the Official Languages Bill, 24 April 1963, *Speeches* 5: 16–32.
98. Or the repellent neologism 'Hirdu', which I can bring myself to use only in inverted commas, and then just. Cf. Kelkar, *Studies in Hindi–Urdu*, pp. 6–7.
99. Diwan and Rajput, *Constitution of India*, p. 372.
100. With Nehru, however, it was never, not even remotely, a 'hate' relationship. He was never apologetic about English or his facility in it. As a typical representative of a certain caste of British intellectual — which Nehru was in this case if not others — he looked darkly on one kind of historical determinism, the loss of ground by British English to its colonial cousin: '[English] is progressively ceasing to be English and becoming American. Personally educated in an English university, I do not myself like many of these Americanisms very much . . . ' However, unlike many others of this persuasion, Nehru at least saw some good in the hateful turn of events: '[I] think these developments are putting new vigour into the English language . . . ' Speech at Osmania University, Hyderabad, 26 Nov. 1948, *Selected Works* II.9: 115–16.
101. *Autobiography*, p. 287.

Chapter 4

Nehru at the Helm

In a story that has never lost its magic nor faded in memory, freedom came to India at midnight on 14 August 1947. A soft light plays over these momentous events. No matter how often the tale is retold there is still an actuality about it, a feeling of suspense and promise and great moment, and although nearly half a century has gone by, everything still seems fated about the day's events. Nehru's biographer concludes this volume of the story of his subject's life:

> The next morning — 'The Appointed Day!' as Jawaharlal had noted in his pocket diary — Mountbatten was invited to continue as Governor-General and he in turn swore in Jawaharlal as the first Prime Minister of a free India. For the next few days Delhi and India seethed with joyous excitement. Only Gandhi celebrated independence in Calcutta by fasting, and was not surprised when the country was overtaken by the disillusion which was round the corner.[1]

The disillusion of which Gopal writes was of course the dreadful communal violence that followed on the heels of Partition. In the maelstrom of events that would now descend on the new India like a plague of hornets, language and its political history on the subcontinent would have been very nearly the last thing on anyone's mind. Creating a country was the order of the day; all else was subordinated to that requirement. But the burden of language India carried on its back, as it were, did not go away. There too, unexpectedly, disillusion was round the corner.

The story of what was now about to happen can be summarized as follows. Within months of Independence Nehru began to back-pedal on the issue of linguistic provinces. He felt that their implementation was among the most trifling of the problems facing the country, and because he knew they would bring dissension he argued with initial success to postpone dealing with linguistic provinces for as long a time as possible. He would succeed in spoking the wheel of the movement for some five years, but by 1952 the political climate in general and a shocking death in the south in particular would force his hand, and in rapid succession the linguistic provinces of Andhra Pradesh, Karnataka, Kerala, Tamil Nadu, and Maharashtra came into existence. Eventually Nehru gave in, unwillingly, to an irresistible force he could only slow down, not halt.

The issue of the national language was neatly finessed by stating in the Constitution of 1950 that Hindi was the official language of the union but that English could continue to be used for fifteen years for all the purposes it had been used for prior to Independence. Though denounced at the time and later as a dithering compromise by Hindi hegemonists who wanted English completely excluded, this clever Solomonic solution was nevertheless acceptable to most of them, and it also satisfied the non-Hindi-speaking areas. Neither side got what it wanted; neither side felt mortally insulted and put upon. 'Sufficient unto the day is the evil thereof' is probably a fair summary of Nehru's attitude: Hindi was in the Constitution, English could continue to be used, and fifteen years is a long time in the life of any country. Nehru was the individual directly responsible for the arrangement: 'He controlled the enthusiasts for Hindi and secured the retention of English as one of the official languages at least until 1965.'[2] And the time he bought ensured that English would become de facto the working language of Indian public life.

Linguistic States

History has not been kind to Nehru for his handling of either of the language problems. He has been especially harshly judged with virtual unanimity on his stance vis-à-vis the movement towards linguistic states.[3] He has few defenders in matters linguistic. His biographers and commentators, even those earnestly sympathetic to him and disinclined to criticize, reckon him weak, indecisive, and unresolved, especially on the issue of linguistic provinces. Michael Brecher: 'Despite his power and prestige, Nehru continues to exhibit a lack of confidence about the right course of action. Perhaps the most notable example in recent years was his weak handling of the vexed issue of States Reorganization [along linguistic lines].' And further: 'It is also clear that his reputation was not enhanced by the episode [States Reorganization].'[4] Frank Moraes says as little as possible about Nehru's role during the language turmoil.[5] Gopal's chapter on 'The Problem of Linguistic Provinces' is crowded with muted criticism and circumlocutions for weakness.[6] Michael Edwardes faults his vacillation and unsteady hand.[7]

Percival Spear: 'The prime minister has been forced to deal with another problem about which he cared less and has certainly been less successful. It is the problem of language . . . '[8] Alfred Apsler: 'Nehru, at times, appeared slow in taking decisive action.'[9] M. Balasubramanian: 'It is obvious that he had not taken any concrete step to solve the language problem.'[10] Walter Crocker: 'Nehru . . . was a man of voltes-faces: he could change overnight. This seems to be true as regards particulars and perhaps as regards a few big things, such as the policy of dividing India into states according to their languages . . . '[11] Rajendra Prasad Dube: 'The controversy over linguistic organization as well as the language problem in general amply illustrate Nehru's vacillation in public affairs.'[12] Denis Judd: '[T]he problem of communalism, provincialism and language usage formed a quagmire into which Nehru sank deeper and deeper as his premiership drew to a close . . . '[13] And Akhileshwar Singh:

In spite of all these explanations given, it cannot be denied that Nehru showed some uncertainty with regard to the issue [linguistic states]. As a matter of fact, the history of SRC [States Reorganization Commission] is one of the glaring examples of Nehru's oscillation on issues of public concern . . . The fact was that Nehru wanted to satisfy everyone, which was impossible.[14]

It is recognized that Nehru was plagued by self-doubt and second and third thoughts about many things — the 'Hamlet of Indian politics', as Lord Salisbury was once called the 'Hamlet of English politics' — but no one accuses Nehru of being a weak man. Foreign policy comes to mind. Why then so much faltering, so many fits and starts, so much foot-dragging, so much 'too little too late' on the language issues, especially on the issue of linguistic states? What should Nehru have done?

Why was Nehru so unenthusiastic about enacting laws and policies on matters of language? Why did he shove to the back of the stove these issues even though they often had broad public support and had been part of the Congress movement's legislative programme for decades?

In a radio broadcast from New Delhi almost a year before the birth of the new nation, 7 September 1946, Nehru addressed the people on the problems India would be facing as Independence inevitably drew nearer.[15] He spoke of the tribulations and opportunities for fulfilment that freedom would bring and of India's future relationship with Britain and other countries. On the domestic front he spoke to only three concerns: (1) raising the standard of living of the 'common and forgotten man in India', (2) continuing the battle initiated by Gandhi against the 'curse of untouchability and other forms of enforced inequality', and (3) conquering the 'spirit of discord that is abroad in India', the reference being of course to the Hindu–Muslim communal disorders associated with Partition. He did not mention language as a potential problem.

A year later, in his first speech as leader of the new India on 15 August 1947 he again spoke eloquently of the challenges then facing the country: 'One first and immediate objective must be to put an end to all internal strife and violence, which disfigure and degrade us and injure the cause of freedom', because, he added, as he so often had and so often would in the years ahead when discussing any form of communal strife, 'they come in the way of consideration of the great economic problems of the masses of the people which so urgently demand attention.'[16] India must change rapidly its 'antiquated land tenure system [and] promote industrialization on a large and balanced scale', ensure fair and equitable distribution of the fruits of production, and build dams and reservoirs to create hydroelectric power. This is all very sensible and unsurprising, but again I note that he did not comment on language. At midnight on 14 August 1947, when, as Nehru put it in the most eloquent speech of his career, India was awakening to 'life and freedom', language problems were nowhere in sight on the horizon.

I do not believe that even the most prescient observer could have predicted in 1947 the degree to which language, in one way or another, would bedevil domestic life and politics in

India from 1947 until well into the 1960s. Certainly Jawaharlal Nehru was not prepared for this; less prepared perhaps than other national leaders of India at the time — and more willing than any of them to accept the opprobrium heaped upon him for not moving as quickly as partisans on the issues would have had him move.

Larger and far more pressing matters than language had priority at the conception and during the birth pangs of the new India, and rightly so. Those were exciting times, momentous. Words of unbounded promise and noble phrases were the rhetorical currency of the moment: 'Tryst with destiny'; 'Soul of a nation'; 'We take the pledge of dedication to the service of India and her people and to the still larger cause of humanity.' But more than thoughts of high purpose occupied India's leaders. Every day dawned to new horrors as the full and terrible effects of the partition of British India into India and Pakistan came home to roost: rioting, massacres, the assassination of Gandhi. It would have been odd, strange, perverse even, had language been any but the very last thing on Nehru's mind.

On 27 November 1947, a scant three months after Independence, Nehru gave before the Constituent Assembly what now, in retrospect, must be considered an extraordinary speech. It was a brief speech — it could hardly have taken more than five minutes, if that, to deliver, — and it attracted no great attention at the time either in the press or among the public. In point of fact, however, Nehru signalled in this speech that he was in no great hurry to move on any of the language fronts, certainly not on linguistic provinces; that alongside matters such as security and economic development, language issues shrank into insignificance; and that he was not about to be rushed into judgment on linguistic affairs. Nehru, in this speech, turned his back, at least for the immediate future, on a quarter of a century's worth of Congress resolutions and actions on the language issues. Since most of what Nehru later did as prime minister in regard to language is but elucidation of the particulars he raised in this little-noticed speech — made, I repeat, barely three months into his administration — I feel obliged to quote from it at considerable length. The occasion for the speech was to reply to a question put by N.G. Ranga about governmental policy regarding the creation of new provinces on a linguistic basis:

Government are fully aware of the demand in some parts of the country for new provinces to be formed primarily on a linguistic and cultural basis. Many years ago this demand was recognized by the Congress and Government accept the principle underlying that demand. In giving effect to that principle, however, many other considerations have to be borne in mind. Apart from linguistic and cultural aspects sometimes also there is no clear demarcation and cultural and linguistic areas overlap . . . Government are anxious not to delay the enquiry or the decision. But, as the House is fully aware, the country has had to face . . . a very critical situation resulting from partition. A living entity had a part severed from it and this unnatural operation resulted in all manner of distempers which have naturally affected the political, social and economic structure of the country . . . The old equilibrium having been shaken up, disruptionist tendencies came to the fore. To a large extent we have faced this crisis and overcome it. But many dangers still surround us. There are numerous urgent demands in the economic and other spheres . . . First things must come first and the first thing is the security and stability of India. Before we can undertake any major schemes we must have a strong state and a smoothly running governmental machinery. The first essential therefore is for India as a whole to be strong and firmly established, confident in her capacity to meet all possible dangers and face and solve all problems. If India lives, all parts of India also live and prosper. If India is enfeebled, all her component elements grow weak.

I suggest to the House that every problem must be viewed in this context today.

It is necessary to have a reconstitution of the provinces, or some of them. But if we tackle this problem in a large way at present, there is grave danger of our energies being diverted from some of the more urgent tasks. In the case of some provinces the problem may be relatively easy, in the case of others it would be very difficult and very controversial . . . It would be desirable not to complicate the issue by having too many simultaneous enquiries.

The demand for the province of Andhra, which, if I may say so, is a perfectly legitimate demand, raises relatively few difficulties and it can be included among the provinces in the constitution as was done in the case of Orissa and Sind under the Government of India Act of 1935 [*see* Ch. 3]. This decision can be implemented soon after the constitution is adopted.

The creation of the provinces of Maharashtra and Karnataka

involves greater difficulties as any marked change will powerfully affect the structure and economy of the provinces concerned . . .

It must be remembered that the creation of a new province inevitably affects all the neighbouring provinces and the interests of these will have to be considered. Every decision must of course be considered from the point of view of the country as a whole.[17]

The questioning that followed upon this brief statement makes inescapable the inference that those present in the Constituent Assembly to hear it did not grasp its implications. Nehru's answers to his interlocutors reveal a certain testiness on his part, however, suggesting that he at least was fully aware of the implications of what he had just said:

Lakshmi Kanta Maitra asked whether the Government would take into consideration the cultural and linguistic affinities of the region before the new provinces were created.

JN: Naturally, Sir, all these questions can be considered at the right time.

Renuka Ray said that there was a strong demand for realignment of Bengal and Bihar on linguistic lines. The issue had not been raised in the Assembly because the Central Government was confronted by more immediate difficulties. She wanted an assurance of sympathetic consideration of the issue when raised later on and not to let it go by default.

JN: I must express my appreciation of the fact pointed out by the Honourable Member that, because of wider considerations, they did not press a certain demand that they had in their hearts or minds. But I must say that the grace of all that has been taken away by a fresh demand for an assurance.

N.B. Khare asked under what section of the Adaptation Act the Boundary Commission would be set up.

JN: I cannot mention any particular Act but without any Act I am quite sure we can appoint any number of boundary commissions.

A committee was then appointed by the Constituent Assembly to study the desirability of creating specifically four, and only four, new provinces: Andhra, Karnataka, Kerala, and Maharashtra. The committee, officially known as the Linguistic Provinces Commission, was commonly referred to as the Dar Commission after its chairman, S.K. Dar. The Dar Commission was not only empowered to enquire into the desirability of creating new provinces but to report on 'fixing their boundaries and assessing the financial, economic, administrative and other consequences in those provinces and the adjoining territories of India'.[18] It is clear from this formulation, which shows unmistakable traces of Nehru's hand, that language was no longer going to be the sole criterion for the reorganization of the map of India. Considerations had now surfaced — 'financial, economic, administrative and other consequences' — which are entirely missing in that measured series of Congress resolutions that had accompanied the momentum of the movement for linguistic provinces (Chapter 3 — 'Linguistic States and the National Language', Linguistic States). What had been so manifestly clear and unequivocal when outside power looking in was now a good deal murkier when seen from inside power looking out.

Nehru became anxious when he discovered, apparently to his surprise, that the Dar Commission was conducting public hearings on the question. He clearly recognized the potential for divisiveness and contention that the question of linguistic states would arouse in public hearings, and took steps — by writing letters, for example, to Rajendra Prasad, a leading Hindi advocate and supporter of linguistic provinces — complaining of the conduct of the Dar Commission, and manoeuvring behind the scenes to restrain the Dar Commission's regrettable penchant for openness.[19] He wrote one member of the cabinet, N.V. Gadgil, on 7 January 1949:

> May I suggest to you that it would be desirable for Ministers not to discuss the very controversial linguistic provinces issue in public? The matter is full of difficulty and has to be handled ultimately by the Cabinet with great care. It would be unfortunate if members of the Cabinet express themselves in different and contradictory ways in public.[20]

Even before the Dar Commission completed its report there were ominous rumblings from the language front. In a speech on 8 November 1948 before the Constituent Assembly in support of Dr Ambedkar's draft of the proposed constitution, Nehru addressed language for the first time at any length since Independence. Specific proposals on both major issues — linguistic provinces and the national language — were included in the draft of the constitution under debate.

Nehru spoke less to the merits of the constitutional proposals than to their timeliness:

> [I]t has long seemed to me inevitable that in India some kind of reorganization of the provinces should take place to fit in more with the cultural, geographical and economic condition of the people and with their desires. We have long been committed to it. I do not think it is good enough just to say linguistic provinces . . . [T]here are more important factors to be considered . . .
>
> Language is and has been a vital factor in an individual's and a nation's life, and because it is vital, we have to give it every thought and consideration . . . Powerful forces are at work in the country which will inevitably lead to the substitution of the English language by an Indian language or Indian languages in so far as the different parts of the country are concerned; but there will always be one all-India language. Powerful forces are also at work in the formation of that all-India language. A language ultimately grows from the people; it is seldom that it can be imposed . . .
>
> Therefore, I would beg of this House to . . . treat it [language, language policy] as a thing which should be settled not in a hurry when passions are roused, but at a suitable moment when the time is ripe for it . . . I would much rather avoid trying to impose my or anyone else's conception and, instead, work to that end in cooperation and amity and see how, after we have settled these major things about the constitution, after we have attained an even greater measure of stability, we can take up each one of these separate questions and dispose of them in a much better atmosphere.[21]

The Dar Commission issued its report on 10 December 1948. The essence of its conclusions was: 'No new provinces should be formed for the present. All things considered, the consideration of linguistic provinces should be postponed for ten years.'[22] That the Commission reached this conclusion was scarcely a surprise, for its report, officially the *Report of the Linguistic Provinces Commission*, was drafted by Nehru himself, even though he was not a member of the committee.[23] The later *Report of the States Reorganization Commission 1955*, an official government document, summarizes the findings of the Dar Commission as follows:

> It [the Dar Commission] not only expressed itself strongly against

any reorganization being undertaken in the prevailing circumstances but also held that the formation of provinces exclusively or even mainly on linguistic considerations would be inadvisable. The Commission felt that in forming provinces the emphasis should be primarily on administrative convenience. The homogeneity of language should enter into consideration only as a matter of administrative convenience. The Commission emphasized that everything which helped the growth of nationalism had to go forward and everything which impeded it had to be rejected or should stand over. Among many other factors which should be given due weight the Commission mentioned history, geography, economy and culture.

In the opinion of the Commission, if new States, formed after taking into consideration all these factors, possessed linguistic homogeneity also, that would be an additional advantage.

The Dar Commission listed certain 'generally recognized' tests which a linguistic area must satisfy before it could be formed into a province. These were:

(i) geographical contiguity and absence of pockets and corridors;
(ii) financial self-sufficiency;
(iii) administrative convenience;
(iv) capacity for future development; and
(v) a large measure of agreement within its borders and amongst the people speaking the same language in regard to its formation, care being taken that the new province should not be forced by a majority upon a substantial minority of people speaking the same language.[24]

One must marvel at this careful elaboration of the complicated issues behind the move towards linguistic states, so reminiscent of the Simon Commission's arguments against moving too quickly to create such units (cf. Ch. 3, *Linguistic States and the National Language*, 'Linguistic States'). How far removed the Dar Commission's language is from the simple, uncomplicated formulations of decades of Congress resolutions, and how far too from Nehru's own laconic — and unenthusiastic even then — acceptance of the principle of linguistic provinces in 1937: 'I might add that my frequent references to linguistic areas and the language of the province necessitate that provincial units should correspond with such language areas.'[25] By 1952 we find Nehru distancing himself even further from his earlier support of the notion, tepid as that support had ever been. In a speech in the Lok Sabha, 7 July 1952, goaded by a hostile comment, Nehru said:

An Hon. member said that I used to go around shouting about linguistic provinces from the house tops and at street corners. I am not aware of having done so at all. In fact, I have never been very enthusiastic about linguistic provinces. My views on our provinces are peculiar. Coming, as I do, from the biggest of India's provinces [Uttar Pradesh], I feel that provinces in this country should be much smaller than they are. It is not necessary to have the whole paraphernalia of a Governor, a High Court and so on for every province.[26]

Shortly after the publication of the Dar Commission report, the Congress, meeting in December 1948, took up the issue. A Congress committee was formed, consisting of Nehru, Vallabhbhai Patel, and Pattabhi Sitaramayya, and charged in effect with modifying the Congress position on linguistic provinces in the light of Independence and the report of the Dar Commission. Nehru, by ensuring his appointment to this committee along with Patel, whom Nehru could trust absolutely on this issue if not others, was not about to leave recommendations on the suddenly explosive topic of linguistic provinces in hands he could not control. This committee, known as the J.V.P. Committee after the initials of the first names of its three members, issued its report which, in the main, not surprisingly echoes themes heard in the language of the Dar Commission report, drafted, as we saw above, by Nehru and themes announced even earlier in Nehru's speech of 27 November 1947 before the Constituent Assembly. As he had done earlier with the Dar Commission of which he was not a member, Nehru himself drafted the report of the J.V.P. Committee.[27] In it he tried even harder to dampen the growing national — or at least Dravidian — ardour for linguistic provinces by putting matters in historical perspective. The report went further too in raising the level of his concerns about hasty action on any language problem:

(a) when the Congress had given the seal of its approval to the general principle of linguistic provinces it was not faced with the practical application of the principle and hence it had not considered all the implications and consequences that arose from this practical application;

(b) the primary consideration must be the security, unity and economic prosperity of India and every separatist and disruptive tendency should be rigorously discouraged;
(c) language was not only a binding force but also a separating one; and
(d) the old Congress policy of having linguistic provinces could only be applied after careful thought had been given to each separate case and without creating serious administrative dislocation or mutual conflicts which would jeopardize the political and economic stability of the country.

The Committee admitted that if public sentiment was insistent and overwhelming the practicability of satisfying public demand with its implications and consequences must be examined. However, it imposed two limitations on the possible satisfaction of such a demand:

(i) that, at least in the beginning, the principle might be applied only to well-defined areas about which there was mutual agreement [meaning primarily Andhra]; and
(ii) that all the proposals which had merit behind them could not be implemented simultaneously [meaning Andhra first, then only later Karnataka and others].[28]

The cold-water therapy of the J.V.P. Committee report slowed things for a while. However, under the surface, events had begun to move beyond Nehru's control. The Andhras in particular felt betrayed and were enraged by the dilatory mood and stately language of the J.V.P. report. We recall that, in his speech before the Constituent Assembly of 27 November 1947, Nehru had as much as conceded the prior right of Andhra to statehood: 'The demand for the province of Andhra, which, if I may say so, is a perfectly legitimate demand, raises relatively few difficulties and it can be included among the provinces in the constitution . . . This decision can be implemented soon after the constitution is adopted.' That was 1947. The new Constitution was scheduled to come into effect on 26 January 1950, and in a bad attack of eleventh-hour nerves Nehru abandoned the idea of including a new province of Andhra in it:

[O]n 6 January 1950 he [Nehru] doubted whether the Province could be formed before 26 January. Two days later he said it could not be formed even before 1 April 1950. By 17 January, it was certain that the Province would not be formed before 26 January. Finally the Government of India stated on 24 January, that it was essential that the outstanding differences and unresolved questions should be settled before the question could be taken up again.[29]

The allusion here to 'outstanding differences and unresolved questions' shows how far wrong Nehru had been in 1947 when he said that the 'demand for the province of Andhra . . . raises relatively few difficulties'. Nothing, it had now become clear to Nehru, raised 'relatively few difficulties' where language was concerned. The rush of events had given him a rapid education in the iconicity of language, but Nehru was nothing if not a quick learner. In the case of Andhra, the difficulties were numerous: there was opposition from the Tamils of Madras state, from which the new province of Andhra was primarily to be carved; opposition from the acerbic Tamil leader C. Rajagopalachari; Andhra demands that Madras city be the capital of Andhra — which was completely unacceptable to C.R. and the Tamils, besides being risible on grounds of demography,[30] finance, and much else besides.[31]

As devoutly as Nehru wanted to defer resolution of language problems until more urgent matters of greater moment had been disposed of, both history and events were against him on this. We saw in Chapter 3 ('Linguistic States and the National Language', Linguistic States) that the movement for redrawing the boundaries of British India had gathered steam as the twentieth century unfolded. The momentum was with linguistic states, and it would have required more of a dictator than Nehru was ever willing to be to block consummation of this wish, even for the ten years Nehru had hoped for when he drafted the Dar Commission report. His hopes in 1947–8 that the reorganization of provinces on linguistic lines could be postponed to calmer times were soon to be dashed.

Nehru simply did not in the early days of Independence appreciate that language was important, not so much to him but to other people, in ways that had nothing to do with words or phrases, eloquence or style; that language had material affect beyond its primary function as a means of communication. Nehru, in other words, did not fully comprehend the surrogate uses of language, that is to say, the non-linguistic uses of language

(Ch. 2 — 'Linguistic Prolegomena', Language as Icon). He understood dimly but did not grasp firmly either the intricate involvement of language with nationalism and local patriotism or the symbolism ('iconicity') of language.

The second aspect of the fight for linguistic provinces not immediately apparent to Nehru in 1947 was the degree to which language was a Trojan Horse in which lay concealed other kinds of non-linguistic demands divisive by nature (cf. Ch. 3, 'Linguistic States and the National Language', Linguistic States, Ulterior Motives). There were glimmerings of understanding, however, as we see from one of his letters to the provincial premiers of 15 November 1947:

> Assam has some trouble with the Bengalis; West Bengal has some trouble with the Gurkhas in Darjeeling . . . ; there is trouble in Orissa between Oriyas and Telugus . . . To some extent, these developments indicate a move for closer cultural ties between men of the same stock and language living in different provinces; and I have no doubt eventually some readjustment will be necessary. But at this stage of our national life any dispersion of our energies in internal schisms of this kind is likely to be dangerous.[32]

By 1952 events had taught him clearly the lesson that language was a convenient cloak for concealing dissatisfactions that had little or nothing to do with language:

> I feel that behind the demand for linguistic provinces there lies something a little more difficult to deal with than the problem of languages. That something is a feeling on the part of the people who make the demand that they have not had a square deal, that if they were left alone to manage their affairs they would see they got it. I cannot say whether there is much justification for the existence of such a feeling but the fact that it exists is not good for us. If we still function in a narrow, provincial way, reserving one group for our favours to the exclusion of another, it is unfortunate.[33]

Nehru's manoeuvrings and his chill public statements distancing himself from the linguistic provinces movement, together, of course, with his immense popularity and prestige and his command of Congress loyalties, combined to prevent action between 1947 and 1952. There were very serious issues foreign and domestic that took precedence over anything to do with language. Difficult as most of these other problems were, they were the kinds of problems far more congenial to a man of Nehru's interests and sensibility than something as purely domestic and vaguely atavistic as redrawing the state lines of India or settling once for all the matter of the national language. The Cold War had broken out. Nehru's non-alignment policy was in gestation. China had gone communist. Hyderabad and Kashmir were near boiling point. Relations with Pakistan were not good. Domestic divisions pulled him in a dozen directions and occasionally brought him into conflict with his comrades from Gandhi days such as Patel and Rajagopalachari; and Krishna Menon — 'aquiline and intense'[34] — was difficult and getting worse, as ever. The Korean War broke out in June 1950. China had begun to make threatening noises about Tibet. Almost all of the problems that would beset India for the rest of the century were foretold in the events of 1947–52.

Apart from all of these frightening and often intractable diversions and dissensions, whenever the air cleared enough for Nehru to have time for reflection on the larger things there remained the plain fact that India was a very poor country with many problems: how to create wealth, how to spread wealth, how to make agriculture more efficient, how to feed the people, and on and on. It is not difficult to understand Nehru's lament in a letter of 10 January 1949 to one of the leading and most zealous Andhra leaders, T. Prakasam: 'I should like to have a little peace or the semblance of peace for some time. After that we can go ahead in many directions.'[35] The phrasing 'semblance of peace' says a great deal.

And peace of a sort he had, for a time, but resentments of prolonged delays and unfulfilled promises on the linguistic provinces festered away, injecting a steady stream of toxic bacilli into the always labile Indian body politic, in particular in south India. Something was bound to happen to force the issue, and something did. It began with the Andhras, who had been pressing for their own 'country' since the dawn of the twentieth century.[36] The demand for a 'land of the Andhras' (Andhra Pradesh) meant to most Andhras the same thing as a demand for a Telugu-speaking state to be carved out of Madras state and other existing political units, primarily out of what had been prior to Independence parts of the Bombay Presidency and the princely states of Hyderabad and Mysore. Caste also played a role, as large a role as language though covertly, as we saw in Chapter 3 ('Linguistic States and the National Language', Ulterior Motives); but the simplest formulation that met the Andhra demands was: 'We want a Telugu-speaking state — and we want it *Now!*'

Nehru's hand was forced by the fast to death on 15 December 1952 of the revered Andhra leader, Sri Potti Sriramulu. Very little has been published in English on Potti Sriramulu; the following account of his life is taken from Narayana Rao's excellent narration of the Andhra movement.[37] I have no doubt that a fuller account would provide a more generous portrait of the man. Sriramulu had been born in 1901 in Madras into a Vaisya family. After a series of personal tragedies — the deaths in rapid succession of his wife, his five-year-old son, and his mother — Sriramulu chose to renounce the world, and joined Gandhi in 1928 in Sabarmati ashram. He became one of the Mahatma's most energetic and committed disciples. He participated in the famous salt march from Sabarmati to Dandi in 1930, was active in civil disobedience, worked for the relief of victims of the 1934 earthquake in Bihar, and devoted himself, especially after the War, to Harijan uplift. Sriramulu appropriated the Gandhian weapon of the fast first in late 1946, when he entered on a fast demanding legislation to open public temples to Harijans. The Madras legislature subsequently passed the Harijan Temple Entry Bill and the Harijan Civil Disabilities Bill, and he called off his fast. The chief minister of Madras at the time was T. Prakasam, a leader of the Andhra movement and supporter of Andhra independence against Tamil domination (whom Nehru had besought for 'a little peace or the semblance of peace'). Sriramulu fasted again in 1948 to protest the snail-like progress towards ending untouchability, was arrested, and released a fortnight later. He resumed his fast 12 January 1949 and gave it up three weeks later on assurances of speedier action on the problem of untouchability. At a time when most followers of Gandhi had relegated the fast to history as a tactic against the British, Sriramulu's enthusiastic renewal of this device of the master was an anachronism, but effective nevertheless.

From this time forward he seems to have become obsessed with the notion that progress in implementing the Gandhi programme — *ahimsa, satyagraha*, abolition of untouchability, *brahmachari* — was impossible so long as there was not an independent Andhra state. After Rajagopalachari, an Andhra opponent, was elected leader of the Madras Legislature Congress Party in 1952, Sriramulu issued an appeal:

In trying to organize the constructive work [the Gandhi programme], I have come across several obstacles and was continuously feeling the want of a separate Andhra province. Now I have come to the conclusion that further work is impossible without an Andhra State. I know that constructive workers [followers of Gandhi] are not satisfied with the policy of the Government in their States almost everywhere in the country. But still they are able to put forward substantial work on account of having people in the Government whom they know and who sympathize with their work, whereas in a multilingual province like Madras, the constructive workers are thrown to the winds, more particularly in Andhra.[38]

He had been weighing the idea of a fast for Andhra independence since 1949, but matters came to a head for him when C. Subrahmanyam, Finance Minister of Madras, and C. Rajagopalachari gave speeches asserting once again that Madras city belonged to Tamils — and the leaders of the Andhra movement failed to respond publicly to these speeches. Moreover, Sriramulu's insistence on a separate Andhra province had now escalated to include the requirement that Madras city be either jointly run by Tamils and Telugus or administered from the centre:

If the country is to remain united and the States should get rid of parochialism, it is necessary that important cities like Bombay, Delhi, Madras, and Calcutta should not belong to any one province but should be centrally administered. These cities owe their prosperity to the efforts of all states . . . Now the question of Andhra Province is tied to the status of Madras City. If the future of Madras is decided immediately the future of other cities gets decided in due course.[39]

Opinion among Andhra leaders was divided on the issue of how strongly to insist upon the inclusion of Madras city in their state, and understandably so. As I indicated earlier, the Andhra claim was quite weak; indeed within the context of linguistic arguments, remarkably so: culturally, historically, and by weight of its Tamil-speaking population vis-à-vis its Telugu-speaking population, Madras city belonged to the Tamils. Negotiations and discussions did not advance the situation. Matters were at an impasse. Nehru would not move until the parties involved — Telugus and Tamils — had reached an agreement, and the parties involved could not reach an agreement. Sriramulu concluded that none of the outstanding Andhra questions would be resolved through the ordinary political process. Consequently, on 19 October 1952, he announced a fast to death until two demands were met: that Andhra Pradesh be created immediately with Madras as its capital, and that Madras city be administered jointly by both Tamils and Andhras. He chose Madras for the location of his hunger fast; it was 'a part of [Sriramulu's] *satyagraha*'.[40] All other agitation for Andhra ceased. A stillness settled over this corner of Dravidian India as the agitators for Andhra awaited they knew not what: capitulation by Nehru, or the death of their beloved leader?

Naturally Nehru was not anxious to be blamed for the death of a follower of Gandhi; most certainly not a death through a means — the fast — that will in India forever evoke memories of Gandhian idealism and his detachment from the normal human desires of this world. On the other hand, Nehru was no different from anyone else in resenting pressure, especially pressure in a form that he regarded as unfair at the least and perhaps unethical or even immoral (as, one supposes, the British had done before him when Gandhi went on one of his fasts). Since Nehru was on public record as early as 1947 in favour of an Andhra linguistic state if not immediately others, he could hardly object in principle to Sriramulu's demand for an Andhra state. He knew, however, that the Tamils and Rajagopalachari would themselves fast to death rather than relinquish Madras city as their capital, nor would they ever agree to a shared capital. That part of Sriramulu's demands Nehru could never have granted; it would have cost him far too dearly in Tamil support and made of Rajagopalachari an implacable enemy instead of an occasional headache.

It was a cleft stick. But by this time Nehru had decided, however reluctantly, to concede Andhra. He had been beaten down, and his was a lonely vigil since none of his associates felt as strongly as he did that the concession of linguistic states was a major threat to Indian unity. By 13 December serious disturbances broke out in Andhra as Sriramulu's physical condition deteriorated. He died on the evening of 15 December 1952; looting and rioting and major destruction of property followed apace.

Hasty decisions now rained down: it was a case of 'scuttle, scuttle, scuttle', in Churchillian language. On the day after Sriramulu's death, 16 December 1952, Nehru announced in the Lok Sabha that the Andhras could have their state. Simultaneously the Vice-President of India, Dr Radhakrishnan, informed the Rajya Sabha that the prime minister was contacting the Madras government with instructions to proceed with the creation of Andhra state out of the undisputed Telugu districts. On 19 December the disturbances in Andhra subsided, and Nehru announced in parliament that the government were prepared to establish an Andhra state, to be carved out of the then-existing Madras state but not including Madras city, and he appointed K.N. Wanchoo, chief justice of the Rajasthan High Court, to advise him on the financial and other implications of the decision.[41]

Andhra state came into existence on 1 October 1953. Prolonged discussions with representatives of 'Telengana', the Telugu-speaking districts of the former native state of Hyderabad ruled over by the Nizam, were then initiated. Hyderabad had been an overwhelmingly Telugu-speaking native state ruled by an Urdu-speaking élite. These discussions culminated in the incorporation of Telengana into Andhra state. The state of Andhra Pradesh, with Hyderabad as its capital, was then inaugurated by Prime Minister Nehru on 1 November 1956.

Why did Nehru delay so long in doing what he eventually did so hastily and in retreat, and would not earlier action have saved Sriramulu's life? What role in all of this did Rajagopalachari play? Historians and chroniclers of the Andhra movement have discussed these questions.[42] The present discussion does not require detailed pursuit of all of these matters, but I should like to briefly take up the question of why Nehru capitulated when he did.

Nehru always denied that Sriramulu's fast had forced his hand on Andhra. Asked the following January at the meeting of the Hyderabad Congress Session about Andhra and Potti Sriramulu, Nehru stated that 'I did not want anyone to compel us or coerce us into taking any action'.[43]

In spite of Nehru's disclaimers, it is plain that Sriramulu's death was precisely the factor that precipitated his actions of

December 1952 concerning Andhra. It was not the only factor, however; it was more like the proverbial final straw that broke the camel's back. We recall that Nehru had very early in his administration (27 November 1947, in his speech before the Constituent Assembly) conceded the justice of the Andhra case in the abstract; thus Andhra, unlike demands for other linguistic provinces, was never for Nehru a matter of principle, only a matter of timing. He had resisted the mounting pressures, and not only from the Andhras, to do finally what he had said all along that he would be willing to do when the time was right for it — to begin to redraw the map of Indian states, starting with the state that had, in his opinion and the opinion of many others, the clearest title to linguistic statehood: Andhra. If there was no principle at stake, then when, people were asking, would the timing ever be right for an Andhra state?

Nehru had paid a very heavy price for his intransigence on implementing linguistic provinces. By the end of 1952 he was a tired, drained man at the end of his tether. In the gruelling election campaign that had concluded earlier that year, in March 1952, Nehru had covered about 25,000 miles and addressed about 35 million people.[44] Congress had gained a majority of seats in the Lok Sabha, but its losses in Rajasthan had been worrisome and its losses in the south, where linguistic grievances were uppermost on many politicians' minds, even more ominous.

With all of this building up and coming to rest on Nehru, the death by hunger fast of a follower of Gandhi appears to have shattered his nerves. The pell-mell flight from his carefully crafted position on the linguistic provinces within a day of Sriramulu's death was not characteristically Nehru. Nothing about his actions of 13–19 December 1952 is in character. This is evident, for example, in the two letters to the province premiers of 19 December 1952. Nehru wrote letters to his lieutenants, called initially province premiers and then, after 1950, chief ministers, on a very regular fortnightly basis almost until he died. The adjectives that might be associated with the typical letter of this genre would be: discursive, expansive, optimistic, scolding, playful, and above all lengthy. They range over whatever was uppermost in his mind. Where did he find the time to compose these essays, for essays they are, not 'reports' or 'position papers' or mere letters? They appear to have been for Nehru a kind of restorative. He enjoyed composing them. He enjoyed letting ideas off the lead to see where they would wander off to.

There are two letters of 19 December 1952 — that two letters were written on the same date in itself is unusual for him — and both are altogether different in every possible way from the normal fortnightly letter.[45] Both are very short; neither comes to more than two pages in the printed copy. The sentences are choppy, the tone sombre and prosaic, the choice of words pedestrian. The first letter of same date does not mention Andhra at all; it does, however, go on about much else disagreeable to Nehru: the Hindu Mahasabha, the Jan Singh, the R.S.S., the Ram Rajya Parishad, Master Tara Singh and the Akali Dal, the problems of Muslims in Bengal. The second announces laconically and without adornment or explanation that he, Nehru, had decided to proceed with the establishment of an Andhra state. The presentation of both letters is decidedly costive and very dark in tone. The man who wrote these letters is tired, dispirited, terse, and depressed.

But he made a remarkable recovery. Only three days later his epistolary style has recovered its verve and dash. In his letter to the chief ministers of 22 December 1952, which true to the norm goes on for about ten pages in the reprinting,[46] he does not deal with Andhra and the recent unpleasantness at all; not even with a single allusion. He writes about world affairs and his plans for India's future. The letter ranges here and there over a wide variety of topics. It is broad and expansive; very much a typical fortnightly letter to his province premiers. He even commends to their attention an exciting new Japanese farming method he has heard about called the 'raised bed seeding method', and would it not be well worth trying in India?

Nehru's capitulation on Andhra Pradesh opened the floodgates of linguistic separatism, as he had known it would do, even as he hoped against hope it would not. The dam broke. Demands for other long-deferred linguistic provinces mounted and became too overwhelming to be resisted or to be delayed in the ways that had worked, if only just, for Nehru between 1947 and 1952. After Andhra state was officially constituted in October 1953, pressure to accede to the demands for other linguistic states became intolerable, and on 22 December 1953 the prime minister announced that a commission would be appointed to examine 'objectively and dispassionately' the question of the reorganization of the states of the Indian Union 'so that the welfare of the people of each constituent unit as well as the nation as a whole is promoted.'[47] The Commission were charged to

> [i]nvestigate the conditions of the problem, the historical background, the existing situation and the bearing of all important and relevant factors thereon. They will be free to consider any proposal relating to such reorganization. The Government expect that the Commission would, in the first instance, not go into the details, but make recommendations in regard to the broad principles which should govern the solution of this problem and, if they so choose, the broad lines on which particular States should be reorganized, and submit interim reports for the consideration of Government.[48]

The Commission were to submit their recommendations to the Government of India by 30 June 1955.

The fat was now fairly in the fire. On 13 February 1953 Nehru wrote to K.N. Katju, the home minister, saying: 'You will observe that we have disturbed the hornet's nest and I believe most of us are likely to be badly stung.'[49] In the near term Nehru's prediction would be true. Many people would be stung, Nehru chief among them. But, paradoxically, as I shall argue in Chapter 7 ('Summing Up'), Nehru had accomplished more than he knew by delaying linguistic provinces and the battles accompanying their creation as long as he had — eight years, from 1947 to 1955 — and thereby laying a groundwork for an accommodation between centre and state, between the language of the centre and the vernacular languages of the states, that would, in the long run, more than compensate for the pain of the short run. By doing little, and that little grudgingly, Nehru would accomplish more for 'unity in diversity' than he dreamt of.

The Commission on States Reorganization had an unenviable task. It held public hearings, received 152,250 documentary communications of one sort or another of which its Report says, with prim rectitude, that 'The number of well-considered memoranda does not exceed 2,000.'[50] The volume of communications and the enthusiasm of concerned parties to make their opinions known required the Commission to extend its deadline to 30 September 1955. When it appeared, the *Report of the States Reorganization Commission 1955* ran to 267 pages and contained four and facilitating a calmer consideration of them. I shall send you a copy, also to Maulana [Azad].[29]

By 3 August 1937 Gandhi had received a draft of the essay, for he sent a letter of that date from 'On the train' to Nehru with comments.[30] Gandhi had no major problems with the text of the essay but did suggest a few amusing changes: 'You have "perhaps" before Pashto and Punjabi [as languages of instruction in the schools]. I suggest your removing the adverb. Khan Saheb for instance will never give up Pashto. I believe it is written in some script I forget which. And Punjabi? The Sikhs will die for Punjabi written in Gurumukhi. There is no elegance about that script.' Gandhi proposed that the unified south Indian language script Nehru endorses be Devanagari, which would never have been acceptable in Dravidian India — iconicity again — and made a few other observations in this vein. As far I can make out, Nehru acceded to Gandhi's editorial advice only to the extent of removing the adverb 'perhaps' before Pashto and Punjabi.

Mahadev Desai also offered some editorial suggestions,[31] all virtually identical to Gandhi's, with whom he had almost certainly gone over the matter since they were in the same train compartment when they wrote their respective letters. Gandhi contributed a foreword for the publication in tract form by the All-India Congress Committee:

I have very carefully gone through Jawaharlal Nehru's essay on the Hindi–Urdu question. The question has latterly become an unfortunate controversy. There is no valid reason for the ugly turn it has taken. Be that as it may, Jawaharlal's essay is a valuable contribution to a proper elucidation of the whole subject considered from the national and purely educational point of view. His constructive suggestions, if they are widely accepted by persons concerned, should put an end to the controversy which has taken a communal turn. The suggestions are exhaustive and eminently reasonable.[32]

In short, 'The Question of Language' owes as much to Gandhi's political need at the time as it does to Nehru's interest in Hindustani. It tracks very closely the points made in Nehru's brief message in Hindi to the Madras Hindi Sahitya Sammelan, which was the acorn out of which the oak grew.

There are considerable differences between Gandhi and Nehru in their entire approach to language and its political

Setting aside Nehru's involvement in and opinions of all this for the moment, I shall summarize here the modifications of the map of India between 1956 and 1995:[53]

1. In Dravidian India were created the linguistic states of Kerala (Malayalam language) and Karnataka (Kannada language), in addition to the previously created Andhra (Telugu language). Telengana, the Telugu-speaking region of Hyderabad, was merged with Andhra to create Andhra Pradesh. Kerala was formed out of Travancore–Cochin with the accession of a piece of the Malabar coast of Madras. Karnataka grew out of the former princely state of Mysore with absorption of the Kannada-speaking areas of former Hyderabad, Madras, and Bombay. The Madras Presidency of hoary British Raj splendour shrank in size to a linguistically homogeneous Tamil-speaking area, hence its new name Tamil Nadu 'Land of the Tamils'.
2. The linguistic states of northern and central India are: Madhya Pradesh (Hindi language), Rajasthan (Hindi, Rajasthani language), Uttar Pradesh (Hindi language), Bihar (Hindi language), West Bengal (Bengali language), Assam (Assamese language), Orissa (Oriya language), and Jammu & Kashmir (Kashmiri language, but also Punjabi). Most of these states were already more or less in existence. Madhya Pradesh was cobbled together out of the Central Provinces with the addition of the Hindi-speaking states of Madhya Bharat, Vindhya Pradesh, and Bhopal, and with the loss of Berar, which went to Maharashtra. Jammu & Kashmir in which both Kashmiri and Punjabi as well as Hindi are spoken, have by unstated common assent been left out of linguistic-state considerations for obvious reasons, with the result that Jammu & Kashmir remains India's most multilingual state.
3. The single bilingual state of Bombay was acceptable to no one, and all parties to the matter were extreme, bitter, and uncompromising. In 1956 Bombay state was partitioned into Marathi-speaking Maharashtra and Gujarati-speaking Gujarat, with Bombay city going to Maharashtra.
4. The older practice of designating states by size and importance as class A, B, or C was eliminated.

5. Until 1961 Punjab remained India's only seriously bilingual state, with both Hindi and Punjabi spoken by almost equal proportions of the population. The difference between the Hindi and Punjabi spoken there was not great linguistically but enormously great symbolically — and iconically, for Punjabi had rightly or wrongly a 'Sikh' identification, Hindi a 'Hindu' identification. Sikhism was in resurgence, and, moreover, to add to the iconic problems, Sikhs were moving more and more towards the Gurmukhi script for Punjabi in place of the Devanagari or Perso–Arabic script. Gurmukhi was the script of the sacred texts of the Sikh religion and thus of sublime iconic implication. In 1966 Punjab was partitioned. The largely Hindu Himalayan foothills were transferred to Himachal Pradesh, which was promoted from territory to state status. The Hindi-speaking areas of the Punjab plains were sheared off into the newly created state of Haryana, and what remained was the now largely Punjabi-speaking Punjab. The Sikhs still did not get their own state. That has been a source of Sikh discontent ever since with periodic demands for a Sikh 'Khalistan' or 'Sikhistan'.
6. Nagaland was formed as a state in 1963, but this had nothing to do with linguistics — Nagaland has many different tribal languages — and everything to do with satisfying the aspirations of tribal peoples in north-east India and elsewhere. Additional changes in these areas came in 1972 with the creation of Meghalaya, Manipur, and Tripura.

The eventual outcome of all this reshuffling of political boundaries is an India today whose state structures correspond astonishingly well, given India's linguistic diversity, to language units. Linguistic minorities within states were reduced to the lowest percentages they had been in modern Indian history. The national average of minority populations within states averaged approximately 22 per cent.[54] (Compare Map 1 with Map 4.)

And where was Nehru during this hectic period of states reorganization of the mid-1950s where he was so often at odds with others? He could not, of course, leave the playing field, being prime minister and leader of the Congress party. The luxury of withdrawal was denied him. He was active both publicly and behind the scenes. He gave lengthy speeches on language problems in the Lok Sabha on 21 December 1955, 23 February 1956, and 30 July 1956, and a shorter speech in the Rajya Sabha on 23 August 1956. He addressed the nation on All-India Radio on 9 October 1955 and 16 January 1956.[55] Throughout he maintained basically the position he had first enunciated in his speech of 27 November 1947 before the Constituent Assembly. It was unwise to rush these matters. Questions of language should be decided in stillness and deliberation, not in passion and haste. Delay would be better than a headlong rush into the unknown: 'What concerned him were the timing, the agitation, and violence with which linguistic provinces were being demanded and the harsh antagonism between various sections of the Indian people that underlay these demands.'[56]

His thinking on these matters never ran along the same tracks as others; his ideas were always more subtle and larger, more 'cosmopolitan'. A province like Hyderabad with its mixture of Urdu and Telugu, of both north Indian and south Indian ambience, and a rich Hindu–Muslim cultural tradition appealed to Nehru, as did Bombay with Marathi and Gujarati and its openings to the West:

> I should have thought that a multilingual State like Bombay or Madras afforded greater opportunities for growth and for developing a wider outlook than the big leviathan of a State like Uttar Pradesh. You will find in history and elsewhere that in some countries, small States are forced to think in large terms. They are forced to learn the languages of other States. Because people live in huge States and countries, they become so complacent that they do not think of people elsewhere . . . I, for my part, would be perfectly agreeable if there were a proposition that Uttar Pradesh, for instance, be split up into four provinces.[57] However, I doubt very much if my colleagues from Uttar Pradesh would relish that idea; on the contrary, they would probably like to have an additional chunk from some other province.
>
> Some hon. Members thought it desirable that Hyderabad should be split up into smaller units. I think such a step would be injurious to Hyderabad and would upset the whole structure of South India. It would be very unwise to do anything that would destroy the

administrative continuity that has been achieved in Hyderabad after so much effort.[58]

However, once the Pandora's Box of linguistic separatism had been opened, there was nothing for it but to let the thing run its course. Nehru's efforts to convince others of the rightness of fewer and larger states came to naught; they were dismissed as utopian and tainted with the aura of cosmopolitanism. Cosmopolitanism commanded no premium in the India of the 1950s. He was inevitably drawn into the dispute over Bombay, which did him no good. It led to the resignation of his finance minister, C.D. Deshmukh, and estrangement from the chief minister of Gujarat, Morarji Desai. His letters and public utterances from the period sound again and again the fundamental note he had first struck shortly after becoming prime minister: in India, in all matters of language, always proceed very, very slowly. We shall see in the next chapter ('The Private Nehru') that Nehru always derided the schoolboy knowledge of Latin he had got from his Harrow days; but one Latin proverb would have been useful to him at the time: *Festina lente*, 'Make haste slowly'. Good advice that, and for Nehru's view of intervention in language matters almost a mantra for him.

With the resolution, in 1956, of most of the linguistic province issues, the great passions they engendered were spent. People had either got what they wanted, or they had got half a loaf, or they had had to come to grips with the fact that they would not get what they wanted. A kind of linguistic ennui, a boredom with language, settled over the country. Nehru had done all he could to avoid linguistic states, and his delays had worked for a time; but after the noise and bother subsided there they were, the linguistic states, and only time would tell whether they had been a good idea or not. India would survive them. Was there anything India had not survived—Mughals, Shivaji, the British, Partition? India had its unity and its weather still, its castes and all of the rest, and time would heal some if not all the wounds inflicted on the country by its language-obsessed past.

It was now time for India to rest and recover, and time for Nehru to turn to those problems so much better matched to his interests and cast of mind such as economics and foreign policy. The latter would soon divert him almost completely from domestic politics, what with the Suez crisis and the Russian invasion of Hungary. It is easy to imagine his relief at being able to leave language and linguistics behind and begin to find a way for India to make its way in a world dominated by America and Russia. Theirs was a Cold War; but how much easier, in some ways, it was for Nehru to deal with the problems of a Cold War than the problems of a very hot war within his own country over linguistic provinces. In that latter war, which like Arjuna he had never wanted to fight, he could at least declare victory and leave the battlefield, bruised, much knocked about, but with his honour and reputation for probity damaged very little. It was, in retrospect, not a victory, not even nearly a victory, but not a complete defeat, and he should have been thankful that he had not been more seriously hurt in this row that had gone on for almost a decade past 1947.

And there was something more that Nehru had learnt from the battle over linguistic provinces. He now had to recognize that his linguist-like approach to language — unemotional, patient, 'scientific', and 'clinical' in the way of the academic linguist — found no favour among his countrymen. It was not a mistake to have dallied as Nehru did in responding to the demands for linguistic states, but he could not have known that at the time. All opinion was against him. However, he would not make the same mistake, as he and his critics saw it, twice — to underestimate the power of language to create mischief and delay the implementation of his larger programme for moving India ahead. 'Like most of those who study history', according to the historian A.J.P. Taylor, 'he [Napoleon III] learnt from the mistakes of the past how to make new ones.'[59] But where Napoleon III was thick as a plank, Nehru was the opposite, and he learnt neither to make the same 'mistake' twice nor to make new ones. Above all, he departed the enfeebling struggle for the linguistic states with the certain knowledge that head-on linguistic battles are best avoided. Wise men know never to confront an icon head-on. And so, when the next great linguistic battle — the national language — rose over the horizon, he was better prepared intellectually to cope with it, to plan his strategy in advance.

> Arjuna, action is far inferior
> to the discipline of understanding;

so seek refuge in understanding — pitiful
are men drawn by fruits of action.
[*Bhagavadgita* 2,49]

HINDI VERSUS ENGLISH

Nehru's management of the other major language problem, that of the 'national language, can be traced much more easily and briefly than his handling of the linguistic provinces. He made it clear from the very outset of his prime ministership that the Hindi absolutists would never have their way as long as he had anything to say about it. English — he insisted on this — would continue to be used officially in India along with Hindi; there would never be compulsion. Apart from his theoretical doubts about compelling the use of a language such as Hindi as the sole national language, which I shall discuss in the next chapter, there was the simple matter of politics, of tallying votes: in the matter of English, Dravidian India would never submit to the imposition of Hindi and the elimination of English. Other non-Hindi-speaking areas of India, Bengal in particular, also shared that view, though less stridently and forthrightly than for example the Tamils. Also the demands of the modern world — Nehru always liked to underscore this point — required educated Indians to have a good command of English.

Already on 8 November 1948, as preparations for the drafting of the Constitution were underway, Nehru spoke at length on what in his opinion should and should not be included in the Constitution. On language he was emphatic: say as little as possible. He might have quoted Churchill on this point, but did not of course; Churchill's famous opinion was that a country's constitution should be 'brief and obscure'. Regarding the imposition of a national language — he is speaking about Hindi though does not say so: his listeners knew what was meant — he said:

> Any attempt to impose a particular form of language on an unwilling people has usually met with the strongest opposition and has actually resulted in something the very reverse of what the promoters thought . . . [T]he surest way of developing a natural all-India language is not so much to pass resolutions and laws on the subject, but to work to that end in other ways.[60]

The themes of 'imposition' and 'compulsion' are always uppermost in his mind. At a meeting of the Congress Party in New Delhi on 7 May 1954 Nehru speaks on the topic of 'Enriching the Languages': 'Wherever this question of language has arisen, there has been difficulty. Languages cannot be put over by compulsion on large numbers of people; it can be done only by agreement, only by consent.'[61] And he goes on in this speech to tell of a recent visit he had had with 'eminent persons from Yugoslavia' who had stressed to him the need for language tolerance. Yugoslavia, the official language of which was Serbo-Croatian, had a problem virtually identical to that of India and Hindi–Urdu. Serbian and Croatian are mutually intelligible. Serbian is written in the Cyrillic alphabet, is identified with the Eastern Orthodox branch of the Catholic church, and borrows its high-culture words from the 'East' — from Russian and Old Church Slavonic. Croatian is written in the Roman alphabet, is identified with Roman Catholicism, and borrows its high-culture words from the 'West' — from German, for example, and Latin:

> One of the languages, Serbian, is the dominant language in the sense that more people speak it and use it and it may in the course of time dominate the others. But the ex-Minister told me they had taken great care that it should not even appear that Serbian was the chief language and others were not as important . . . I asked him whether they did not make Serbian compulsory in all the areas. He said, 'No, we don't even make it compulsory as a second language, because we want to create an impression of full freedom for every language to develop. As a matter of fact, Serbian does gain.'[62]

No one could fail to see that Nehru was drawing from the status of Serbian in Yugoslavia a lesson directly applicable to the situation of Hindi in India.

He never did so abrupt a volte-face in regard to Hindi as the national language as he had done on the linguistic provinces. Even at the end of his life, in 1963, when he was more than seventy years old, he still refers in his speeches to Hindi as 'a national language' or 'one of the national languages'; for example in a speech of 24 April 1963 in the Lok Sabha on the Official Language Bill.[63] But he never backed away from his steadfast belief that English would always be not only the language linking official India but a signpost for the future. The salvation of India would be science and technology, and English, the language of science and technology, was the beacon that beckoned him until the day he died. His philosophy on the linking language once he had become prime minister belonged always to the benevolent category of both–and rather than the restrictive either–or: both Hindi and English and all the regional languages of India for their purposes; never strictly either Hindi or English. Hindi for symbolism — iconicity; English for the great world: 'English today is by far the more widespread and important world language and probably two-thirds of the scientific and technical books in the world are published in English.'[64] There was also his concern that, by going over to Hindi altogether, India would become intellectually insular and isolated:

> I have mentioned above . . . the necessity of knowing English or any other foreign language for scientific and technological purposes. Also, if I may say so with all respect, we are a narrow-minded people and are apt to live in our own shells. There is the danger of our getting cut off from the world of thought in all its aspects and becoming complacent in our own little world of India. For this reason also contacts with foreign languages are essential.[65]

It was Nehru who crafted the joint constitutional provisions that Hindi should be the 'official language of the union' — not quite the same thing as 'national' language, but sufficiently imprecise to meet the need of the case — and that English could continue to be used for all official purposes for fifteen years past ratification of the Constitution, which is to say until 1965.

It was Nehru who contrived to ensure that the statement 'The form of numerals to be used for the official purposes of the Union shall be the international form of Indian numerals' not only appeared in the Constitution but followed directly, in the very next sentence, the provision in §343 stating that Hindi in Devanagari script should be the official language of the union. The story behind the curious business of the numerals is that certain Hindi supporters wanted to confer official status on the Devanagari form of the numerals. The Devanagari numerals do not look like '1, 2, 3'; they are quite different. What eventually happened was that use of the Devanagari numerals was allowed, and the question was to be reconsidered after fifteen years. It was more of 'sufficient unto the day is the evil thereof'. Anyone familiar with Nehru's thought and cast of mind can without difficulty imagine the contempt which a matter so trivial to him — though iconically important to others — would evoke. He made his strong preference for the international form of numerals clear in a letter of 24 August 1949 to N. Gopalaswami Ayyanger, minister without portfolio;[66] and, leaving no doubt of his attitude towards this matter, in a letter of 10 September 1949 to Ayyanger he says: 'I am very tired of all this business.'[67]

A theme Nehru played on many times was that Hindi needed to develop more as a modern language before it could serve adequately as an all-India language. We shall see in Chapter 5 ('The Private Nehru') that he had concerned himself since the 1930s with the inadequacy of Hindi for technical and state purposes, and he had always argued that it must evolve further in these areas before it could assume the functions of English as a linking language. In his statement 'The Place of English' on 8 September 1956, he says:

> We can build up our technical terms in Hindi, as we are doing. But we cannot produce the vast and complicated thought that lies behind this technical and industrial age by translating a few books or having a list of terms . . . Personally I think that even from the cultural point of view in addition to the point of view of developing and widening the scope of Hindi and our other languages it is necessary for us to keep in intimate touch with, and have adequate knowledge of, foreign languages . . . This will enrich Hindi and gradually make it a vehicle of this new thought . . . Thus I think that Hindi must be given every encouragement to grow and to be used for educational administrative purposes, provided always that it grows on sound lines and not on superficial, journalistic lines.[68]

And even close to the end of his life he is still speaking of this in the Lok Sabha debate on the Official Language Bill:

> It is claimed that Hindi might have become a link language if the Government had encouraged it enough. There may be some justification for this remark. But I think that most people will agree with me when I say that at the present moment Hindi cannot take up all this work of administration. I do not, therefore, think that there is much truth in the criticism that the Government has not helped its growth. The reasons (for Hindi not growing faster) are far deeper than Government help or lack of help.[69]

It would have been particularly apt for Nehru to have cited here the example of the Irish language, where, as we saw in Chapter 2, the Irish government did virtually everything in its power to encourage its use. It availed nothing. 'The reasons (for Irish not growing faster)', Nehru might have said, 'are far deeper than government help or lack of help.' Indeed they are — whether Hindi or Irish.

I have mentioned several times that the original constitutional provision for English was that it could be used for all official purposes 'for a period of fifteen years from the commencement of this Constitution'.[70] As 1965 drew nearer, the implications of this provision began to sink in. Would not Indians whose native language was Hindi — some 35 per cent of the population, mostly in the north of the country — have a considerable advantage with the replacement of English altogether by Hindi: in competition for government jobs, in the foreign service, indeed in private firms with pan-Indian aspirations? How could a deputy in parliament effectively argue for or against a bill if he had to speak a language he did not know well or know at all? Not to put too fine a point on it, would not non-native-Hindi-speakers be handicapped in every possible way? The answer to these questions is Yes, of course: Hindi speakers would indeed have all the advantages; Indians whose native language was not Hindi would indeed start every race a step or several behind. Let us have no nonsense about that. No amount of soothing reassurance, of tedious explication, on the part of Hindi hegemonists could change the fundamental inequality: without English as an official language, Hindi speakers would have a better chance in every all-India arena of competition. Nothing could hide that stark reality. A decision made in 1950 — that Hindi would replace English in fifteen years — looked altogether different by 1960, and to the Indians whose native language was not Hindi, a good deal darker and more threatening.

In 1959 Nehru promised that Hindi would not be imposed on the country and that English would continue as an associate, additional language for official purposes indefinitely. This was a great annoyance to Hindi absolutists and, while reassuring to non-Hindi-speakers, it did not have the power of law behind it. Nehru was again in a cleft stick, as he had been on the issue of linguistic provinces, but regarding the mandatory imposition of

Hindi on the country his mind was made up and his position unambiguous. There would be none of the vacillation that had allowed him to be so battered about on the issue of linguistic provinces. He was solid, immovable. Unlike Napoleon III, he had not learnt how to make new mistakes.

In the early 1960s serious disorders over the approaching deadline of 1965 broke out, principally in south India and especially in Madras. Tempers flared. Newspaper headlines were inflammatory. On 18 February 1963, when President Radhakrishnan rose to deliver the annual President's Address to a joint session of both houses of parliament, socialist and right-wing deputies interrupted the speech and demanded that he deliver it in Hindi, not English. Some six of the objectors left the hall. Radhakrishnan, a Telugu speaker by birth and a master of the English language, refused to give his speech in Hindi. The incident troubled Nehru a great deal. In his fortnightly letter of 18 February 1963 to the chief ministers he wrote:

> The incident at the time of the President addressing the Joint Session of the two Houses of Parliament, to which I have referred earlier, was meant to be in connection with the agitation in favour of Hindi and against English. It was an exceedingly foolish thing to do because this kind of thing injures the cause of Hindi more than anything else . . .[71]

He then addressed the Official Language Bill, which had been drafted but not brought before parliament at the time he wrote his letter to the chief ministers. This bill provided that English may continue to be used, in addition to Hindi, after 27 January 1965 for all official purposes of the union and for the transaction of business in parliament:

> We certainly hope to bring the Bill or an amendment of the Constitution in regard to English being an associate language during this session . . . I have made this perfectly clear . . .
>
> But pledge apart, I am quite sure this is the right thing to do, both for wider reasons and even in the interests of the growth of Hindi. The wider reasons are obvious, because in the world today English is becoming an even more important language than previously, and all the development in science and technology depends upon our knowledge of a foreign language. Hindi is growing pretty fast and will grow. The one thing that will come in the way of its

growth is a heated controversy on this language issue. That will surely impede its growth and injure us in many other respects also.

There is another and, I think, deeper reason for our being associated with English for some time more at least. We in India live in a large country and have been to a great extent, inward-looking . . . If we discard English, we will . . . be cut off from the outer world, to a large extent. I have referred to some reasons for our continuing English as an associate language while at the same time developing Hindi as fast as we can. But essentially the overriding reason for it is the necessity of not encouraging any disruptive tendencies in India.[72]

The Official Language Bill was brought before the Lok Sabha and debated in the early months of 1963 and passed by the Lok Sabha on 27 April and by the Rajya Sabha on 4 May 1963. It provided that English may continue to be used past 1965, in addition to Hindi, for all official purposes of the union and in parliament.

With the passage of the Official Language Act, Nehru rendered his last service to the cause of progressive language policy in India, and a very great service it was. No country that turns its back on the international language of science, commerce, and technology — English — can avoid becoming a fever swamp of backwardness, excessive inwardness, isolation, and intellectual stagnation. By securing the place of English in India indefinitely into the future, Nehru guaranteed a foundation for progress that will always remain one of his most enduring legacies. No other Indian leader would have placed the full weight of his prestige behind the cause of English or been so highly resolved to secure a permanent place in the foundation of India for the English language.

The Common Thread

It is clear now what was the paramount, the overarching reason, for Nehru's reluctance to move decisively on the language issues once he had become prime minister. That reason was his consuming determination to preserve the union, to oppose anything, to refuse to initiate anything, that would weaken India's unity. The unity of free India had been too recently acquired and too dearly purchased to be put at risk. The primordial passions unleashed by Partition had shaken him to the bottom of his soul, as they had Gandhi.[73] Nehru's letters and statements from this period repeatedly and eloquently express his horror, his disbelief, that such things — what he saw before his eyes — actually could be happening; his dispirited hopelessness as he saw what Hindu–Muslim enmity could come to.

This theme — the unity of India — had been an invariant in his thinking since his earliest involvement in the freedom movement. It suffuses his autobiography *(Toward Freedom)* and *The Discovery of India*. It was the title given to his collected writings from 1937–40, assembled by his friend V.K. Krishna Menon. Whether he is writing about events of great political moment, or whether — always with a softer, gentler stylistic touch than that of his political essays — he is writing about the Ganga, the Surma valley, Khali, Kashmir, Garhwal, or the monsoon coming over the Arabian Sea to Bombay with a whimper instead of a bang,[74] the operative sentiment is always unity. Unity first, unity all the time; never, never yield on Indian unity. 'My profession', he once said, 'is to foster the unity of India.'[75]

Nehru never quite came to grips with the fundamental contradiction wrapped within the notion of the 'unity of India'. No foreigner spends any time in India wondering about what India is; the average Indian does not fret himself about it. That there is a unity is plain to see and impossible not to feel. What constitutes that undoubted unity has spawned volumes of exegesis. British observers of an earlier date were fond of denying that there was a unity. John Strachey, very blimpish about it, asserted 'that there is not, and never was an India,'[76] a sentiment very close to that of the editors of *Hobson-Jobson*: 'We use the adjective *Indian*, but no modern Englishman who has had to do with India ever speaks of a man of that country as "an Indian".'[77] Vincent Smith in the *Oxford History of India* captured something in the famous and convenient phrase 'unity in diversity'.[78] Nehru was fond of the notion 'unity in diversity', but that clever formulation is more a cover symbol for a mystery than it is an explanation of that mystery.

Ainslie Embree summarizes the range of views authoritatively and asserts that:

Smith's identification of 'unity in diversity' as the characteristic feature of Indian society, despite its widespread acceptance, is not very satisfactory. It leaves unanswered some crucial questions, for while it is true that the complex structures of Hinduism differentiate Indian civilization from the other great world cultures, it is not at all clear that in the past it ever acted as a unifying factor in the political realm . . . When Smith said that India possesses a 'deep underlying fundamental unity', attributable to Hinduism, it would have been more accurate to have said that the institutions and beliefs that he identifies as Hindu — caste, the place of Brahmans, the cow, sacred geography, and so on — make it distinctive. It is not Hinduism but one element of it, Brahmanical ideology, that has been a unifier in Indian civilization and a powerful force in maintaining its integrity in the face of tremendous onslaughts of two other great civilizations, the Islamic and the European . . .

Hinduism is here understood to be correctly applied to the whole complex of religious and social practices that developed in the subcontinent over a very long period of time and which have many regional and local manifestations, varying greatly in time and place, while by Brahmanism is meant the much more coherent and consistent intellectual statements of the great classical texts.[79]

All speculation along these lines would have been profoundly uncongenial to Jawaharlal Nehru, the great secularist. Where in 'Brahmanical ideology' and 'Brahmanism' is there room for the Muslim minority, for the Sikhs and the Jains, for the Parsis? 'Nowhere' is the only answer — which is why Nehru avoided pursuing to its rational end any definitive answer to the question: wherein resides the unity of India? He would, I suspect, happily have taken refuge in the observation of F.T. Jannuzi, an economist: 'Regional identities are shaped not only by shared language, culture and political consciousness, but also by economic variables.'[80]

But these are academic quibbles foreign to Nehru's sensibility; he was after all both politician and intellectual. The forces unleashed by linguistic regionalism and linguistic chauvinism threatened the unity of India; therefore Nehru opposed them. All else is footnote. As one of his biographers put it: 'When freedom came, however, Jawaharlal Nehru changed his mind [on linguistic provinces and the national language question]. Partition had so affected him that he would not be party to any decisions which he felt encouraged fissiparous tendencies.'[81] It is a measure of the gratifying extent to which language as a major divisive force had faded from the domestic scene by the 1980s that Akbar's biography of Nehru needed to devote only a handful of pages to either of the linguistic issues.

In virtually every speech he gave from Independence to his death that dealt with any language problem, any question of the reorganization of states, any dispute between Hindi and English, between Hindi and Urdu, with the role of Sanskrit, the emphasis on unity is never absent. The association in his thoughts of language with disunity and unity is almost reflexive, automatic:

8 November 1948, Constituent Assembly:

We all know that reference has been made . . . to linguistic provinces and to the question of language in this Assembly and in the country . . . [T]he glory of India has been the way in which it has managed to keep two things going at the same time: that is, its infinite variety and at the same time its unity in that variety.[82]

7 July 1952, Lok Sabha:

Speaking for myself, I have been overburdened with the thought that we must give the topmost priority to the development of a sense of unity in India because these are critical days. Any decision that might come in the way of that unity should be delayed till we have laid a strong foundation for it. Because of that, I for my own part have frankly . . . not taken any aggressive or positive step in regard to the formation of linguistic provinces . . . The idea of linguistic provinces will intensify provincial feelings and that, undoubtedly, will weaken the concept of a united India.[83]

9 October 1955, All-India Radio:

This Report [of the States Reorganization Commission] deals with a vital and most important issue for our present and future and, therefore, it deserves the most careful consideration by all of us. It should be considered not only in its separate parts dealing with special problems but even more so as a whole because of the interrelation of each of these separate problems and areas. Above all, we have to consider these questions from the point of view of the unity, strength and prosperity of India.[84]

16 January 1956, All-India Radio:

The idea of any State standing by itself is, of course, absurd apart from its being opposed to the basic conception of India's unity. I would earnestly appeal to all our countrymen and comrades to consider these matters in a spirit of peaceful cooperation. India appeals today to the world for peaceful coexistence between nations. How much more is that necessary within the broad confines of our dear country.[85]

7 August 1959, Lok Sabha:

There are certain risks and dangers in the Indian languages becoming autarkies or developing a separateness. We should fight any such tendency . . . We shall get over the danger of linguistic separatism as long as we encourage the right tendencies and one language group does not try to impose its will on other groups.[86]

31 March 1963, Sahitya Akademi:

I think the Sahitya Akademi has done fairly good work in encouraging our languages and eminent writers in them, and in bringing them nearer to one another and thereby contributing not only to the variety of India but also to its essential unity. Both the variety and the unity are essential. Persons who think that unity can be maintained by suppressing variety are, I think, completely wrong. On the other hand, mere variety means separateness and breakup of the unity, which is fatal even for the diverse aspects of India.[87]

And less than a year before his death:

22 July 1963, Central Institute of English, Hyderabad:

So, while the regional languages must enjoy a basic position in our education and ordinary usage, English and, of course, Hindi have also a very important position. That is why a year or two ago the three-language formula was evolved . . . [I]t is a good formula keeping in view the various aspects of this problem and the need to bring about a sense of unity in the political and cultural spheres and a common understanding all over India.[88]

I do not find that Nehru ever quite put it this way — the formulation would have been uncomfortable to him — but it would be fair to say that Nehru's destiny was to create and leave behind him a strong, stable, and above all a *united* India. All his life had been but prologue for this monumental task. The clarity of motive I perceive — that Nehru was driven by his determination to preserve the unity of India at all costs and therefore instinctively distrusted all linguistic separatist demands — comes most clearly from retrospect and is aided by the passage of time. Immediately before and after 1947, nothing concerning the language issues was particularly clear; nor was it clear precisely what if anything Nehru had accomplished by his withdrawn and remote handling of the language problems.

There were those who, like Selig Harrison in 1960, as much as prophesied that India would not last as a unified country, and language was among the premises on which he based his gloomy reasoning.[89] Harrison was proved wrong, and part of the reason he was wrong was his and others' failure to recognize that Nehru's dawdling had served a purpose. Nehru's 'dawdling' had gained time for independent India's political institutions to mature and its unity to be proved in practice as well as in theory. Nehru's method had pulled the country through language battles that, under a different prime minister more responsive to popular demands, could have poisoned the wells of Indian unity for all time to come.

> Always perform with detachment
> any action you must do;
> performing action with detachment,
> one achieves supreme good.
> (*Bhagavadgita* 3,19)

Notes and References

1. Gopal, *Biography* 1: 362.
2. Ibid., 2: 78.
3. The most judicious summary account of Nehru's actions in regard to linguistic states is Ch. XII ('The Problem of Linguistic Provinces'), vol. 2, of Gopal's *Jawaharlal Nehru: A Biography* (Gopal, *Biography* 2: 256–71). A full account of the movement behind Andhra Pradesh — the first linguistic state to be created — is given in Narayana Rao, *The Emergence of Andhra Pradesh*, and much of Narayana Rao's account is useful for the background of linguistic states other than Andhra. The *Report of the States Reorganization Commission 1955 (SRC)*, though an official document and itself part of the political process which brought about the linguistic states, is useful, as are relevant parts of Ram Gopal, *Linguistic Affairs of India* and Mukerji, *Reorganization of Indian States*. An excellent account is that of the geographer Joseph E. Schwartzberg, 'Factors in the Linguistic Reorganization of Indian States', whose maps lucidly trace the developments.
4. *Nehru*, pp. 2, 489.
5. *Jawaharlal Nehru: A Biography* (New York: Macmillan, 1956).

6. *Biography* 2: 256–71.
7. *Nehru* (London: The Penguin Press, 1971), pp. 253–6.
8. *India*, p. 440.
9. *Jawaharlal Nehru* (New York: Julian Messner, 1963), p. 166.
10. *Nehru: A Study in Secularism* (New Delhi: Uppal Publishing House, 1980), p. 54.
11. *Nehru* (New York: Oxford University Press, 1966), p. 71.
12. *Jawaharlal Nehru: A Study in Ideology and Social Change* (Delhi: Mittal Publications, 1988), pp. 212–13.
13. *Jawaharlal Nehru* (Cardiff: University of Wales Press, 1993), p. 74.
14. *Political Leadership of Jawaharlal Nehru* (New Delhi: Deep & Deep, 1986), p. 93.
15. 'The Interim National Government', *Speeches* 1: 1–5.
16. 'First Servant of the Indian People', *Speeches* 1: 29–31.
17. 'Linguistic Provinces', *Selected Works* II.4: 530–1.
18. *SRC*, p. 15.
19. Gopal, *Biography* 2: 257. See also the letter of 4 Feb. 1949 to Pattabhi Sitaramayya, *Selected Works* II.9: 139–40.
20. *Selected Works* II.9: 137.
21. 'The Last Lap of Our Long Journey', *Speeches* 1: 36–8.
22. B. Shiva Rao, *The Framing of India's Constitution* (New Delhi: Indian Institute of Public Administration, 1966–8), vol. 4, p. 439f.
23. Gopal, *Biography* 2: 257.
24. *SRC*, pp. 15–16.
25. 'The Question of Language', *Unity*, p. 258.
26. 'Linguistic States', *Speeches* 2: 34.
27. *Selected Works* II.10: 128–37, esp. 128n.
28. *SRC*, pp. 16–17.
29. Narayana Rao, *The Emergence of Andhra Pradesh*, p. 216.
30. Ibid., pp. 124–225.
31. The largely unedifying story is told from different perspectives in Gopal, *Biography* 2: 258–9 and Narayana Rao, *The Emergence of Andhra Pradesh*, pp. 199–269.
32. *Letters to Chief Ministers*, vol. 1, pp. 15–16.
33. Lok Sabha, 7 July 1952, 'Linguistic States', *Speeches* 2: 40.
34. Campbell-Johnson, *Mission with Mountbatten*, p. 50.
35. *Selected Works* II.9: 137.
36. Narayana Rao, *The Emergence of Andhra Pradesh*, pp. 1–78.
37. Ibid., pp. 330–3.
38. Ibid., p. 331.
39. Ibid., p. 332.
40. Ibid., p. 248.
41. Ibid., p. 249.

42. Cf. Gopal, *Biography* 2: 258–9 and Narayana Rao, *The Emergence of Andhra Pradesh*, pp. 249–53.
43. *The Indian Express*, 18 Jan. 1953.
44. Gopal, *Biography* 2: 161.
45. *Letters to Chief Ministers*, vol. 3, pp. 198–9, 200–1.
46. *Letters to Chief Ministers*, vol. 3, pp. 203–13.
47. *SRC*, p. i.
48. Ibid.
49. NMML, Nehru correspondence.
50. *SRC*, p. ii.
51. Gopal, *Biography* 2: 261.
52. The story is told in Gopal, *Biography* 2: 262–71.
53. Cf. Schwartzberg, 'Factors in the Linguistic Reorganization of Indian States', pp. 164–7.
54. Ibid., p. 165.
55. *Speeches* 3: 167–208.
56. Gopal, *Biography* 2: 260.
57. Nehru rarely let pass an opportunity to needle his colleagues on their small-bore obsessions with language boundaries.
58. Lok Sabha, 7 July 1952, 'Linguistic States', *Speeches* 2: 40–1.
59. *Listener*, 6 June 1963.
60. *Speeches* 1: 37.
61. *Speeches* 3: 393–4.
62. *Speeches* 3: 394.
63. *Speeches* 5: 16.
64. 'The Place of English', 8 Sept. 1956, *Speeches* 3: 422.
65. *Speeches* 3: 425.
66. *Selected Works* II.13: 47–50.
67. *Selected Works* II.13: 145–6.
68. *Speeches* 3: 422–6.
69. 24 April 1963, *Speeches* 5: 28.
70. Diwan and Rajput, *Constitution of India*, p. 372.
71. *Letters to Chief Ministers*, vol. 5, p. 579.
72. *Letters to Chief Ministers*, vol. 5, pp. 579–80.
73. J.M. Brown, *Gandhi* (New Haven: Yale University Press, 1989), pp. 372–82.
74. 'In the Surma Valley, In the Valley of the Brahmaputra', 'Escape', 'A Visit to Garhwal', 'The Monsoon Comes to Bombay', 'Flying during the Monsoon', 'A Holiday in a Railway Train', 'Kashmir', *Unity*, pp. 184–240.
75. *National Herald*, 10 Feb. 1956.
76. *India* (London: Kegan Paul, 1888), pp. 5–8.
77. H. Yule and A.C. Burnell (eds), *Hobson-Jobson: A Glossary of*

Colloquial Anglo-Indian Words and Phrases (London: Routledge & Kegan Paul, 1968), *vide Indian*. (This famous linguistic simulacrum of Anglo–Indian life and language was first published in 1886 edited by William Crooke.)

78. *Oxford History of India*, pp. viii–ix.
79. 'Indian Civilization and Regional Cultures: The Two Realities', pp. 22–3.
80. 'Land Systems, Economic Growth and Social Justice: The Permanent Settlement Region', *in* P. Wallace (ed.), *Region and Nation in India* (New Delhi: American Institute of Indian Studies, 1985), p. 183.
81. M.J. Akbar, *Nehru: The Making of India* (New York: Viking, 1988), p. 509.
82. 'The Last Lap of Our Long Journey', *Speeches* 1: 36–41.
83. 'Linguistic States', *Speeches* 2: 35, 39.
84. 'The S.R.C. Report', *Speeches* 3: 168–9.
85. 'Appeal for Goodwill', *Speeches* 3: 187.
86. 'English and the Indian Languages', *Speeches* 4: 53–4.
87. 'Dialogue between Indian Languages', *Speeches* 5: 15.
88. 'Future of English in India', *Speeches* 5: 37.
89. *India: The Most Dangerous Decades*.

Chapter 5

The Private Nehru

The preceding chapter, 'Nehru at the Helm', was concerned with what I shall call 'the public Nehru' — his actions in regard to language as leader of independent India, what he did and thought about language as a matter of public policy in his official capacity as prime minister. But there was also a 'private' Nehru, of course. The 'public Nehru' grew out of the 'private Nehru', as any man's policies once in high office are influenced and formed by his privately held beliefs.

Nehru did a very good job of handling the language crises of his country, in part because he did not react in haste or accede easily to the demands of those who placed language near the top of their political agendas. He always wanted to move slowly into these uncharted waters. He feared the passions that language aroused: they were too much like the passions that religion and racial hatred aroused. They were too much like communal division. They were too much like hate. He doubted a government's ability to legislate advantageously in regard to language.

Nehru thought, in other words, much like a linguist in the modern academic sense of the word. He possessed a sophistication, a subtlety in his beliefs about language, whether consciously formulated or inchoate, that went well beyond his contemporaries. In this chapter I wish to delve deeper into the origins and development of his ideas about language, into his love of language and his fascination with what he could accomplish by means of language.

Nehru worshipped language — perhaps more than was good for a man at the helm of a language-troubled nation. Nehru the literary man did not easily make the leap to Nehru the statesman and politician required to deal with language as a political problem. It requires a strenuous conceptual leap from 'language-as-means' (means of self-expression, for example, or of literary effect) to 'language-as-object' (the object of domestic policy, for example, or of law-making). This was one of the topics of Chapter 2 ('Linguistic Prolegomena', The Linguistic Way). No one could possibly make that leap easily, and Nehru was no exception.

Nehru loved language. He was gifted in his use of language, especially of the written word. With the exception of Winston Churchill no national leader in the English-speaking world in this century has had as fluent and sensitive a way with words as Jawaharlal Nehru, or written as much. It is surely one of the more amusing ironies of the British Raj that English prose would be the poorer had the British not imprisoned Nehru so often and for such long periods, for it was in prison that he had the time and the freedom from distraction to nourish and then sustain his longer literary efforts such as *Glimpses of World History*, his autobiography *(Toward Freedom)*, and *The Discovery of India*.

It is not just that he wrote so well, but the volume of his production that astonishes. Not only essays and books and speeches and political documents, but a continuous stream of letters — letters cajoling, scolding, persuading, all very personal, never formulaic or repetitive. It would have been an impressive literary achievement for anyone; for a man totally immersed in his country's affairs for almost half a century it is extraordinary.

I said that Nehru worshipped language, and this is only a slight exaggeration. Occasionally, in both his earlier and later writings when he touches on language, a lyrical, even moving, quality comes over his prose. It is often not far from poetry. In 1950, after the Constitution had been ratified and the Hindi–English controversy put on the shelf for fifteen years, G.V. Mavalankar, speaker of the Lok Sabha, wrote to Nehru about translating the Constitution from English into Hindi and the other languages recognized officially in Schedule VIII of the Constitution. Nehru wrote back responding to various mundane points Mavalankar had raised; but then he steps back, as it were, from the politics of the thing and writes about language with a grace and perception that come in equal measure from the heart and the intellect:

I fear my views on the language question do not represent what might be called the majority opinion in India and are not very popular [the allusion is to Nehru's lukewarm support of Hindi as national language]. But it has been a matter of sorrow to me that in such a vital question as language we should forget all artistry and all beauty and become the slaves of some paedagogues and grammarians who have no conception of art or beauty or the music of words. Each word is a thing of power with a history behind it, calling up images in one's mind. No word can ultimately be translated with accuracy into any other language. One can only find some synonym for it which does not convey the exact sense. Translation becomes, therefore, if it is to be good, something divorced from the grammarian and the man with a literal mind. Otherwise it is dull and without effect or even real meaning. It seems to me a tragedy that our beautiful languages should be strangled in this way. A language, more than anything, represents the character of a people. Milton wrote long ago: show me the language of a people and I shall tell you who and what they are without knowing more about them. I think this is perfectly true.[1]

The man who wrote this was no ordinary man to whom language was simply a means of communication — a sequence of words arranged in sentences and paragraphs and organized for maximum functionality. There is depth of understanding of language here, reverence even. And let us recall that this man was prime minister of a great country with mountains of problems lying in its path, his days taken up with wearying details of governing. Let us recall, too, how few men of state in the English-speaking world in the twentieth century would be capable of thinking about language as Nehru did, let alone writing about it with such composed elegance. Churchill is one, and there may not be another — and what great irony there is in this! Churchill, the diehard on Indian independence, the icon of British Empire irredentism, joined with Nehru in one thing if virtually nothing else: a surpassing love of language. Whatever else lay between these two great men, devotion to language they had in common, though I should argue that Nehru's understanding of language went well beyond Churchill's, who was a great writer but not a student of language as Nehru was off and on throughout his life. Because of their reciprocal love of language and their shared gift of using it so well, it has always given me secret pleasure to know that in the end, Churchill and Nehru were writing to each other in a spirit of warmth and reconciliation:[2]

30 June 1955

My dear Nehru,

[I] was much touched by what you said. One of the most agreeable memories of my last years in office is our association. At our conferences your contribution was a leading and constructive one, and I always admired your ardent wish for peace and the absence of bitterness in your consideration of the antagonisms that had in the past divided us. Yours is indeed a heavy burden and responsibility, shaping the destiny of your many millions of countrymen, and playing your outstanding part in world affairs. I wish you well in your task. Remember 'The Light of Asia!'

With warm personal regards,

I remain,
Yours sincerely,

Winston S. Churchill

The origins of Churchill's skilful way with language go back to his childhood, and equally it is from Nehru's childhood in Allahabad that we can begin to trace the course of his maturation in language and linguistic understanding.

From First Steps to Maturity

From earliest childhood Nehru had formed the habit of writing long and frequent letters to members of his family. Letter-writing was expected in the Nehru family. The letters from father to son easily comprise several good-sized volumes. Their number goes well beyond even the late Victorian norm, when letter-writing was so compendious an enterprise. The phrase 'late Victorian' is odd and perhaps even jarring in an Indian context, but nonetheless not a wrong description of Motilal Nehru's family and of Motilal himself. I think Motilal would have been secretly pleased to be called 'Victorian', at least prior to his increasing involvement in the freedom movement in the 1920s and in consequence his withdrawal from the world of upper-class Anglo–Indian gentility he had so successfully conquered years before:

A cheerful extrovert, full of the confidence and inner balance that come from self-made success, he set about living the life of an English gentleman. A photograph taken in 1894 shows him attired in English style, his wife, who was from an orthodox family of Lahore, in traditional Kashmiri dress, and his five-year-old son in a sailor suit. It is the kind of photograph a bourgeois English family would have had taken on a visit to Brighton.[3]

The letters between Jawaharlal Nehru and his daughter Indira have been collected in two large volumes totalling over a thousand pages and edited by Sonia Gandhi.[4] Nehru's letters to his younger sister, Krishna Hutheesing, were assembled in a collection published in 1963.[5] There were numerous letters throughout the years to his older sister, Vijayalakshmi Pandit. Beyond the family letters, Nehru wrote book after book during the 1930s and 1940s, all in addition to essays, newspaper articles, political position papers, speeches, and a constant stream of letters to his friends and associates in the freedom movement, and above all to Mahatma Gandhi.

Both the felicity of Jawaharlal Nehru's mature style and the sheer volume of his writings give the impression that writing came easy to him, and so it probably did by his late twenties; but this easy way with words was not his by birthright. He was not a language prodigy — a Macaulay or a John Stuart Mill. Nehru always judged his linguistic ability harshly, but the truth is that he did not as a boy have a facility for learning languages nor did he reveal skill in the intricacies of grammar. 'The great Sanskrit scholar, Pandit Ganganatha Jha, tried, with no noticeable success, to teach Jawaharlal Sanskrit.'[6] Nehru himself wrote many years after the fact:

> The only other tutor [besides Ferdinand T. Brooks] I had at the time was a dear old Pandit [Jha] who was supposed to teach me Hindi and Sanskrit. After many years' effort the Pandit managed to teach me extraordinarily little, so little that I can only measure my pitiful knowledge of Sanskrit with the Latin I learned subsequently at Harrow. The fault no doubt was mine. I am not good at languages, and grammar has had no attraction for me whatever.[7]

However, under the tutelage of Brooks, who harboured a theosophical bent and encouraged his charge's reading interests, the young Nehru's literary horizons broadened: 'I also developed a liking for poetry, a liking which has to some extent endured and survived the many other changes to which I have been subject.'[8] This is more than conventional obeisance towards a youthful enthusiasm for poetry. Nehru is not normally thought of as a poet and did not, so far as I know, write poems in the strict sense, but so often in his prose one detects the soul and sensibility of the poet concealed behind the text. His will and testament is eloquent — and poetic:

> The Ganga, especially, is the river of India, beloved of her people, round which are intertwined her racial memories, her hopes and fears, her songs of triumph, her victories and her defeats. She has been a symbol of India's age-long culture and civilization, ever-changing, ever-flowing, and yet ever the same Ganga . . . Smiling and dancing in the morning sunlight, and dark and gloomy and full of mystery as the evening shadows fall, a narrow, slow and graceful stream in winter and a vast, roaring thing during the monsoon, broad-bosomed almost as the sea . . .[9]

The rhythm and word-sense are those of a poem. A word more here, a word less there, a different arrangement on the printed page, and the result would be a poem in the conventional sense. It has been suggested that Nehru's deeper conception of India is poetic in origin. As the author of a major study of Nehru as writer has said: 'Nehru has a poetic rather intuitive grasp of the invisible thread, the inner unity, which holds together the apparent contradictions [in] the life of her people and prepares the charming wreath that is India.' [10]

He had copied out and kept on his table the lines of Robert Frost:[11]

> The woods are lovely, dark and deep,
> But I have promises to keep,
> And miles to go before I sleep,
> And miles to go before I sleep.

His was the soul of a poet. Nehru had it right in his autobiographical reflections: grammar was not his forte; no question about it. He wrote in a letter to his father, Motilal, from Harrow:

> In the school report the only subject in which I am supposed to be bad in [sic], excepting of course the Old Testament, is Latin. I suppose this means Latin Composition for I did rather well in the translations. Even the form master remarked that I had done well in them. But I am quite hopeless at Latin composition . . . As for the German it was not difficult last term and I was quite easily top of my div . . . I am about 3 divs above many who were as many divs

above me last term in French Prose. So I suppose I must have done well.[12]

Nehru's love of language always remained primarily aesthetic. His talent during the Harrow days lay in style — translation into English — rather than the technical aspects of grammar such as parsing sentences and memorizing endings. That he received such high marks for translation suggests that his feeling for good style in English was formed early. Feeling for style, yes, but not yet ease in the use of language whether written or spoken. One of his earliest written forays into political life, undertaken in 1919 when he was twenty-nine, is described by his biographer as 'rather stilted'.[13]

His speaking ability was also slow to develop. At Cambridge he was 'wincingly shy'[14] and suffered badly from fear of public speaking:

Frequently I went to the Majlis [a society formed by Indian students at Cambridge], but during my three years I hardly spoke there. I could not get over my shyness and diffidence. This same difficulty pursued me in my college debating society, 'The Magpie and Stump', where there was a rule that a member not speaking a whole term had to pay a fine. Often I paid the fine.[15]

In the summer of 1912 he was called to the Bar, and that autumn he returned to India, as he famously put it, 'a bit of a prig with little to commend me'.[16] He was called upon to speak in public first in 1915, though the precise date is not clear; nor is much else clear about his early rhetorical appearances, partly because there were not that many of them, perhaps also because he felt 'that public speeches should not be in English', and he doubted his 'capacity to speak at any length in Hindustani'.[17] Even as late as 1920 he dreaded public speaking, declaring himself 'frightened at the prospect, especially if the speaking was to be done in Hindustani, as it almost always was [at what he called "peasant gatherings"]'.[18] His first appearance on the national stage, at a meeting of the All-India Congress Committee in Bombay in May of 1923, opened to decidedly mixed reviews. 'Simplex' in *The Bombay Chronicle*, 30 May 1923 did not like very much what he saw and heard:

He is no orator, has no tricks of manner of speech. He is sparing in the use of words, but the words are carefully chosen, for which his Harrow and Cambridge education are perhaps responsible. His voice is feeble and low, and he should make an effort to raise it, for it is possible, and should not expect his audience to do the impossible and intensify their power of hearing. When he speaks [however], sincerity exudes from him as perspiration from the body in the month of May in Bombay. He succeeds in impressing his audience probably because he does not consciously try to do so . . . His modesty is a virtue; he should be careful not to convert it into a vice. He is sometimes impatient when the audience does not rise to his intellectual level but let him remember there are hordes of people in this world who have to manage with a lower level of mental equipment than himself and he should sympathize with them.[19]

Did Jawaharlal read that dreadful commentary? ('. . . sincerity exudes from him as perspiration from the body'). If so, it did not derail his political career though it might have a lesser man's. Speech-making would never be an easy thing for him, and, unlike both Winston Churchill and Franklin Delano Roosevelt, Nehru is not remembered for great speeches. The exception that proves the rule was his richly eloquent address on the death of Mahatma Gandhi:

[T]he light has gone out of our lives and there is darkness everywhere . . . The light has gone out, I said, and yet I was wrong. For the light that shone in this country was no ordinary light . . . [T]hat light represented something more than the immediate present, it represented the living, the eternal truths, taking this ancient country to freedom . . . A great disaster is a symbol to us to remember all the big things of life and forget the small things of which we have thought too much. In his death he has reminded us of the big things of life, the living truth, and if we remember that, then it will be well with India . . .

And at the appointed time for cremation . . . people should go to the river or to the sea and offer prayers there. And while we pray, the greatest prayer that we can offer is to take a pledge to dedicate ourselves to the truth, and to the cause for which the great countryman of ours lived and for which he has died. That is the best prayer that we can offer him and his memory. That is the best prayer that we can offer to India and ourselves. JAI HIND.[20]

Though trained to the law, he was in every fibre of his being unsuited for its practice. His father — Motilal was one of India's leading and most successful lawyers — seems not to have noticed this at first. I picture Motilal Nehru somehow less as a person than as a commotion, all activity and movement, and one does not know how much patience he had to 'read' his son's moods. Motilal wrote to his brother, Bansi Dhar Nehru, on 30 January 1910: '[I]f my knowledge of human nature does not deceive me I think he is bound to rise in his father's profession. He has already begun to like it and in deciding that he should devote his energies to the study of law I have only followed the bent of his own mind.'[21] But arguing a case before a jury cannot have been easy for a young man who only shortly before had paid a forfeit rather than summoning the courage to speak in his Cambridge debating society. Writing briefs bored him, and he loathed the tedium attendant upon everyday legal life. 'To go back to the profession of law', he wrote of his state of mind in 1924, 'was . . . out of the question for me. My dislike for it had grown and kept on growing.'[22]

Nehru began to make his way in the public sector, dipping a toe into the political waters initially in Mrs Besant's campaign for Home Rule. He had spoken in public on 20 June 1916 against the Press Act.[23] Later the same year he met Gandhi for the first time at the Lucknow meeting of Congress.[24] It was preordained that he would gravitate into Gandhi's orbit — few there were who did not — and by the early 1920s, in the wake of Jallianwala Bagh, he had become the Mahatma's follower and would remain devoted to him throughout his life, though not without reservations and occasional mutterings.[25]

Motilal was by no means unhappy to see a political interest igniting his son's life — it cannot have given the hyperkinetic Motilal much pleasure to have Jawaharlal mooning about discontentedly in the family law offices — but the father was always more concerned than the son about where the money would come from to support the very comfortable Nehru family lifestyle. The contrasts between father and son were great. Money never much mattered to Jawaharlal.[26] It did to his father. Motilal was the man of affairs, hugely successful and ambitious, gregarious, never introspective; Jawaharlal was then and always would be his exact opposite. Genes account for much but not everything, though Motilal, for what it is worth, wrote English very well. His was a sturdy journeyman's prose, down-to-earth. He had a straightforward way with words, not given to frills and flights of fancy. Motilal's style was a well-crafted instrument for the use of a distinguished, successful lawyer.

The 1920s were for Nehru a time of increasing immersion in the dramatic political movements sweeping over India. My concern here, however, is not with his rise into the political life of his country but with its effect on his language skills. His involvement honed his writing and forensic abilities. Speeches and documents are the daily habit of politics, and so gradually Nehru overcame his shyness and withdrawn ways as he assumed ever greater responsibility in the independence movement. Also, by this time he had become more sensitive to the language issues that were beginning to impinge upon politics. We recall from Chapter 3 that by the early 1920s the Congress had begun to organize itself according to the regional languages, and Gandhi had come out in favour of Hindustani as the national language. All of this had its effect upon Nehru.

In 1923 he was elected chairman of the Allahabad Municipal Board. It was not a very lofty position from which to make and influence policy, but Nehru did his bit where language issues were concerned. On 28 January 1924, on behalf of the Allahabad Municipal Board, he sent the following resolution to the Commissioner, Allahabad Division:

> Sir,
>
> The following resolution was passed by the Board on the 16th January:
>
> Resolved that wherever the word 'vernacular' appears in the byelaws and regulations of the Board it be replaced by the word 'Hindustani' . . .
>
> It was felt by the Board that it was not desirable to use the word 'vernacular' for 'Hindustani' as the ordinary use of that word is for the vulgar tongue or the *patois* and not for a literary language.[27]

The Annual Administration Report for 1923–4, Allahabad Municipal Board Records, 30 May 1924, notes that 'The use of Hindustani is on the increase.'[28] In 1923 Nehru gave a speech in Hindi before the 38th session of the Indian National Congress in Kakinada. The record shows the following exchange: 'Mr

President and Gentlemen, [Cries of "English, English"]; JN: "Please allow me to speak in Hindi".'[29] I wonder whether Nehru recalled that incident when President Radhakrishnan was interrupted during the delivery of the President's Address on 18 February 1963; the latter episode, so similar to the events of Nehru's 1923 speech yet linguistically of reverse polarity, was discussed in Chapter 4 ('Nehru at the Helm', Hindi Versus English).

Writing became an increasingly important part of his life, and by the end of the 1920s he had become a skilled, prolific, and sensitive writer. Imprisoned in Almora Jail in 1934, his wife Kamala nearing the end of her long, sad struggle against tuberculosis, Nehru plunged out of nervous desperation into writing his autobiography. He wrote it between June 1934 and 14 February 1935[30] — a remarkable *tour de force* in itself, given the great length of the manuscript (976 pages). He originally gave it the title *In and Out of Prison*, but upon publication in the spring of 1936, shortly after Kamala's death, by the British publisher The Bodley Head, the title became simply *An Autobiography*; later reprints bore the title *Toward Freedom*. *An Autobiography* became a best-seller, running into repeated editions within weeks.

The reasons for the great success of the book have been set out by Gopal in some detail.[31] Perhaps the paramount reason for its triumph was its portrayal of the psychic toll that colonial status in an empire, even in an empire as fundamentally decent as the one the British ran, took on a sensitive, intelligent, worldly man such as Nehru. Not many of the British or American public would have viewed it from such a perspective, as indeed not many of them would have given much thought to India at all.

Writings by Indians had enjoyed success in the West before, but they were quite different from what Nehru had produced in his autobiography. Quite apart from the portrayals by visitors to the subcontinent of 'exotic' India, its picturesque and profligate maharajahs and otherworldly sadhus, writing by Indians tended toward to the philosophical and religious. At the upper end of the scale were the books and essays of a major intellectual figure such as Radhakrishnan. His was a superior mind, subtle, as familiar with indigenous Indian philosophy as with the great books of the West, and Radhakrishnan became the principal and far and away the most sophisticated explicator of India's ways to

Western audiences.[32] Among Radhakrishnan's books that had appeared prior to 1936, when Nehru's *Autobiography* came out, were: *The Ethics of the Vedanta and its Metaphysical Presuppositions* (1908); *The Philosophy of Rabindranath Tagore* (1918); *The Hindu View of Life* (1927). Rabindranath Tagore was of course known in the West, having been the first Indian to receive the Nobel prize for literature in 1913 for his poetry, which is sensually absorbed by reverence for beauty, by universality, by love of the simple things, and a consciousness of God almost childlike in its conception. And perhaps above all his poetry is profoundly Bengali, which is to say that it conveys a sensibility that is recherché even for other Indians, let alone Westerners. Much of what appeared in the West out of India had what might be called a 'theosophical' aspect: spiritual, mystic, syncretic, profoundly different — Eastern, mysterious, forbidden.

Nehru's *Autobiography* was different. Here was an Indian not writing about the meaning of life and how to gain mastery of the mind over the body, or about the *Gita*'s rejection of dualism. Nehru wrote as an Indian secularist about what it meant, what it felt like, to be ruled in one's own country by other people, and why this was so bad a thing for him and his countrymen. The prose was supple, not hard to follow; 'Western', yet informed by a profoundly Indian sensibility. It was invigorating for educated Western readers. The voice was 'authentic'. Of course by then, the 1930s, percipient observers knew that change was afoot. The days of the British Empire were numbered; it was one centre that 'could not hold', as William Butler Yeats had it in 'The Second Coming'. E.M. Forster in *A Passage to India* had begun to grapple in fiction and correspondence, some two decades earlier, with the reasons why the days of the British in India were numbered. The idea of independence for India was no longer unthinkable, certainly not to American readers, whose ancestors had evicted the British a century and a half before. The Nehru of the *Autobiography* was a passionate nationalist; but his was a nationalism that, unlike German and Italian nationalism of the 1930s, found favour in intellectual circles in Britain and America. It was possible to envision a future in which Indians would be in charge of their destiny, their country. It was the vision of this future, seen through the eyes of an unusual man and expressed in commanding English, that made of Nehru's *Autobiography* a best-seller.

It is, however, primarily the literary qualities of the book on which I wish to focus here rather than its cultural or historical value. It demonstrated conclusively how far Nehru had come in gaining the upper hand over English prose:

The book was characteristic of Jawaharlal. It was honest and introspective. Standing almost outside himself he commented frankly on the society and age in which he lived, on the people he had known, and on his own mental development. The book is not a wooden narrative of events; nor is it, like Gandhi's autobiography, a part of confessional literature . . .

What further helped to gain a wide audience for the *Autobiography* was its prose style. It was a clear, fluent book, 'an excellent substitute for a novel' (*The Statesman* (Calcutta), 10 May 1936), written with terse, nervous elegance and control of phrase and with a wide knowledge of English writing, old and new. It showed a mind of intellectual and moral quality, free of clichéd emotions, but attractively replete with half-tones, subtleties, and diffidences. In later years, Jawaharlal often spoke of the *Autobiography* as having 'dated'. It has, of course, 'dated' in the sense that it deals with a period that is dead. But the book has not lost its freshness as a piece of craftsmanship and as the expression of a sensitive human being.

Moreover, Jawaharlal wrote with detachment. There was self-scrutiny and self-criticism but no self-pity. The hardships he had opted for were taken for granted. The attempt was not at self-justification but at justification to himself. Estranged from his own people by being soaked in the exploiter's culture, he was a mixed-up being, yearning for roots and struggling to work out his own destiny. Tortured by doubt, impressive in his indecision, agonizing over all sides of every question, always asking to what end the long, wearying struggle was directed, he provided a picture of warm and vulnerable humanity . . .

Jawaharlal was not strong in analytic thought and the book provides no profound ideas or philosophy. Such ideas as he had were intellectual impulses rather than logical constructions. Even his Marxism was vague and confused, for his ideology was to a large extent based more on sympathy than on conviction. But he bore witness to a passionate commitment to nationalism, though in no narrow sense, to an awareness of world forces, and to a total personal integrity.[33]

In sum, by the 1930s Nehru had become a man of parts in

whose life writing — language — played a large and important role.[34] By this time he earned an income from his book royalties,[35] the rest deriving from shares given or bequeathed to him by Motilal. The drain on his finances during the 1930s was heavy. There were the medical bills for the treatment of Kamala for tuberculosis, part of which had to be conducted in Switzerland and Germany. There was the expense of maintaining the familial home of Anand Bhawan in Allahabad. Like many a politician-statesman not awash in great inherited wealth — like Disraeli, for example, or Nehru's great adversary Winston Churchill — Jawaharlal Nehru depended on his writing talent to keep the family supplied in the accustomed manner. We have it on the testimony of one witness that later, after Independence, Nehru planned to live by his pen should he be retired from politics.[36]

Jail Time

It is ironic and perverse, and not a little sad, I suppose, but there is no question that part of Nehru's facility with words derived from the time he spent in jail, courtesy his British rulers. There were nine different periods of confinement between 1921 and 1945, totalling about nine years altogether.[37] We have little detail of how he spent his time during his first imprisonment from December 1921 to March 1922.[38] His second stay in prison came on the heels of the first, and though the stay in Lucknow District Jail was relatively brief — from May, 1922 to January, 1923 — it is at this time that Nehru established the programme of reading, self-discipline, and writing that would remain constant during later and much longer confinements. He exercised and minded his body well. He did yoga; his favourite posture was the *shirshasana* — the headstand.[39] He always seems to have had two left thumbs where the *charkha* was concerned but usually managed to accomplish his obligatory daily quantum of spinning in piety to the Mahatma.[40]

However, more to the point, he read voraciously and improved his mind variously.[41] Indeed, the sheer quantity and variety of reading material he took with him into confinement at this time and later is extraordinary. Nehru kept a detailed account of his reading in prison diaries and journals. The exquisite record-keeping of these early days hints at a successful career as accountant, did one not know otherwise. He had 163 books sent to him in jail, of which he notes that he read 55.[42]

He also initiated another favourite jail-time project of improving his Urdu, which though he spoke reasonably well he read and wrote poorly: '[M]uch of my time is taken up with spinning & Urdu. I am not making as much progress in Urdu as I would wish . . .'[43] He read two daily newspapers, *The Leader* and *The Englishman*, until the prison authorities cut them off. He read the *Nation*, the *New Statesman*, and the *Modern Review* as well as the *Qur'an* and the *Bhagavadgita*. He began to interest himself in India's past and in world history, reading Havell's *Aryan Rule in India*, Bryce's *Holy Roman Empire*, the memoirs of the Mughal emperor Babur, and Bernier's account of his travels through India during the Mughal period. Easily noticeable here are the beginnings of what later became the collection of observations he wrote for his daughter, Indira, and published as *Glimpses of World History*.

He once wrote, in reference to Gandhi's detentions, that 'Jail has indeed become a heaven for us, a holy place of pilgrimage since our saintly and beloved leader was sentenced.'[44] There can be no doubting Nehru's sincerity here; but jail was for him a 'heaven' of a different sort too, of a refuge from the petty aggravations and the trivial catastrophes of outside life. His prison diary from Alipore Central Jail, Calcutta, contains this entry for 30 June 1934 after an interview with family members: 'Kamala full of Allahabad trouble & bickerings. I told her to keep out of them. How our people go to pieces at the least provocation. I am glad I am not out . . .'[45] Prison was no bed of roses for Nehru — he hated the lack of privacy more than anything.[46] But prison became a time for reflection, for reading, for writing, an imperfect sanctuary of course, at times indeed almost ridiculous; nevertheless a place and an opportunity to devote himself to a life of the mind not easily sustainable outside prison, where he had to swim upstream against the trials and minor tribulations of everyman's daily life and its wearisome details:

> It is those who work and labour outside who deserve sympathy, not we who laze and eat and sleep. Soon the pleasant autumn days will come and it will be delightful to be under the trees. And what can be pleasanter than freedom from worry? We have no appointments

to keep, no piling up of work with which we cannot cope, no speechifying, no hurry. Time almost ceases to have significance and life moves on like a gently flowing river.[47]

And again, to his father, 15 November 1922:

Indeed I wish I could convince you how well I am here and how pleasantly my days pass. Selfishness would hardly favour a quick discharge but I do feel sorrow when I think of you labouring away and I, basking in the sun, wrapped up in my reading and spinning.[48]

Nehru used his time in prison for writing; but he also took advantage of the enforced idleness to teach himself Hindi and Urdu, especially the latter. In Chapter 3 ('Linguistic States and the National Language', The National Language) I discussed the complex of problems subsumed under the rubric of Hindi–Urdu–Hindustani. To recapitulate here, Hindi and Urdu are variants of the same language which, in its common spoken form, used to be and on occasion still is called Hindustani, a word which fell into a kind of political limbo with the division of what had been north-western India into India and Pakistan. Hindi has 'Hindu' overtones; Urdu has 'Muslim' connotations. Hindi is written in Devanagari script, and Urdu is written in a script derived from Persian, which is itself originally derived from Arabic script. Learned variants of Hindi go to Sanskrit for inspiration and enrichment of vocabulary, learned variants of Urdu to Persian and Arabic. Hindi and Urdu diverge from each other cumulatively, mostly in vocabulary, as one moves upward from the bazaar to the higher reaches of literature, and in the highest — and therefore most artificial — literary forms the two languages can be mutually incomprehensible. Spoken Hindustani Nehru knew from childhood and had grown up with it in the Allahabad household. As a boy he wrote postcards to his mother in Hindi in Devanagari script.[49] Almost always Nehru used the term 'Urdu' or 'Hindustani' rather than 'Hindi' to denote his cradle language.

As I stated earlier, he embarked on a programme to improve his knowledge of Urdu during his very first imprisonment in Lucknow District Jail in 1922, where he had been interned for his part in the disorders following Jallianwala Bagh.[50] Of the books he read in jail in 1922–3, most are in English, but there are several Hindi and Urdu titles and also a Hindustani–English dictionary.[51] He wrote to his father at this time: 'I am learning Urdu these days, and hope to write to you soon in Urdu. Please send me an Urdu dictionary.'[52] Written Urdu was always a chore for Nehru from early on,[53] and it never grew easy.

His jail-time interest in improving his Urdu, rather than in learning say Sanskrit or French or German, better foretells his later staunch advocacy of Urdu after he had become prime minister. The 'public' Nehru is always a reflection of the 'private' Nehru. Urdu was to Nehru a symbol of tolerance of the Muslim minority; an icon of the secular India which was Nehru's greatest aspiration.

Language continued to be a major preoccupation of Nehru's while imprisoned during the Second World War in Ahmadnagar Fort. He resumed his study of Urdu, this time with Maulana Azad as his instructor. Nehru liked Azad, who was his favourite Urdu teacher in prison, in any case for his general roundedness of character: 'He was a strange mixture of mediaeval scholasticism, eighteenth-century rationalism, and the modern outlook.'[54] Azad was not known for his sense of humour, but he managed to put up with some fond teasing from his comrade-in-jail Jawaharlal: '[A]bul Kalam Azad has especially cultivated a look of venerable age to give a suitable background to his great learning.'[55] He admired Azad's chaste Urdu — 'chaste' being for some reason the adjective of choice of the subcontinent for describing elegant, spruce Urdu:

> Abul Kalam Azad spoke in a new language to them [Indian Muslims] in his weekly *Al-Hilal*. It was not only a new language in thought and approach; even its texture was different, for Azad's style was tense and virile, though sometimes a little difficult because of its Persian background. He used new phrases for new ideas and was a definite influence in giving shape to the Urdu language as it is today.[56]

His diaries and letters from Ahmadnagar Fort Prison during wartime, especially those letters to his daughter Indira between 7 May 1943 and 18 February 1944, are sprinkled with quotations of mostly Urdu poetry written both in Urdu and Hindi in their respective scripts. Almost every second letter has quotations from the Urdu of Ghalib, Mir, Hali, Wazir of Lucknow, or Zauq.[57]

Language was always uppermost in his mind in jail. In the preface to *The Discovery of India*, written in prison in Ahmadnagar Fort in 1944, it is language to which he turns in the second paragraph in characterizing his companions in prison:

Nearly all the principal living Indian languages, as well as the classical languages which have powerfully influenced India in the past and present, were represented, and the standard was often that of high scholarship. Among the classical languages were Sanskrit and Pali, Arabic and Persian; the modern languages were [Hindi], Urdu, Bengali, Gujarati, Marathi, Telugu, Sindhi, and Oriya.[58]

What an extraordinary statement for its time and place! When one speculates on everything else Nehru might have said in this preface — about the British, about Gandhi, about the War, about communal tensions, about the deadening effect of prison life — it becomes quite remarkable that it is *language* that is near the front of his mind. I cannot think of another Indian leader — or for that matter, any political leader at any time, any place — who would have devoted the major part of the preface to such a book, written in prison, to language.

It is the more remarkable because this, his last stay in a British prison, was not only very long but not very pleasant. Nehru's imprisonment in Ahmadnagar was his longest — 1,040 days, almost three years, from 9 August 1942 to 15 June 1945.[59] That is a very long time to be incarcerated even for someone to whom jail was not abhorrent. His closest fellow inmates were comrades from the freedom movement, who had, as Gopal says, 'in common only dedication to a common cause and acceptance of Gandhi's leadership . . . and by the time of their release some were hardly on speaking terms.'[60] Quite aside from the natural frictions that came of living in close quarters with other people, no matter how agreeable in disposition and personal habits they may have been, Nehru occasionally vented secret feelings quite bitter and out-of-character for him, often about the British:

I had always looked forward in the past to a visit to England, because I have many friends there and old memories draw me. But now I found that there was no such desire and the idea was distasteful. I wanted to keep as far away from England as possible, and I had no wish even to discuss India's problems with Englishmen.[61]

He wrote his sister Vijayalakshmi Pandit on 23 October 1944:

I do not fancy being treated like a wild beast in a cage with occasional rope allowed so that I can move a few feet if I behave myself. I dislike being the plaything of others and to have my movements and my emotional life regulated by others. Where force prevents me from acting as I wish, I have to accept it, but I prefer to retain such freedom of mind and action as I possess. If it has been thought fit and proper to prevent us from seeing even those one cares for during these 2 ¼ years or so, well and good; anyway perforce I had to adapt myself to it. But I see no reason why I should adapt myself to all the new vagaries of those who keep us in prison or stabilize myself in new positions.[62]

And to his younger sister, Krishna Hutheesing, he wrote on 3 October 1944:

[O]f the men we see the range is limited and I fear we grow less and less fresh to each other. And women? It struck me as an odd and arresting fact that for nearly 26 months — for 785 days to be exact — I had not seen a woman even from a distance. Previously it was not so for even in prison we had interviews occasionally. And I began to wonder — what are women like? How do they look — how do they talk and sit and walk?[63]

There is a soddenness of spirit that pervades this period of wartime imprisonment. Nehru's pitiful journal entries speak volumes:[64]

15 January 1943	I have been keeping unwell.
30 January 1943	Sowed carnation seeds in box. New canvas shoes.
12 April 1943	New canvas shoes.
13 April 1943	Rain — rain — continuous rain! The monsoon.
5 May 1944	The cat tragedy! Poor Chando hit inadvertently over head by cook — concussion of the brain. Hovering between life and death.
14 May 1944	Cat Chando died in hospital.
20 June 1944	New canvas shoes.
26 June 1944	My blood pressure today 125 Systolic; 83 Diastolic; 42 Pulse pressure.

Nehru's salvation lay in intellectual work, as it had before during his imprisonments. He threw himself into the writing of *The Discovery of India*. On 13 April 1944, after reading material had been restored to the prisoners, he once again took up the book he had started in jail in Dehra Dun in 1941. It was completed a short five months later, on 7 September 1944. The manuscript ran to a thousand handwritten pages.

The Discovery of India, described by Gopal as 'a great jumble of a book which bears the marks of haste and tension',[65] badly needed the services of a ruthless copy-editor. It is very long and rambling, full of long quotations and poorly baked ideas:

> So, in an astonishingly narrow nationalist tradition, he put together a version of India's cultural history derived from secondary sources and studded with testimonials from European observers. It was not just the hurry and the atmosphere in which the book was written but the thesis itself which led to woolly writing. All his ideas about race, for example, make little sense. 'We are an old race, or rather an odd mixture of many races, and our racial memories go back to the dawn of history' —just one of many meaningless sentences of which Jawaharlal himself would later have been ashamed . . . Yet, if the book is lacking in analysis, elegance and clear thinking, it had a purpose. It sought to portray an emotional comprehension of Indian nationalism and to stress the necessity of revitalizing the Indian people . . . *The Discovery of India*, written in the dark years of Indian nationalism, carried not a precise, scientific argument but a buoyant message.[66]

However, there are passages here of great lyricism, especially in the early portion of this very large book:

> Time seems to change its nature in prison. The present hardly exists, for there is an absence of feeling and sensation which might separate it from the dead past. Even news of the active, living and dying world outside has a certain dreamlike unreality, an immobility and an unchangeableness as of the past. The outer objective time ceases to be, the inner and subjective sense remains but at a lower level, except when thought pulls it out of the present and experiences a kind of reality in the past or in the future. We live, as Auguste Comte said, dead men's lives, encased in our pasts, but this is especially so in prison where we try to find some sustenance for our starved and locked-up emotions in memory of the past or fancies of the future.
>
> There is a stillness and everlastingness about the past; it changes not and has a touch of eternity, like a painted picture of a statue in bronze or marble. Unaffected by the storms and upheavals of the present, it maintains its dignity and repose and tempts the troubled

spirit and the tortured mind to seek shelter in its vaulted catacombs. There is peace there and security, and one may even sense a spiritual quality.[67]

Not bad, not bad at all for a man who only a short time before had been writing of carnation seeds, canvas shoes, rain, and his blood pressure.

Influences

John Gunther, the American journalist whose travel-and-area books were hugely popular in the 1930s and 1940s, spent time with Nehru in the late 1930s. In his book *Inside Asia* Gunther logs the books that Nehru took with him when he went on holiday in the Himalayas: Aldous Huxley, *Ends and Means*; Bertrand Russell, *Which Way to Peace*; John Dewey, *The Quest for Certainty*; Edward Thompson, *Life of Lord Metcalfe*; J.R. Firth, *The Tongues of Man* ('a book on comparative philology', Nehru noted); Hyman Levy, *A Philosophy for a Modern Man*.[68] Most of this reading material is unsurprising for a well-educated man of the world in that period. However, the name J.R. Firth will not be known to the average reader. John Rupert Firth (1890–1960) was among the leading linguistic theoreticians, arguably *the* leading theoretician, in England during the 1940s and 1950s, and *The Tongues of Man*, published in 1937, was his major popular work, a general introduction to the modern science of linguistics. Firth had also worked in India, and to the end of his days maintained a keen interest in Indian matters.[69] Gunther had got his information by asking Nehru to fill out a questionnaire: what magazines he subscribed to, who his closest friends were, what books he was reading at the time. Nehru replied in a letter dated 16 March 1938 from Khali. Among his answers to Gunther's question 'What books do I read?' was 'J.R. Firth: *The Tongues of Man* (a book on the development and use of language) and a number of pamphlets, etc.'[70]

The knowledge that Nehru had read Firth is useful in exploring the origins of Nehru's knowledge of linguistics. Firth's *The Tongues of Man* was quite slender and easy to read, and I shall cite later in this chapter a specific phrase Nehru used that is almost certainly 'Firthian'. And this carries some weight in inferring a

'Firthian' intellectual influence on Nehru, for Firth, a charismatic figure in the British linguistic world, was known for the vigour of his assertions, as Braj Kachru, who was his student, points out.[71]

What has impressed me from the beginning of my study of Nehru and language was not only how important language was to him, or how often he thought about it, but how preternaturally advanced he was in his understanding of so many rather technical aspects of language. There is not a great deal in, for example, his essay 'The Question of Language' which he wrote in 1937,[72] that a modern linguist would feel obliged to correct on technical grounds. This essay, 'The Question of Language', is slightly 'off key' for reasons I shall discuss in Chapter 6 ('Nehru's Essays on Language'), but it is linguistically sound. Likewise in *The Discovery of India*, which has extensive references to language and discussions of many linguistic issues contemporary and historical, there are few ideas so seriously wrong or so imperfectly framed that a modern-day linguist would have to drastically reorganize. This is noteworthy primarily because even smart people are prepared to believe every form of rot when it comes to language.[73] I cannot recall in all my reading of Nehru a single stupid thing he wrote about language.

Otherwise intelligent men and women still can be found who believe one or two or all of the following assertions: that there are 'primitive' languages with only a few thousand words; that race and language have something to do with one another; that dolphins possess language in the way humans possess language; that some languages are intrinsically 'better' than other languages; that some languages are, objectively, 'prettier' than other languages; that children would not learn to speak their language if their parents did not teach them. Not a single one of these assertions is true; not one! But the educated ranks of the world are populated by intelligent, well-meaning, decent people who believe such things. This is one of the reasons why linguists continue to plow their lonely furrow, hoping to bring the same kind of enlightenment to the public understanding of language that others have brought in unrelated areas of human activity such as sex, mental illness, and alcoholism.

It is not only in his writings about specifically language issues that Nehru shows a kind of detailed, specialized knowledge —

a linguistic sophistication or at the very least an inborn receptivity for the linguistic way of regarding language. It is in his general *laissez-faire* approach to language as a public, political problem: live and let live. I am thinking especially of his stand on the question of the national language (Chapter 3, 'Linguistic States and the National Language'). His position, on which he never faltered, was that language and language policies cannot and should not be forced down a people's throat. It might be said 'Of course, how obvious; how could it be otherwise?', but in point of fact the history of language planning in multilingual countries that have emerged from colonial rule teaches us that this reasonable point of view is anything but a commonplace (cf. Ch. 2, 'Linguistic Prolegomena'). Most people believe that if legislatures pass laws relating to language, the populace will simply change its linguistic behaviour to accord with the new laws. That is not the way it works. Democratic governments are very largely powerless to effect major changes in linguistic attitudes and habits.

I would not expect Jawaharlal Nehru to have agreed with all that I say here and in Chapter 2 regarding the powerlessness of governments in free societies to enforce language policy choices and to impose national languages over opposition, but he would have enthusiastically agreed that language usage cannot be coerced in a free society; a point that is virtually axiomatic in modern linguistics. It requires a very heavy hand, to put it mildly, to change people's language habits significantly if they themselves see no reason to change.

There is no way to know whether Nehru was encouraged in his 'hands-off' view of language policy by his reading of Firth, and I rather doubt that he 'got it' from anywhere except perhaps from his reading of Lenin in the late 1920s — a point I shall return to shortly. It is so at one with everything else Nehru believed that one need not posit any direct influence on him to account for it. It is but a short step from being a secularist in religion to being a non-dogmatist in language. At least some notions and terms, however, Nehru did almost certainly get from Firth. When, for example, Nehru refers to Chinese as a 'picture language', as he does in a Lok Sabha speech in 1963,[74] there is no doubt in my mind that he had acquired this way of putting it from Firth, who had used the same word, 'picture', to describe Chinese writing.[75]

This is a clever and plastic description of the Chinese writing system, in which individual symbols stand for words rather than sounds or syllables, but it is not the standard technical term that linguists use in describing Chinese — in linguistic terminology Chinese is said to have a 'logographic' writing system, and a layman would know nothing about Chinese script.

In Chapter 4 ('Nehru at the Helm') I argued at some length that the unity of India was the controlling reason for Nehru's innate suspicions about the language movements. A somewhat ironic consequence of his unyielding stand for unity was his steadfast defence of Urdu. I say 'somewhat ironic' because the greatest enemy of unity in India has always been communalism, and understandably the form of communalism that grieved him most sorely was Hindu–Muslim antagonism. He thought nothing of scolding Hindu politicians for their near-sightedness and inability to rise above themselves. One exchange from parliamentary debate is illuminating (and amusing). It is from a speech during debate on the Report of the States Reorganization Commission, Lok Sabha, 21 December 1955:

> [NEHRU]: Now take two of the major problems — the question of Bombay and the Punjab.
> AN HON. MEMBER: Bihar also.
> SHRI JAWAHARLAL NEHRU: With the greatest respect for our friends in Bihar and Bengal and Orissa, I would say that nothing is more unimportant than their problem . . . What does it matter if a patch of Bihar goes this way and a patch of Bengal or Orissa goes the other way?[76]

One cannot but be beguiled by the image of Nehru flinging about 'patches' of Bihar, Bengal, and Orissa this way and that, the better to show his contempt for the political opposition on linguistic states. This is Nehru the modern-day Mughal at his most autocratic.

Imperious as he was prepared to be to 'AN HON. MEMBER' of the (Hindu) opposition, he was never guilty of 'insensitivity' towards the Muslims. He never let pass an opportunity to speak out for Urdu:

1937, 'The Question of Language':

> We have had during recent months a revival of the old controversy between Hindi and Urdu . . . A subject eminently suited

for calm and scholarly consideration and academic debate has been dragged down to the level of the market-place, and communal passions have centred round it.[77]

21 December 1955, Lok Sabha:

Quite frankly, I do not understand the way some people are afraid of the Urdu language. I am proud to speak Urdu and I hope to continue to speak Urdu. I just do not understand why in any State in India people should consider Urdu a foreign language or something which invades their own domain. Urdu is a language mentioned in our Constitution. I object to any narrow-mindedness in regard to Urdu.[78]

24 April 1963, Lok Sabha:

Language is something bigger than offices and clerks. I shall give you an example. Take Urdu. I think it may broadly be said that no great encouragement has been given to Urdu and yet, such is the vitality of this language that today Urdu is growing faster than many other national languages of India . . . [I]t is extraordinary how fast Urdu has grown. This is because Urdu is a dynamic language.

I think that if Hindi is really to grow very fast, it should ally itself with Urdu . . . It will get vitality from Urdu while retaining its own genius and nature. Urdu is vital.[79]

That Nehru regarded his own mother tongue as Urdu — though he ordinarily wrote it in Devanagari script rather than the Perso–Arabic script traditional to Urdu — had nothing to do with his unflagging defence of Urdu which, after all, gained him no support except among Muslims in the Congress Party: 'Jinnah had also demanded that Urdu be made the national language. While Nehru was opposed, his views on the language question were closer to Jinnah's than to most Congressmen's.'[80]

I do not, as I say, believe that Nehru's untiring defence of Urdu had anything to do with the role of Urdu in his own life. On the contrary. I think he would have gone as much out of the way to defend Urdu if his childhood language had been Bengali, Oriya, or Kannada. It was a question of preserving the unity of India and of assuring the Muslims who had remained in India after Partition that India was their home in every possible sense of the word: 'In the long run, the most significant aspect to Nehru of the language problem, even more important than the role of Hindi or English, was the future of Urdu, for it was tied up with the place of the Muslim minority in India.'[81]

Nehru was always proud of his own family's legacy of Persian and Urdu from their Kashmiri past:

[I]t is true that my father had grown up in an Indo-Persian cultural atmosphere, which was the legacy of north India of the old Delhi court, and of which, even in these degenerate days, Delhi and Lucknow are the two chief centres. Kashmiri Brahmans had a remarkable capacity for adaptation, and coming down to the Indian plains and finding that this Indo-Persian culture was predominant at the time, they took to it, and produced a number of fine scholars in Persian and Urdu.[82]

I note in passing the irony of Jinnah's support for Urdu as the national language. English was Jinnah's language. He spoke no Urdu beyond the ritual greeting or two that politicians were wont to work into their speeches, and he read no Urdu whatsoever. Politics, it is said, make strange bedfellows. Language and politics, in language-sensitive countries, create even stranger alliances.

I do not care to overplay the argument here of 'influences' that may have contributed to Nehru's instinct for assuming positions on language issues so close to those that modern linguists adopt. After all, he was an intelligent, well-educated man who read deeply and widely throughout his life. Books played an important part in his life. The overwhelming impression received from an intimate reading of Nehru's writings and speeches was how much language *mattered* to him. This is particularly evident in the letters he wrote to his daughter Indira, the future prime minister. If language mattered a great deal to him, it mattered also that Indira should acquire as many languages as possible, Indian and non-Indian, during her school and university years.

He began writing to her regularly when she was about five years old. At first there were postcards, mostly in Hindi, from 17 October 1922, off and on, down to 23 August 1928.[83] After she had reached her teens and had learnt French and German in Europe, he freely sprinkled foreign phrases and long stretches of French poetry in letters such as that of 23 March 1932 from Bareilly District Jail.[84] Typical salutations in his letters to his daughter were 'Indu, *bien aimée*' and 'Indu, *carissima mia*'.

His concern for her language development is in evidence throughout the letters from the mid-1930s, when he was in various jails and she was pursuing her schooling in Santiniketan, Rabindranath Tagore's ashram near Calcutta, in Europe, and subsequently at Somerville College, Oxford. From Alipore Jail, 15 June 1934, to 'Dear Indu':

I am sending you a prospectus of Santiniketan. This will give you a great deal of information. On p. 13 the subjects are given. Among the compulsory subjects, I think, you should choose Hindi (as an Indian language) and French (as a modern language).[85]

From Almora District Jail, 4 February 1935, to Indira in Santiniketan:

Languages are also desirable and languages are tricky things after a certain age. You will find it far easier to learn a new language now than say five years later. As one grows the capacity for learning languages weakens tremendously. The best time of course is babyhood. As Miss Spiegel (I refuse to call her by any other name. Why should people's names be changed?) is a good linguist, take advantage of this. I do not know what languages you are taking at present. Of the Indian languages I understand you are taking up Bengali and Hindi. French of course you are taking and presumably English literature. Are you taking German also?[86]

Indira, devoted and dutiful daughter that she was, never complained to her father in the face of these onslaughts of linguistic advice, though it would have taken a heart of stone to blame her if she had fussed a bit: '. . . Bengali and Hindi . . . French of course . . . English literature. Are you taking German also?'

In Almora Jail in 1935 Nehru devoted himself for a time to reading extensively and even writing in Hindi, as I shall discuss in Chapter 6, and the letters from this period show it. 'Darling Indu', 4 April 1935:

You ask me about your reading Hindi literature. Why, of course you should do so. Hindi poetry is very beautiful but I find it a little monotonous and it seems to deal with a few limited topics. Old Hindi literature is good and it is not only desirable but necessary that we should know it. Only then can we build on it and develop it and make it absorb modern ideas. My own limited knowledge of that literature has been a great drawback to me . . .

I am inclined to agree with the U.P. boys at Santiniketan about the Hindi translation of the *Glimpses [of World History]*. There are some very obvious howlers in it . . . I hesitate to interfere as I am no scholar of Hindi.[87]

By the end of the summer of 1935 Indira had gone to Europe for further schooling. Still detained in Almora, her father wrote: 'I am very happy to learn of your progress in the German language. Evidently you have a linguistic bent which certainly you have not inherited from your father.'[88] But Hindi, English, Bengali, French, and German were not enough. On 14 August 1935 he wrote: '[Y]ou should try to improve your knowledge of languages, French, German, and if possible Russian.'[89]

After a visit to Mathura he wrote her on 2 December 1939 from Anand Bhawan in Allahabad:

I regretted nothing so much in Muttra [Mathura] as my ignorance of Braj Bhasha [the dialect of Hindi in the Mathura area]. I felt how cut off I was from the life of the people and the roots of their culture and how much I had missed because of this. And straightaway I resolved that when I have to put up with my next period of enforced retirement I shall devote myself to the study of Hindi and Urdu literature. After all, it is the language that is the closest bond between people and is the mirror where one sees their minds and hearts.[90]

The Urdu theme in his correspondence with his daughter grew stronger during wartime imprisonment, mirroring the growth of Nehru's own interest in learning Urdu better, especially written Urdu. I mentioned earlier that he inserted couplets of classical Urdu poetry regularly in his letters to her from Ahmadnagar Fort Prison. Even earlier, in Dehra Dun District Jail, he had written her on 29 June 1941: 'I am writing today to Dr Zakir Husain of the Jamia Millia of Delhi to send you some elementary books in Urdu . . . Apart from Urdu and Hindi, it might be worthwhile for you to start on a voyage of discovery of India.'[91]

In the context of the extremely large volume of correspondence with his daughter — Sonia Gandhi's compilation of letters between them makes up two very large volumes — I would not like to leave the impression that language was Nehru's principal preoccupation. These letters were extremely wide-ranging, and it would seem that a large number of them, especially the early ones, were written with an eye on publication, as indeed they were published in a narrative form in *Glimpses of World History* (1934) and the earlier *Letters from a Father to his Daughter* (1929). Language was but one of the many topics Nehru returned to repeatedly in the correspondence with Indira. Nevertheless, I remain impressed by his concern with languages and language issues over decades of voluminous correspondence. He writes about language and language history, about the importance of learning languages, about Sanskrit and its place in Indian history. He often reproaches himself for not having learnt more languages and having learnt them better. He writes of Hindi and Hindustani and Urdu. The excerpts I have given above are only a small sample from the letters he wrote his daughter.

THE LARGER PICTURE

In Chapter 4 ('Nehru at the Helm') I argued that Nehru's reluctance to rush into linguistic battle was fuelled overwhelmingly by his passionate determination to oppose anything that would weaken India's unity. There was in this passionate conviction something almost theological, so firmly did he hold to it through rough and smooth waters alike.

If it was one kind of belief — belief in the unity of India — that stayed Nehru's hand in yielding forthrightly and without delaying tactics to the demands for linguistic states; it was another kind of belief that made him peculiarly ill-equipped to regard any kind of language or religious dispute as anything more serious than a childish tantrum. I am referring to his belief in rationalism and in its handmaiden, science.

Nehru was nothing if not a thoroughgoing rationalist. There was in him no yielding to the dark side, to the passions of unreason, to cynicism. From reason was derived his belief in science, not only as the means to progress but more especially in the sense, common during most of his lifetime in English and American intellectual circles, that science was the antidote to reactionary beliefs such as religion, narrow nationalism, and tribalism. 'My early approach to life's problems had been more or less scientific, with something of the easy optimism of the science of the nineteenth and early twentieth century';[92] 'Who indeed can afford to ignore science today? At every turn we have to seek its aid and the whole fabric of the world today is of its making';[93]

'[T]he literature of science is, indeed, his favourite reading — almost a passion with him. In part this must be traced to his education at Cambridge . . .'[94] 'Religion', said Nehru, 'though it has undoubtedly brought comfort to innumerable human beings and stabilized society by its values, has checked the tendency to change and progress inherent in human society.'[95]

Science was always one of the strongest motifs in Nehru's intellectual life. He liked to write about science and work it into his speeches, even as early as the 1930s;[96] and after he became prime minister he missed few opportunities to speak out on science and its promise for the upliftment of India. Einstein's theory of relativity fascinated him: in one passage in *The Discovery of India* his mind jumps from Sir James Jeans to the teachings of the Upanishads, from the 'transcendent and the immanent' to Einstein and the modern meaning of religion, with a diversionary footnote on Vivekananda along the way.[97] There is a certain amount of dilettantism here, the 'Two Cultures' attraction of the 'mysteries' of science for the humanist, but Nehru was more than a dilettante in his understanding of science, which had come from very wide reading.[98] It is all very much of a piece, Nehru's belief in science, the rule of reason, and Indian history. Science was for Jawaharlal Nehru the light of hope that beckoned him throughout his life. In a letter of 27 June 1933 from Dehra Dun Jail to his daughter, Indira, he wrote: 'If more people had a scientific training, there would be far less of unreason and bigotry and conflict in the world.'[99] Those of us who have grown up in the post-Hiroshima, post-Auschwitz world can be forgiven for having drifted from this pious faith in the benevolence of science, but in this belief Nehru was a member of a much larger fraternity of progressive thinkers of the intellectual community prior to the Second World War.

His belief in reason and rationality lies at the heart not of what Nehru did about language but why he wished to do so little about it once he came to power. He had seen what religion could do to India in the terrible scenes of violence associated with Partition. He looked upon religion as a force of darkness, an atavistic agent of reaction — irrational, unscientific. Nothing in Nehru's background prepared him for the shocking things that men did to one another in the name of religion, nothing in his peaceful, mildly secular upper-class upbringing in Allahabad, nothing in his genteel education at Harrow or Cambridge where he was, as he said, 'vaguely attracted to the Fabians and socialistic ideas',[100] nothing in the *ahimsa* and *satyagraha* that he had absorbed from Gandhi. He was, in part because of the novelty of the thing, still less prepared for the divisiveness caused by language, which must have struck him as an even more superficial and questionable core loyalty than religion.

Language as a political issue, like religion, belonged for Nehru to the pre-rational impulses. They engendered passion, pointless bickering, deflection from higher purpose. In his speech of 8 November 1948 before the Constituent Assembly on the language legislation proposed for the new Constitution, where Nehru argued in favour of delaying discussion of the vexed language issues until other, more important problems had been resolved, he says:

> There are various problems, important problems, on which there is little controversy and we pass them with unanimity. There are other problems, important no doubt, possibly of a lesser importance, on which we spend a great deal of time and energy and passion also, and do not arrive at agreements in the spirit with which we should arrive at agreements . . . It [the question of linguistic provinces] is eminently a question which should be settled in an atmosphere of goodwill and calm and by scholarly discussion of the various factors of the case. I find, unfortunately, that it has raised a considerable degree of heat and passion, and when heat and passion are there, the mind is clouded . . .
>
> The same argument, if I may say so, applies to the question of [the national] language . . . Language is and has been a vital factor in an individual's and a nation's life . . . A language ultimately grows from the people; it is seldom that it can be imposed . . . I would beg this House to consider the fact and to realize, if it agrees with me, that the surest way of developing a natural all-India language is not so much to pass resolutions and laws on the subject, but to work to that end in other ways.[101]

Heat, passion, 'the mind is clouded'; it is not rational to get lost in language controversies; discussion of these matters should be deferred until there is 'goodwill and calm'. This statement is pure Nehru, ever the rationalist. Few things in life mattered as much to Nehru as clear thinking.[102]

This speech early in his administration before the Constituent Assembly sounds themes that occurred over and over again in his thinking about language and its role in national life. There is in it first of all his absolutely correct and commonsensical insistence that a language cannot be forced on people against their will in a free society — and to do so is dangerous and destabilizing even in totalitarian societies. It cannot be done; to attempt to do so is to ignite the passions and invite trouble. Here too are intimations of his lifelong perplexity that language could arouse such 'heat and passion' among his countrymen, his barely concealed vexation that other people could not see as clearly as he did that language was not particularly important alongside the far graver challenges facing the country. Nehru knew a good deal about the Irish and Turkish histories described in Chapter 2.[103] From Ireland he would have learnt that government wishes do not make things come true; certainly they do not make a language grow and prosper. From Turkey he learnt how hard a man he would have to become to accomplish what Mustafa Kemal had accomplished in the way of radical language reforms. It cannot have been an enticing prospect for Nehru.

I have spoken of Nehru's commitment to rationalism and science as being largely responsible for his utter inability to understand the affect and strength of forces such as language and religion in free India. There is a third element in his belief system which has a bearing on his attitude to language, and that is socialism.

Rationalism, science, and socialism were for Nehru the trivium that had replaced the mediaeval lower division consisting of grammar, rhetoric, and logic. A thoroughgoing commitment to rationalism was the central belief. Nehru's commitment to socialism — though never unquestioning or doctrinaire — grew in turn out of his belief in the rule of reason and the conviction that science provided the key to economic progress; over and above this, he believed that economic disputes were basically the cause of domestic miseries. Social progress, all forms of social progress — tolerance, secular thinking, liberation from language chauvinism — would follow from economic progress. Socialism, for Nehru the sum of rationalism and science, was as much the application of moral reasoning to the distribution of economic goods as it was doctrine.

Nehru had acquired his belief in socialism during his schoolboy and student days in England from the writings of thinkers such as George Bernard Shaw, H.G. Wells, and Sidney and Beatrice Webb. It was the soft, benign British strain of socialism that goes under the name of 'Fabianism'. Fabianism was a very different sort of socialism from the sharper versions of Marxism that evolved on the Continent and clashed so violently on the Republican side during the Spanish Civil War. 'A vague, confused socialism was already part of the atmosphere of India' when he returned from his trip to the Continent in 1927. 'Marxian theory was influencing them [Indian socialists] increasingly.'[104] Nehru's socialism always had something of the London School of Economics about it.[105]

His socialism could be called by other names such as fairness, hope, and rationalism, and part of it too was a naïve faith in the Soviet way:

> I am convinced that the only key to the solution of the world's problems and of India's problems lies in socialism, and, when I use this word, I do so not in a vague humanitarian way but in the scientific, economic sense. Socialism is, however, something even more than an economic doctrine; it is a philosophy of life, and as such also it appeals to me . . . If the future is full of hope, it is largely because of Soviet Russia and what it has done . . .
>
> Socialism is thus for me not merely an economic doctrine which I favour; it is a vital creed which I hold with all my head and heart.[106]

Nehru's socialism was not creed but ethos; it had no hard edges:

> The Marxian philosophy appeals to me in a broad sense and helps me to understand the processes of history. I am far from being an orthodox Marxist, nor does any other orthodoxy appeal to me. But I am convinced that the old Liberal approach in England or elsewhere is no longer valid. *Laissez-faire* is dead, and unless far-reaching changes are made with reasonable speed, disaster awaits us, whether we live in England or India. Today the community has to be organized in order to establish social and economic justice. This organization is possible on the Fascist basis, but this does not bring justice or equality, and is essentially unsound. The only other way is the Socialist way.[107]

It was all so much simpler in the 1940s, when human progress and economic progress seemed so much more interdependent. Nehru saw the violence of Partition as economically determined:

> If I may draw on my Socialist background, what is happening now is to a large extent an upheaval in the lower middle classes . . . Undoubtedly there has been a communal trend in what has happened, but the trend now is away from killings and towards increased looting . . . In a sense this is worse, but in another way it is a hopeful sign. It is something we can deal with by persuasion or force, and that is the way we must deal with it.[108]

He never passed up an opportunity in the early days of Independence to preach the economic gospel — to stress the overriding need for economic progress and greater production before the other problems facing India could be tackled.[109] Economic development — five-year plans, hydroelectric power schemes — became his refuge from the unredeeming factionalism of the domestic scene. 'It was in taking these first steps in dealing with the economic problem, which to his mind was more vital than anything else, that Nehru recovered a little of his old enthusiasm [in the summer of 1948].'[110] In a 1955 radio broadcast to the nation, the major purpose of which was supposed to be the presentation of Nehru's position on the *States Reorganization Commission Report* recommending linguistic states, Nehru actually devotes most of the speech to the recent floods and their disruption of development.[111] It is not difficult to discern where his heart *really* lay.

Nehru basically placed his faith in economic progress as the ultimate solution to communal fracas of every shape and form.[112] Naturally then as a socialist Nehru hoped to delay discussion of the linguistic proposals, certain to be divisive, bitter, and unrewarding, until greater economic progress had been made and given a chance to work its magic: *primum vivere deinde philosophari*. Economics was always at the head of Nehru's plans. Just prior to Independence, 'Mountbatten next asked what Nehru thought was the biggest single problem facing India today, and he replied at once, the economic one.'[113]

Yet another aspect of Nehru's thinking about solutions to India's language problems went hand in hand with his belief in socialism, and his feeling that Russia could be a model for India in addressing the many-language situation. Nehru's affection for the Soviet Union is well known. Even though it was a very brief visit[114] he had paid there in 1927, it had had a profound effect on him:

I had long been drawn to socialism and communism, and Russia had appealed to me . . . With all her blunders, Soviet Russia had triumphed over enormous difficulties and taken great strides toward this new order . . . Russia, following the great Lenin, looked into the future and thought only of what was to be, while other countries lay numbed under the dead hand of the past and spent their energy in preserving the useless relics of a bygone age.[115]

Lenin had too much else lying before him to spend much time fretting about language or allowing it to become a source of ethnic unrest in post-1917 Russia. In countries with many languages, once linguistic fires break out anywhere they tend to break out in rapid succession everywhere. The basic premise of Lenin's policy, at least in theory, in regard to language and nationality was:

Absolutely no privileges for any one nation or any one language . . . The liberals . . . are completely at one with the reactionaries on the point that a compulsory official language is necessary . . . What we do not want is the element of *coercion*. We do not want to have people driven into paradise with a cudgel; for no matter how many fine phrases about 'culture' you may utter, a *compulsory* official language involves coercion, the use of the cudgel.[116]

Nehru in 1952:

The language problem is almost always exceedingly important from the psychological point of view . . . It is absolutely clear to me that the Government must encourage the tribal languages. It is not enough simply to allow them to prevail. They must be given all possible support and the conditions in which they can flourish must be safeguarded. We must go out of our way to achieve this. In the Soviet Republic we have the example of a country that has adopted such a policy with success. Lenin and other leaders in his time were exceedingly wise in this respect . . . In the matter of languages there must be no compulsion whatever.[117]

Nehru held unswervingly to these Leninist views of language — no coercion, tolerance; there were more important things to worry about — when he was forced to deal with the national language issue as a leader in power and not as an observer on the sidelines as he was in British India.[118] When he had served as Chairman of the Allahabad Municipal Board in 1923, he had encouraged 'the use of Hindi or Urdu in official transactions but rejected suggestions that these be made obligatory'.[119]

There was much in Soviet Russia he disliked, such as 'the ruthless suppression of all contrary opinion, the wholesale regimentation, the unnecessary violence (as I thought) in carrying out various policies'.[120] Nehru, along with most intellectuals of the West and East at the time, took the Soviet leaders at their word when they proclaimed that they had solved, once for all, such intractable problems as illiteracy among their minority peoples.[121] In a letter to his sister Vijayalakshmi Pandit dated 12 November 1927 written during his Russian visit he explains to her that the Soviet Union had 'successfully tackled' the problem of illiteracy.[122]

It is only since the Soviet Union broke up that we have seen how much of this idyllic picture was a sham — an ethno-linguistic Potemkin Village. We note the insistent demands for greater ethnic — and frequently linguistic — autonomy that have broken out like fires on the steppes throughout the vast domain of what was until the early 1990s the Soviet Union. It became almost impossible for the Soviet Union in its waning days to keep the lid on ancient ethnic animosities once totalitarianism had been supplanted by glasnost.

In the 1920s and 1930s the overall perception was that the Soviet Union had resolved the problems of nationalism and minorities, virtually the only 'developing' country in the world to have done so, and the Soviet Union became a model and beacon of hope for the newly independent and multilingual countries that have emerged in this century. It was to India's powerful neighbour to the north that Nehru looked for guidance in these matters: 'It is difficult to draw any final conclusions about anything Russian at this stage, but it would certainly appear from the progress made in the last five years that the problem of minorities has been largely solved there.'[123] 'Only Soviet Russia is said to have solved its problem of nationalities and minorities by creating what is called a multinational state.'[124]

The Soviet Union had followed a policy of benign neglect of language from the Revolution to the early 1930s, and the policy had been successful so far as anyone outside the country could see. The liberal language policy of the early Soviet regime was nativization (*korenizacija*). Every possible latitude was granted the constituent languages of the USSR. Book publishing was subsidized by the state. Instruction in the local language was permitted at all levels of education. This was the legacy of Leninist language policy; it was to be liberal, tolerant, large-minded. Under Stalin *korenizacija* came to a screeching halt in the mid-1930s. Stalin adhered to the Leninist doctrine only as long as it suited his purposes. He was ruthless in squashing languages whose speakers had become, for one reason or another, hateful to him: Yiddish, German, Ukrainian, Belórussian. But certain knowledge of all this heavy reality lay in the future during the period of Nehru's greatest infatuation with the Soviet Union, the late 1920s and early 1930s. Few were those percipient enough to see how things truly were beneath the surface in the Soviet Union.

In *The Discovery of India* Nehru wrote:

> A study of Marx and Lenin produced a powerful effect on my mind and helped me to see history and current affairs in a new light. The long chain of history and of social development appeared to have some meaning, some sequence, and the future lost some of its obscurity. The practical achievements of the Soviet Union were also tremendously impressive.[125]

In summary, Nehru admired Russia, and he thought that India had much to learn from the Russians about tolerating linguistic diversity and permitting regional languages to flourish while insisting upon a strong central government operating, for all practical purposes, with a single official language for government business. But with time, Nehru felt, India could resolve its language problems as Russia had done; or so it seemed to him at the time of his visit and for a long time afterwards.

Sanskrit

To round out the picture of the 'private Nehru' there remains only consideration of Nehru's reverence for Sanskrit. Such 'reverence' is far from unusual even among highly 'Westernized' Indians:

I often wonder which is the most important of the many things that have distinguished India in the past in its history of thousands of years. I have no doubt in my mind that it is the Sanskrit language. I think it is that which has embodied the genius of our race, the wisdom of our race and almost everything that has come out in later years can somehow be found to have sprung from that magnificent language.[126]

The Sanskrit language always conjured up for Nehru the theme of the unity of India, never far from his thoughts when language was discussed:

Hardly any language in the world has probably played that vital part in the history of a race which Sanskrit has. It was not only the vehicle of the highest thought and some of the finest literature, but it became the uniting bond for India, in spite of its political divisions. The *Ramayana* and the *Mahabharata* were woven into the texture of millions of lives in every generation for thousands of years. I have often wondered, if our race forgot the Buddha, the *Upanishads* and the great epics, what then will it be like! It would be uprooted and would lose the basic characteristics which have clung to it and given it distinction throughout these long ages. India would cease to be India.[127]

The Discovery of India has a striking tribute to the Sanskrit language — moving, and factually accurate — entitled 'The Vitality and Persistence of Sanskrit' which begins: 'Sanskrit is a language amazingly rich, efflorescent, full of luxuriant growth of all kinds, and yet precise and strictly keeping within the framework of grammar which Panini laid down two thousand six hundred years ago.'[128] One can quarrel with Nehru's date; but even scholars are not agreed on when Panini lived and wrote his *Astadhyayi*. Sir William Jones properly comes in for his share of praise, and Nehru quotes the famous Third Anniversary Discourse before the Asiatick Society in Calcutta on 2 February 1786 in which Jones drew attention to the similarities in structure and 'forms of grammar' between Sanskrit and Latin and Greek. This 'Discourse' delivered before the Asiatick Society, which Jones had founded in order to increase the store of knowledge about India among the British, is generally reckoned to be the starting-point of the great intellectual enterprise of nineteenth-century comparative and historical linguistics in western Europe, especially Germany. In a later section of *The Discovery of India* Nehru accurately relates the account of how Jones obtained his instruction in Sanskrit despite Brahmanical opposition to the idea of a *mleccha* (foreigner, generally used pejoratively) learning the sacred language of the Hindu scriptures.[129]

Sanskrit never failed to bring out the language romantic in Nehru:

> A language is something infinitely greater than grammar and philology. It is the poetic testament of the genius of a race and a culture, and the living embodiment of the thoughts and fancies that have moulded them . . . It is difficult to capture the meaning, much less the spirit, of an old word or phrase . . . The richer and more abundant the language, the greater the difficulty. Sanskrit, like other classical languages, is full of words which have not only poetic beauty but a deep significance, a host of associated ideas, which cannot be translated into a language foreign in spirit and outlook. Even its grammar, its philosophy have a strong poetic content . . .[130]

I said earlier that Nehru's tribute to Sanskrit in *The Discovery of India* is factually accurate. That is true, and slightly amazing at that, for Nehru had gathered his technical knowledge of Sanskrit and Sanskrit literature from an unsystematic variety of sources — he cites 'Sylvain Lévi, *Le théâtre Indien* (Paris, 1890), A. Berriedale Keith, *The Sanskrit Drama* (Oxford, 1924), and E.H. Johnstone's translation of Ashvaghosa's *Buddhacarita* (Lahore, 1936)'. But Nehru manages to get things largely right for all his eclectic browsing. I should argue that Nehru somewhat overplays the theme that the 'continuing use of Sanskrit has undoubtedly prevented the normal growth of the modern Indian languages. The educated intellectuals looked upon them as vulgar tongues not suited to any creative or learned work, which was written in Sanskrit, or later not infrequently in Persian. In spite of this handicap the great provincial languages gradually took shape . . .' The point was of more than passing interest to Nehru: '[E]very cultured person was supposed to know one of these [Sanskrit or Persian]. These two classical languages played a dominating role and prevented the growth of the popular provincial languages.'[131] The vernacular languages of India would have developed pretty much as rapidly as they did, certainly as spoken languages and not very far behind as written languages, wherever Sanskrit was in the picture. But Nehru is right — and it is generous of him to say so — when he observes that 'The early Christian missionaries, especially of the Baptist mission at Serampore, helped in this process greatly [the process of development of prose literatures in the vernaculars]. The first private printing presses were set up by them, and their efforts to translate the Bible into prose versions of the Indian languages met with considerable success.'[132]

However, the principal point is how much Sanskrit meant to Nehru, and that is made abundantly clear from the numerous references to the language in his letters, writings, and speeches over his entire adult life. It is clear that a part, perhaps even the biggest part, of Nehru's respect for Sanskrit derived from its unifying power in Indian history and culture; Sanskritic learning at least was one thing that joined Aryan and Dravidian India, even as much else divided them. Both south Indian Hindus and north Indian Hindus could agree upon the enduring value and richness of the Sanskrit language. It was a point of unity.

Nehru returned to the theme of Sanskrit in a number of speeches throughout his years in power. One of his most graceful and informed tributes was a speech delivered on 1 August 1956 at the Bhandarkar Oriental Research Institute, Poona.[133] He praises the work being done by the Institute in preparing a critical edition of the *Mahabharata*, which 'may have a greater significance in the scheme of things than much that we passing politicians of the day do'. He goes on to the theme of language and thought of which he often spoke and which, as we shall see in the following chapter, he devoted an essay to:

> What is language, Sanskrit or any other language? Thought represented in words . . . Thought has been and will be the greatest thing in the world, and everything else comes out of thought. But thought has to take shape in words, words of power, and in this language of our race, the most magnificent thoughts are clothed in words of power. And so, this language, out of which again came this greatest of our books [the *Mahabharata*], was probably the strongest cultural manifestation of the Indian people.

And Nehru once again weaves Sanskrit into his vision of the oneness of India:

The Governor mentioned that the city of Poona has been a great centre of scholarship. It is so. But we know how the Sanskrit language has been nurtured in all parts of India, certainly in and round about Benares but in the far north in Kashmir also . . . Devoted service was paid there to this great language of ours. In the far south of India great scholars arose and did service to it; and so in Poona and in the east and the west. However India may have been split up in the past in terms of political entities and whatever it may have suffered through the ages, this basic language, the thoughts that it represented, the dreams of our race that it has embodied, have continued to condition all of us equally . . . It is extraordinary that this language . . . which I suppose has not been a spoken language in the normal sense of being the mother-tongue of the people ever since Buddha's day, and perhaps earlier, has yet been a vital and a vivid language throughout these centuries. It is extraordinary that a language which ceases to be the language of the common people should still have the enormous vitality which Sanskrit has possessed during these thousands of years. And so, this Sanskrit language, with its offshoots, of course, the daughter languages, but even more so with the force of thought and dreams and search for truth and wisdom that it contains, has been the inheritance of not only you and me but of everybody living in this country, whether in the north, or south or west or east . . . I have no doubt that whatever shape th[e] future may take, one of the biggest, the strongest and most powerful and the most valued of our legacies will be the Sanskrit language and this great epic.

Nehru's devotion to Sanskrit did not end with eloquent tributes. He concludes his speech at the Bhandarkar Oriental Research Institute by saying that 'this work will not suffer in future for lack of money'. The same year, in 1956, a Sanskrit Commission was constituted under the Ministry of Education and chaired by the distinguished scholar of the history of language in India, Professor Suniti Kumar Chatterji, who had a towering reputation among the world's linguists. The report of the Sanskrit Commission under Chatterji's chairmanship came to 439 pages.[134] The overall tenor of most of the recommendations was: what can the government do to further the study of Sanskrit in the country? Proposals were offered to make the study of Sanskrit mandatory in schools, to allow Sanskrit to count as one of the required languages of instruction under the 'Three-Language

Formula',[135] to create more academies devoted to Sanskrit, and so on. Here though we are once more up against the problem I discussed in Chapter 2 ('Linguistic Prolegomena', The Linguistic 'Free Market'): you can lead a horse to water but you cannot make him drink no matter how well you reward him for drinking the water or punish him for not drinking it. The number of speakers considered 'native' of Sanskrit declines inexorably, as does the number of speakers considered 'native' of Irish. Instruction given in Sanskrit continues to deteriorate, even at universities with 'Sanskrit' in their name and dedicated, therefore, to the propagation of Sanskrit — for example, Varanasi Sanskrit University.[136] There is nothing any Indian government in power might do that would have any serious impact on the use of Sanskrit in the country.

Postscript

Nehru's legacy of linguistic *laissez-faire* did not die with him. It was bequeathed intact to his daughter, Indira, prime minister of India from 1966–77 and then again from 1980 until her assassination in 1984. By the time she became prime minister the worst of the language conflicts were past or quiescent. The reorganization of states to correspond to regional language groupings was complete, and all but Hindi extremists were content with the tacit policy of letting sleeping dogs lie regarding the question of the national language. This is not of course to say that there were no longer problems. The Sikhs have continued to demand a state of their own, Khalistan, in Punjabi 'Land of the Pure', and while this might be regarded as a purely communal or religious demand we have seen that such demands in India are almost always intimately intertwined with linguistic demands: a Sikh Khalistan means not only a land for the Sikhs but a land for the Punjabi language and presumably for the Punjabi language written in the Gurmukhi script sacred to the *Granth Sahib*. The Gurmukhi script for ordinary Punjabi, which is to say the Punjabi not of the Sikh sacred writings, competes with the Devanagari and Perso–Arabic scripts.

In a speech at the conference of State chief ministers in New Delhi on 8 April 1967, prime minister Indira Gandhi put her position as follows:

The language question arouses deep emotion. But it should not become a divisive force. As far as the centre is concerned, we view all languages listed in the Eighth Schedule as national languages. They are the cultural streams that together constitute the grand river of Indian thought and tradition . . . Yet we need a link language and it is for this purpose that our Constitution-makers suggested Hindi. Knowledge of a language has to grow; it is a gradual process which takes time. Therefore, we have agreed that English should continue as an associate official language till such time as necessary.[137]

And in a Lok Sabha debate on the President's address, 23 February 1968: 'I think the less said about it [Hindi versus English] from now until tempers cool down, the better it is.'[138]

Where have we heard this before? In substance, in style, in temper, it is impossible to distinguish these familiar statements from ones that Jawaharlal made on scores of other occasions. All those letters from father to daughter with their hundreds of references to language and their pervasive message of linguistic tolerance had had their effect. They did their job. Jawaharlal would have been quite pleased.

Notes and References

1. 17 March 1950, *Selected Works* II.14, 1: 341.
2. Gopal, *Biography* 2: 236–7.
3. Ibid., 1: 18.
4. *Freedom's Daughter; Two Alone, Two Together.*
5. *Nehru's Letters to His Sister.*
6. Gopal, *Biography* 1: 18.
7. *Autobiography*, p. 28.
8. Ibid.
9. NMML. Nehru's will and testament is published in Gopal, *Biography* 3: 269.
10. R.K. Thakur, *Jawaharlal Nehru: The Man and the Writer* (New Delhi: Bahri Publications, 1989), p. 134.
11. Gopal, *Biography* 3: 267.
12. 30 Jan. 1907, *Selected Works* I.1: 17.
13. Gopal, *Biography* 1: 36.
14. Ibid., 1: 23.
15. *Autobiography*, p. 35.
16. Ibid., p. 39.
17. Ibid., p. 43.

18. Ibid., p. 60.
19. Gopal, *Biography* 1: 72–3.
20. 30 Jan. 1948, 'The Light has Gone Out', *Speeches* 1: 42–4.
21. *Selected Works of Motilal Nehru*, vol. 1, p. 144.
22. *Autobiography*, p. 96.
23. Gopal, *Biography* 1: 32.
24. *Autobiography*, p. 44.
25. Cf. ibid., pp. 143, 189, 309–26; 'From Lucknow to Tripuri', *Unity*, pp. 104–7; and Gopal, *Biography* 1: 109.
26. *Autobiography*, p. 95.
27. *Selected Works* I.2: 40.
28. Ibid., I.2: 45–6.
29. Ibid., I.2: 87.
30. Gopal, *Biography* 1: 189.
31. Ibid., 1: 197–8.
32. S. Gopal, *Radhakrishnan: A Biography* (London: Unwin Hyman, 1989).
33. Gopal, *Biography* 1: 197–8.
34. Thakur, *Jawaharlal Nehru: The Man and the Writer*.
35. Gopal, *Biography* 1: 190.
36. M.O. Mathai, *Reminiscences of the Nehru Age* (New Delhi: Vikas Publishing House, 1978), p. 81.
37. *Freedom's Daughter*, pp. 28–9.
38. Gopal, *Biography* 1: 63–4.
39. *Autobiography*, p. 305.
40. Ibid., p. 170.
41. Gopal, *Biography* 1: 68–9.
42. *Selected Works* I.1: 299–306.
43. Letter to Motilal Nehru, 17 Aug. 1922, from District Jail, Lucknow, *Selected Works* I.1: 327.
44. Circular to Secretaries of District Congress Committees and Members of the United Provinces Congress Committee, 5 May 1922, NMML, cf. *Selected Works* I.1: 249–50.
45. *Selected Works* I.6: 261.
46. *Autobiography*, p. 88 *et passim*.
47. Letter to Motilal Nehru, 1 Sept. 1922, *Selected Works* I.1: 338.
48. *Selected Works* I.1: 350.
49. Reproductions of these postcards from 1903 and 1905 can be seen in *Selected Works* I.1: 1–2.
50. Gopal, *Biography* 1: 68.
51. 'Books Read in Jail', *Selected Works* I.1: 305.
52. 13 July 1922, *Selected Works* I.1: 321.
53. Letter to Syed Mahmud, 21 March 1924: 'I have not read wholly

your Urdu letter yet as it takes me some time to read Urdu . . .' (*Selected Works* I.2: 217).

54. *Discovery*, p. 350.
55. *Autobiography*, p. 146.
56. *Discovery*, p. 350.
57. *Two Alone, Two Together*, pp. 193–332.
58. *Discovery*, p. v.
59. Gopal, *Biography* 1: 295.
60. *Biography* 1: 297.
61. *Discovery*, p. 495.
62. *Selected Works* I.13: 501–2.
63. *Nehru's Letters to His Sister*, pp. 166–7.
64. *Selected Works* I.13: 44–439, cf. Gopal, *Biography* 1: 297.
65. *Biography* 1: 298.
66. Ibid., 1: 299.
67. *Discovery*, p. 8.
68. *Inside Asia* (New York and London: Harper & Brothers, 1939), p. 418.
69. B.B. Kachru, *The Indianization of English: The English Language in India*, pp. 4–7.
70. *Selected Works* I.8: 868.
71. *The Indianization of English: The English Language in India*, pp. 4–7.
72. *Unity*, pp. 241–61.
73. The classic work on this perplexing conundrum was written by one of the founders of modern American linguistics, Leonard Bloomfield, 'Secondary and Tertiary Responses to Language', *Language*, 20 (1944), pp. 45–55.
74. 'The Official Languages', 24 April 1963, *Speeches* 5: 25.
75. *The Tongues of Man; and Speech* (London: Oxford University Press, 1964), pp. 42–3 (rpt. of original 1937 edn).
76. 'Coexistence at Home', *Speeches* 3: 180.
77. 'The Question of Language', *Unity*, p. 241. The article was written in 1937 though the collection in which it appeared, *The Unity of India*, was first published in 1941.
78. 'Coexistence at Home', *Speeches* 3: 174.
79. 'The Official Languages', *Speeches* 5: 24–5.
80. Brecher, *Nehru*, p. 233.
81. Gopal, *Biography* 3: 26.
82. *Autobiography*, p. 130.
83. *Freedom's Daughter*, p. 33f.
84. Ibid., pp. 59–60.
85. *Selected Works* I.6: 258.
86. Ibid., I.6: 316. 'Miss Spiegel' was Dr Margarete Spiegel, disciple

of Gandhi, who renamed her Amala. He liked giving his disciples new names.

87. *Selected Works* I.6: 339–40.
88. *Selected Works* I.6: 399.
89. Ibid., I.6: 406.
90. *Freedom's Daughter*, p. 454.
91. *Selected Works* I.11: 639.
92. *Discovery*, p. 13.
93. 'The Progress of Science', *Unity*, p. 178.
94. Brecher, *Nehru*, p. 13.
95. *Discovery*, p. 522.
96. See, for example, 'Science and Planning' and 'The Progress of Science', *Unity*, pp. 175–83.
97. *Discovery*, p. 571.
98. C.D. Narasimhaiah, *The Swan and the Eagle* (Simla: Indian Institute of Advanced Study, 1969) has an interesting analysis of the interplay between science and humanism in Nehru's writings that develops this topic further.
99. *Freedom's Daughter*, p. 96.
100. *Autobiography*, p. 38.
101. *Speeches* 1: 36–7.
102. There is a revealing and unintentionally amusing sentence in a letter from Nehru to Sheikh Abdullah, 28 June 1953 (NMML): 'Nothing is more depressing than confused thinking in any vital matter.'
103. Cf. *Autobiography*, pp. 44, 279 and *Discovery*, p. 352.
104. *Autobiography*, p. 139.
105. Campbell-Johnson, *Mission with Mountbatten*, p. 197.
106. *Autobiography*, pp. 400–1.
107. 'From Lucknow to Tripuri', *Unity*, p. 117.
108. Brecher, *Nehru*, p. 365.
109. Cf. Gopal, *Biography* 2: 97.
110. Ibid., 2: 33.
111. 'The S.R.C. Report', 9 Oct. 1955, *Speeches* 3: 167–70.
112. P.P. Kapoor, *Economic Thought of Jawaharlal Nehru* (New Delhi: Deep & Deep, 1985), pp. 61–165.
113. Campbell-Johnson, *Mission with Mountbatten*, p. 44.
114. '[J]ust three or four days in Moscow, decided upon at the last moment', *Autobiography*, p. 12.
115. *Autobiography*, p. 29.
116. V.I. Lenin, *Collected Works* (Moscow: Progress Publishers, 1964), vol. 20, pp. 20, 22, 711–12.
117. 'The Tribal Folk', 7 June 1952, *Speeches* 2: 581.

118. See, for example, his Lok Sabha speech ('Coexistence at Home') of 21 Dec. 1955, *Speeches* 3: 170–83.
119. Gopal, *Biography* 1: 90.
120. *Autobiography*, p. 229.
121. Ibid., p. 279; cf. also *Selected Works* I.2: 396.
122. *Selected Works* I.2: 374.
123. 'Soviet Russia', *Selected Works* I.2: 426.
124. *Discovery*, pp. 247–8. It is a matter of speculation what lay behind these cautious, almost lawyerly formulations: 'it would certainly appear' and 'is said to have solved'. Had his sensitive nostrils begun to detect a whiff of the stench of mendacity of the cultural party line he and other foreign visitors to the Soviet Union had been given in the 1920s?
125. *Discovery*, p. 17.
126. 'The Sanskrit Language', speech at the Bhandarkar Oriental Research Institute, Poona, 1 Aug. 1956, *Speeches* 3: 419.
127. 'Synthesis is Our Tradition', the Azad Memorial Lectures, New Delhi, 22–23 Feb. 1959, *Speeches* 4: 1.
128. *Discovery*, pp. 156–61.
129. Ibid., p. 317. On Sir William Jones and his acquisition of Sanskrit, *see* King, 'West from India: The Odyssey of Sir William Jones'.
130. *Discovery*, p. 157.
131. Ibid., p. 318.
132. Ibid.
133. 'The Sanskrit Language', *Speeches* 3: 418–21.
134. V. Kumar, *Committees and Commissions in India, 1947–73* (Delhi: Concept Publishing Company, 1975), vol. 2, pp. 185–98.
135. The idea behind the 'Three-Language Formula' was that every Indian schoolchild should learn three languages: Hindi, the vernacular, and a third language which in the normal scheme of things would be English though other languages such as French, German, or Sanskrit could be substituted.
136. H.H. Hock, 'Spoken Sanskrit in Uttar Pradesh: Profile of a Dying Language', *in* E.C. Dimock, Jr., B.B. Kachru, and Bh. Krishnamurti (eds), *Dimensions of Sociolinguistics in South Asia: Papers in Memory of Gerald B. Kelley* (New Delhi: Oxford & IBH Publishing Co., 1992), pp. 247–60.
137. *Selected Speeches of Indira Gandhi*, pp. 68–9.
138. Ibid., p. 38.

Chapter 6

Nehru's Essays on Language

Nehru's most intense focus on language tended to coincide with his enforced periods of idleness in jail. This would sound like a joke in bad taste if it were not for the practical consideration that it was really only in jail that he had the time to pursue his bookish interests without constant interruption. He read widely over a striking variety of subjects when behind bars, and during his later terms of imprisonment, reading and language improvement were linked to the enormous amount of writing he managed to do while in jail. A surprising body of his writing during these periods had language, in one sense or another, as its subject.

There are three essays of Nehru's on language that are particularly intriguing and suggestive of a deeper penetration into the essence of language than is usual in men of state. They are 'The Meaning of Words' and 'The Question of Language'. Two quite different essays with the latter title appeared, one dating from 1937, the other from 1949. What these essays demonstrate is not that Nehru was always right or wise about language or about the relationship between politics and language. They do show that his involvement with language was more than casual and occasional. It went deeper; it was very nearly a preoccupation, especially during the mid-1930s.

'The Meaning of Words'

When Nehru was not in jail he did not pursue his language studies systematically. It would have been surprising if he had, given all the other claims on his time and energy. But as soon as he was back in prison, among the first books he requested were almost always Hindi and Urdu dictionaries and grammars. In prison at Dehra Dun in 1933 he renewed his study of Hindi and

Urdu, and 'he set himself to writing articles in English and Hindi'.[1]

The years 1935–7 were Nehru's period of greatest concentration on language and its problems, in particular on Hindi as a national language. He wrote a letter to his daughter Indira on 4 April 1935 complaining about the shortcomings of Hindi writers:

> Very few writers in Hindi, as far as I can make out, pay real attention to the artistry of language, the beauty and significance of words and the images they convey. They get lost in high-sounding and vague language; there is little precision about it, and hence there is always want of sincerity in the written word. They have not realized yet that true style comes from simplicity and sincerity.[2]

A short time later, between July and August 1935, when he had been transferred to Almora District Jail, he composed a number of rather insubstantial essays in Hindi: 'Our Literature', 'Literature in Hindi and Other Languages', and 'Bhai Parmanand and Swaraj'.[3] He does not appear to have concerned himself subsequently with these essays, which are on the whole rather schoolboyish. He however expands upon the theme he had complained about in his letter to Indira — the shortcomings of Hindi writers — in a short essay originally composed in Hindi dated 1 August 1935 which he later translated into English himself under the title 'The Meaning of Words'.[4] The dominant theme of the essay is 'sincerity' as a vital ingredient of good writing; bad writers, he says:

> [h]ide their weakness in long, confusing and to some extent meaningless words. That prose in which [imprecise] words are used profusely becomes weak. Such writing has not the razor's edge nor can it attain its objective as does an arrow from a bow.[5]

Not much attention has been bestowed by Nehru scholars on this obscure piece which has something of the flavour of a *jeu d'esprit* about it, but I do not think it should be dismissed on that account.[6] Nor, on the other hand, do I think that too much should be made of it. I submit it not only as one more piece of evidence of Nehru's unusual interest in language but as additional support for my imputation of a turn of mind in him that is not far from that of a 'linguist' in the technical sense I discussed in Chapter 2.

'The Meaning of Words' is initially concerned with the problem of translation:

To translate from one language to another language is a very difficult task. The fact is that real translation of even slightly profound thought is just impossible. What is the function of a language? It helps us to think. Language is semi-frozen thought — imagination converted into statues.[7]

What Nehru has raised here is a question of ancient origins that occupied linguists, especially from the 1930s through the 1950s: the question of the relationship, if any, between language and thought ('semi-frozen' or not). Does thought precede language? Or does language precede thought? What is the relationship between language and our perception of reality? What is the effect, if any, of language upon behaviour? Do people who speak radically different languages think about life and see the world in radically different ways?

He continues:

Even an ordinary phrase produces many pictures in the mind and it is possible that in the listener's mind different pictures are produced . . . This difficulty can arise between two persons who speak the same language, are literate and civilized and brought up in the same culture . . . But these difficulties look small when compared to two persons who speak two different languages and do not know much about the cultures of each other. Their mental ideas and images differ as heaven and earth. They hardly understand each other.[8]

This statement and the preceding one from 'The Meaning of Words' have for the linguist unmistakable resonances of what is called the 'Whorf–Sapir Hypothesis'. There is in Nehru's essay no explicit reference to this hypothesis by the name 'Whorf–Sapir' or any other, and there is not the slightest reason whatsoever to believe that Nehru could ever have heard of it in its explicit formulation or read about it or been told about it. At the time in question, the 1930s, speculation about the relationship between thought and language was found mostly in obscure articles buried in scholarly language journals. Nehru refers to 'a philologist, Prof. J.S. Mackenzie', his only suggestion of a source:

A philologist, Professor J.S. Mackenzie, who has deeply studied languages and their relations, has written, 'an Englishman, a Frenchman, and an Italian cannot bring themselves to think quite alike, at least on subjects which involve any depth of sentiment: they have not the verbal means.' This despite the fact that an Englishman, a Frenchman, a German and an Italian are the products of one culture and their languages are closely related. Even so, it is said that on any abstract topic, they cannot by any means think alike because their languages differ. If this is their condition, what will be the relation between the languages of an Indian and an Englishman? By wearing a *dhoti* and *kurta* an Englishman does not start thinking like an Indian just as the latter cannot understand the civilization of Europe by putting on a coat and trousers and by eating with a knife and fork.[9]

I am uncertain who the 'philologist, Professor J.S. Mackenzie', was. This is the only reference I have found to anyone named 'J.S. Mackenzie' in any of the *Selected Works of Jawaharlal Nehru* or in any of Nehru's other writings. There was a John S. Mackenzie who was professor of logic and philosophy at the turn of the century at University College of South Wales, formerly fellow of Trinity College, Cambridge, author of a number of philosophical textbooks: *Outlines of Metaphysics, An Introduction to Social Philosophy*, and *A Manual of Ethics*. It would be entirely in character for Nehru to have read any of these books — he was fond of philosophy. However, none of these books by J.S. Mackenzie is found among the 188 books Nehru lists in his prison diary under the rubric Books Read in Prison between 15 February 1934 and 2 September 1935.[10] Moreover, J.S. Mackenzie was not a philologist but a philosopher, not that anything hinges on the designation of his academic speciality. The books of J.S. Mackenzie's that I have had access to do not deal with language at all; rather with philosophy in a rather traditional sense, so I remain unclear whether Nehru simply misidentified Mackenzie's academic discipline ('philologist') or had been able to read something written by the philosopher, J.S. Mackenzie, in which the latter touched on language and thought, but which I have not seen nor Nehru noted down. It might after all have been an article in a popular magazine where Nehru came across J.S. Mackenzie's speculations about how Englishmen, Frenchmen, Germans, and Italians think.

The Whorf–Sapir Hypothesis is the view — labelled a hypothesis since it is not proved — that language conditions our view of reality.[11] The claim can be found in one form or another from very early times. Aristotle touched on it, as did Leibniz and Wilhelm von Humboldt. Samuel Johnson, in his *Lives of the English Poets*, says that 'Language is the dress of thought.' These rather general speculations gave way in the 1930s to more interesting and specific claims of various kinds which we call the 'Whorf–Sapir Hypothesis'. Common to all versions of the hypothesis is the claim that language is a filter through which we perceive the world. In its weakest formulation it makes the benign claim that language has something to do with the way we see and react to the events of the world around us. In other words, the weak form of the Whorf–Sapir Hypothesis simply states that language affects behaviour. In this version the hypothesis is trivially true, as anyone who speaks two languages knows without having to be told. In its most extreme form the Whorf–Sapir Hypothesis asserts that we are virtually prisoners of our language; that language creates our view of the world, our reality: what we see, perceive, feel is completely governed by the structure of the language we speak. The speaker of Chinese sees the world 'out there' in one way, the speaker of Japanese in another, the speaker of Malayalam in yet another.

The hypothesis usually bears the names of Benjamin Lee Whorf, an early (1930s) American linguist, and Edward Sapir, one of the founders of modern structural linguistics as well as of modern anthropology. Sapir had suggested the possibility of a causal connection between thought and language as part of his ongoing research interest in personality and culture.[12] Whorf, a chemical engineer by training but an insurance investigator by profession, had attended lectures by Sapir at Yale University and, as a result, become fascinated with language. He was so successful in his work that his firm gave him time off to conduct linguistic fieldwork among the Hopis, a Native American tribe of the American south-west.[13]

Whorf's study of Hopi had persuaded him that the structure of the Hopi language made the Hopi see the world and behave in the world in a dramatically different way from speakers of what he called an 'SAE' language: 'SAE' was Whorf's acronym for 'standard average European' language, for example, English, German, French, Italian, Spanish, and the like, all of which are remarkably similar in their deeper structure. Whorf's fieldwork among the Hopi convinced him that the language had no tenses — no past tense, no future tense — and he concluded that the Hopis did not think about the passing of time in the same way as speakers of SAE languages do: such and such happened yesterday; we shall go to town tomorrow.[14] For the Hopi, as Whorf saw it, life was a process, a kind of 'happening', rather than a passage of time, a sequence of events: we plant, we harvest, we hunt; but not 'we planted yesterday' and 'we shall reap next autumn'. His conclusion:

> Concepts of 'time' and 'matter' are not given in substantially the same form by experience to all men but depend upon the nature of the language or languages through the use of which they have been developed . . . Our own 'time' differs markedly from Hopi 'duration'. It is conceived as like a space of strictly limited dimensions, or sometimes as like a motion upon such a space, and employed as an intellectual tool accordingly. Hopi 'duration' seems to be inconceivable in terms of space or motion, being the mode in which life differs from form, and consciousness *in toto* from the spatial elements of consciousness. Certain ideas born of our own time-concept, such as that of absolute simultaneity, would be either very difficult to express or impossible and devoid of meaning under the Hopi conception . . .[15]

Subsequent research has shown that Whorf was wrong about the Hopi language not having tenses. Verb tense in Hopi is not immediately evident the way it is in most other languages, and in the bother and minutiae of data collection Whorf simply missed the tense markers or did not recognize the forms and endings he had elicited as tense markers. His conclusions, as summarized above, do not therefore follow because his premises are wrong. Nevertheless, such were his inferences at the time based on what he thought he knew, and his speculations about concepts and language enjoyed a linguistic and anthropological vogue from the 1930s into the 1960s. Something about the human mind there is that is seduced by the notion that language and thought are the two faces of Janus. As Sapir put it in his no-nonsense way: 'Language and our thought-grooves are inextricably interrelated; are, in a sense, the same.'[16]

Linguistic interest in and tacit belief in the Whorf–Sapir Hypothesis peaked during the period immediately before and after the Second World War. Most contemporary linguists do not believe that the Whorf–Sapir Hypothesis is true in any formulation as strong as 'our language is a filter through which we perceive reality'. There are several reasons for our scepticism. A great many languages have grammatical gender — masculine, feminine, neuter sometimes — and this is reflected in the choice of definite and indefinite article, adjectival endings, and so on. But a great many languages do not have grammatical gender. English is one such language. In English the 'gender' of nouns like *apple, table*, and *moon*, is not learnt for there is none. In French, Spanish, and German, on the other hand, the gender of each noun needs to be learnt. Hindi has two genders in its nouns, masculine and feminine. While grammatical gender is commonplace in languages, there is no reason to think that the grammatical use of gender carries over in any way to our perception of 'gender'. German assigns the word for 'girl' (*Mädchen*) to the neuter gender, not to the masculine or feminine gender; but no one has ever detected any tendency among Germans to behave as if girls were sexless objects.

A further and more compelling argument against the Whorf–Sapir Hypothesis is the universality of basic terms for colour. That is, even though languages have different numbers of words for basic colours — some languages have only two, whereas English has eleven (black, white, red, yellow, blue, green, orange, brown, purple, pink and grey) — people from different language backgrounds apparently 'see' the same colours whether they have names for them or not. This is not what the Whorf–Sapir Hypothesis predicts.[17]

A current assessment summarizes contemporary linguistic opinion regarding the Whorf–Sapir Hypothesis:

> The repeated failure of experimental attempts to uncover systematic shaping effects for language has drastically reduced the credibility of the Sapir–Whorf Hypothesis. This is not to say that languages do not represent reality in different ways. Clearly, they do. Thus, French distinguishes between knowing someone *(connaître)* and knowing something *(savoir)*, a distinction that is not made in the verb system of English. On the other hand . . . English has an extremely fine set of contrasts involving light *(glimmer, glitter, glow, gleam*, and *glisten)* that are not found in other languages. What is in doubt is whether such differences in the linguistic description of

reality reflect deeper, language-induced differences in patterns of thought or perception.[18]

This is, however, the contemporary view. It was not the received view in the 1930s and 1940s. The possible relationship between language and reality was an idea drifting round the thought world of the 1930s. However, as I said earlier, there is no reason to suppose that Nehru had ever heard of the Whorf–Sapir Hypothesis, whether under that name or some other name in use such as the 'Linguistic Relativity Hypothesis'. Yet this brief essay of his on 'The Meaning of Words' deals precisely with the issues that Whorf was wrestling with at the same time. The impetus for Nehru's thinking along these lines must surely have grown out of his concentrated efforts to improve his writing skill in Hindi. It is only speculation, but I should imagine that his compositions in Hindi were basically translated from the English he was most comfortable with and in which he thought. The problem of carrying his thoughts back and forth between English and Hindi obviously got him off onto the thought groove of the possible relationship between language and concepts.

Quite apart from the suggestion throughout this essay 'The Meaning of Words' of a nascent Whorf–Sapir Hypothesis, Nehru is interesting — and in part completely wrong-headed — in his general commentary on words and the pitfalls in their uses:

All the same, we laymen should not forget that words are dangerous things and the more abstract, the more deceiving. And the most dangerous words, perhaps, are *dharma* and *mazhab*. Everyone in his heart understands them in his own way. In everyone's heart they form new impressions. Some will think of a temple, mosque or church; the others of a few books, or of some religious oblations, statues, philosophy, customs or of mutual disagreements. In this way one word will produce hundreds of different pictures in the minds of men, and that will bring out a variety of thoughts. It seems to be the weakness of the language that one word can produce such a varied effect. A word should, actually, connote just one picture. It means that *dharma* or *mazhab* has a dozen facets, each of which should have a separate word for it. They say there were more than two hundred words used for making love in the old American Maya language. How can we now translate all those words correctly?[19]

He is right about words provoking many different images in different speakers. That is what good writing is about; that is what good poetry is about. But his idea about it being a 'weakness of the language that one word can produce such a varied effect' is not well thought out; is in fact nonsense. I rather doubt that he really believed what he wrote, or at least that he had seriously thought through the consequences of what he wrote: who among us is not guilty of writing sentences in the white heat of exigent creativity that, on sober reflection next day, are rubbish? And I say the same of his further comment that 'A word should, actually, connote just one picture.' That will not do. True, Nehru — ever the rationalist — eschews ambiguity in his prose. We have all been taught to say what we mean: write clearly! Nehru laid great weight on clarity of expression. He would not have had much use for William Empson's famous defence of ambiguity.[20] But ambiguity is a necessary and useful component of poetry and prose alike. Every accomplished writer knows that, and knows too when ambiguity is needed and when it should be avoided. I cannot believe that Nehru, a very accomplished writer when he wanted to be, felt otherwise. As for the Mayan language and its two hundred words for making love, well I shall merely say that it is not true, alas, and leave it at that.

This essay also contains a slyly amusing comment on Gandhi's expository style:

> In general whatever he [Gandhi] speaks or writes is precise and effective — no superfluous words and no attempt at a flowery style. This trimness is his power. But whenever he speaks of God, the truth or ahimsa — and he does this often — then that mental precision is lessened. God is truth, truth is God, nonviolence is truth, truth is nonviolence — all this he has said. It must mean something but it is not quite clear what. To me at least, such use of words suggests that injustice is being done to them.[21]

I cannot but wonder what the Mahatma thought about such *lèse-majesté* on the part of his favourite disciple or the passage in the *Autobiography* in like vein: 'As for Gandhiji himself, he was a very difficult person to understand; sometimes his language was almost incomprehensible to an average modern.'[22] Gandhi was very puckish about affronts to his dignity, and so I rather imagine he would have had a chuckle or two over these and like misdemeanours on the part of his errant *chela*. Gandhi knew the uses of ambiguity as well as anyone, better actually than almost anyone — he could turn ambiguity on and off like a spigot, as it were — and so I suspect he and Nehru would have agreed, amiably of course, simply not to talk about matters of language so exquisitely refined.

'The Question of Language'

Language was very much on Nehru's mind during the mid- and late-1930s, as I have pointed out. Released from prison he wrote an essay 'The Question of Language', which appeared in *The Bombay Chronicle* in August 1937. Later it was published as a pamphlet by the All-India Congress Committee with a foreword by Gandhi, about which more later.[23]

This was his longest sustained effort to come to grips with the national language problem of India. His major thrust was to argue in support of Hindustani as the national language and how Hindustani could be spread among the masses, how its technical vocabulary could be modernized and the language tarted up for its use as the common language of modern India. This essay continued themes Nehru had first started working out in a piece he wrote in Hindi while in Almora in 1935, 'Literature in Hindi and Other Languages'.[24]

The tone and topic of 'The Question of Language' are set in the opening sentences:

> We have had during recent months a revival of the old controversy between Hindi and Urdu, and high excitement has accompanied it and charges and counter-charges have been flung about. A subject eminently suited for calm and scholarly consideration and academic debate has been dragged down to the level of the market-place, and communal passions have centred round it.[25]

Nehru's intent then is to bring reason to bear on this issue so rich in its iconic potential for whipping up communal mischief. He quotes Milton to the effect that no empire, no state could flourish without 'liking and care for its language'. The policy of the state in regard to language should be that of the 1931 Congress Resolution on Fundamental Rights: 'The culture, language, and script of the minorities and of the different linguistic areas shall be protected.' English is the language only of the élite in India; it can never be the language of the great mass of people, who should receive their education in the regional languages which should be modernized and developed in the area of technical, scientific vocabulary. A common script for India's languages should be designed, perhaps two or even three: a 'Devanagari–Bengali–Marathi–Gujarati' script, the Perso–Arabic script of Urdu, and 'if necessary, a southern script' (for the Dravidian languages). Hindustani, in either of its scripts, should be the national language. Hindi and Urdu can only enrich each other; there should be no antagonism between them. Would it not be possible and desirable to create a 'Basic Hindustani' after the fashion of Basic English? This he got directly, of course, from Ogden and Richards.

The linguistic views expressed by Nehru in 'The Question of Language' are on the whole unexceptionable and even mushy in places, though expressed in elegant prose. He poses the question: what is Hindustani? His answer:

> Vaguely we say that this word includes both Hindi and Urdu, as spoken and as written in the two scripts, and we endeavour to strike a golden mean between the two, and call this idea of ours Hindustani. Is this just an idea with no reality for its basis, or is it something more?[26]

'Vaguely' is perhaps the operative word here. This conception of Hindustani is of a piece with Gandhi's equally vague notions which I laid out in Chapter 3 ('Linguistic States and the National Language', Gandhi's Position, and Nehru's). At that time I pointed out the essential weakness of the Gandhi–Nehru position on Hindustani, which was to deny the iconic importance of script. And of course the cavalier manner in which Nehru suggests radical changes of script tradition — a 'Devanagari–Bengali–Marathi–Gujarati' script, a 'southern script' for Dravidian — will not do at all. People do become attached to their scripts; it takes an Atatürk and threats of force to wean people from their writing systems.

I do not call the views expressed in 'The Question of Language' whimsical or superficial. I do call them conventional and rather predictable; tired actually, and certainly not linguistically subtle or sophisticated — different, in other words, from much of Nehru's other writing about language. They are 'off key' for

Nehru, and it turns out that there is a reason for this: Nehru did not write 'The Question of Language' of his own volition. He did so at Gandhi's request and for the specific purpose of pouring oil on the troubled waters of Hindu–Muslim religious antagonism qua Hindi–Urdu language antagonism: in pre-Partition India, battles between the Hindi and Urdu languages were never much more than the continuation of Hindu–Muslim 'warfare' by other means.

The story behind 'The Question of Language' is interesting in its own right for the light it throws on Gandhi's and Nehru's relationship. On 6 July 1937 Nehru sent a message in Hindi to a meeting of the Madras Hindi Sahitya Sammelan entitled 'On the Hindi–Urdu Controversy'.[27] The main points of this brief message were: (1) the rivalry between Hindi and Urdu is harmful to both; (2) Hindi literature is at present very backward; (3) we desire progress in all the languages of India as well as Hindi and Urdu; (4) Hindi or Hindustani is certainly the national language of India and it ought to be; (5) we require a Hindustani midway between Hindi and Urdu, neither too Sanskritized nor too Persianized; (6) both scripts, Devanagari and the Urdu Perso–Arabic script, must coexist peacefully; and (7) 'One thing more. It is essential that the famous books of Europe be translated into Hindi. Only thus will we be able to bring here the ideas prevalent in the world and derive advantage from foreign literatures.'

Gandhi, much involved at the time in trying to keep the peace between Hindus and Muslims and much put upon by Hindi and Urdu fanatics, read Nehru's brief message and decided it could be used to aid the cause of Hindu–Muslim rapprochement. Gandhi asked Nehru to develop his ideas at greater length for wider dissemination: 'I expect you will write on the Hindi–Urdu topic at an early date. Yours sincerely, BAPU.'[28] The phrasing of Gandhi's letter presupposes additional contact between them on this matter beyond what we find in the archives. That contact could have been orally transmitted or otherwise communicated through an intermediary, such as Mahadev Desai, Gandhi's assistant and secretary. On 13 July 1937 Nehru wrote Gandhi from Allahabad:

About the Hindi–Urdu matter I shall write something within a few days. It will not be very deep. But it may help in clearing the issues and facilitating a calmer consideration of them. I shall send you a copy, also to Maulana [Azad].[29]

By 3 August 1937 Gandhi had received a draft of the essay, for he sent a letter of that date from 'On the train' to Nehru with comments.[30] Gandhi had no major problems with the text of the essay but did suggest a few amusing changes: 'You have "perhaps" before Pashto and Punjabi [as languages of instruction in the schools]. I suggest your removing the adverb. Khan Saheb for instance will never give up Pashto. I believe it is written in some script I forget which. And Punjabi? The Sikhs will die for Punjabi written in Gurumukhi. There is no elegance about that script.' Gandhi proposed that the unified south Indian language script Nehru endorses be Devanagari, which would never have been acceptable in Dravidian India — iconicity again — and made a few other observations in this vein. As far I can make out, Nehru acceded to Gandhi's editorial advice only to the extent of removing the adverb 'perhaps' before Pashto and Punjabi.

Mahadev Desai also offered some editorial suggestions,[31] all virtually identical to Gandhi's, with whom he had almost certainly gone over the matter since they were in the same train compartment when they wrote their respective letters. Gandhi contributed a foreword for the publication in tract form by the All-India Congress Committee:

I have very carefully gone through Jawaharlal Nehru's essay on the Hindi–Urdu question. The question has latterly become an unfortunate controversy. There is no valid reason for the ugly turn it has taken. Be that as it may, Jawaharlal's essay is a valuable contribution to a proper elucidation of the whole subject considered from the national and purely educational point of view. His constructive suggestions, if they are widely accepted by persons concerned, should put an end to the controversy which has taken a communal turn. The suggestions are exhaustive and eminently reasonable.[32]

In short, 'The Question of Language' owes as much to Gandhi's political need at the time as it does to Nehru's interest in Hindustani. It tracks very closely the points made in Nehru's brief message in Hindi to the Madras Hindi Sahitya Sammelan, which was the acorn out of which the oak grew.

There are considerable differences between Gandhi and Nehru in their entire approach to language and its political entanglements. Gandhi was far less knowledgeable and sophisticated about language than Nehru. If Nehru was not, at least not initially, attuned to the iconic uses and misuses of language for political purposes, Gandhi was as a babe in the woods regarding such worldliness. The English language, of which he was so wicked a master? — 'I speak to you, brothers, in that broken Hindi of mine, because even if I speak a little of English, I have the feeling that I am committing a sin.' Scripts? Filial attachment to a language? Love of a language and its literature? All such questions put as purely linguistic questions, arising out of ignorance of the iconicity of language, were no more than provocations for the Mahatma, causes for exasperation, flies to be swatted away (if the Mahatma had allowed flies to be swatted away in his presence).

All this otherworldliness about language was too much for Nehru. Nehru sympathized with the political need to calm Hindu–Muslim tempers. But he had very little patience for Gandhi's imprecision and vague wooliness in matters of language. As Nehru had written in 'The Meaning of Words' (see above): 'In general whatever he [Gandhi] speaks or writes is precise and effective . . . This trimness is his power. But whenever he speaks of God, the truth or ahimsa — and he does this often — then that mental precision is lessened . . . It must mean something but it is not quite clear what.'

Gandhi, at the time he asked Nehru to write 'The Question of Language', was gingerly negotiating his way through the treacherous terrain of Hindu–Muslim animosity with its outworks of Hindi–Urdu language conflict, trying very hard to find consensus, to smooth ruffled feathers, and to broaden areas of agreement between warring parties. Gandhi always tried harder than Nehru did to accommodate the more radical of the Hindi organizations, hoping thereby to moderate their positions.[33] In his letter to Nehru of 3 August 1937, Gandhi writes: 'I take it that my endorsement of your suggestions does not mean that I must ask the Hindi Sammelan to give up the use of the word Hindi.' Nehru had used the word 'Hindustani' rather than 'Hindi' as Gandhi himself normally did; but at this particular moment Gandhi was anxious not to provoke the Hindi Sahitya Sammelan. This organization was committed to 'Hindi', not 'Hindustani'. Tonnes of iconic import hinged on the difference.

Nehru, on the other hand, was not bothered in the least by the word 'Hindustani', even at the risk of exacerbating the always touchy feelings of the Hindi Sahitya Sammelan. Nehru never had a high opinion of Hindi journalists and authors, who had attacked him severely for his moderate views on the national language.[34] Indeed, the text of 'The Question of Language' is rife with thinly veiled sarcasms about the narrow provincialism of both Hindi and Urdu partisans. Speaking of Hindi and Urdu literary societies and their tendency to emphasize the differences between the languages over their commonalities, they 'accuse each other of encouraging separatist tendencies. The beam in one's own eye is not seen, the mote in the other's eye is obvious enough.' 'Scratch a separatist in language and you will invariably find that he is a communalist, and very often a political reactionary.' Sounding a theme he would often return to after Independence — the inadequacy of the languages of India, Hindi and Urdu included, for the intricacies of modern life — Nehru wrote: 'Hindi and Urdu are both at present inadequate for the proper expression of modern ideas, scientific, political, economic, commercial, and sometimes cultural . . .'[35]

More generally, Nehru voiced here his perceptions, which we encountered first during his imprisonment in Almora Jail in 1935, that Hindi writers — and Urdu ones too, though he never criticized Urdu writers as harshly as he did Hindi ones — were timorous, inward-looking, excessively refined, and élitist:

> I am no expert in this matter, but my own impression is that the average writer in Hindi or Urdu does not seek to take advantage of even the existing audience. He thinks much more of the literary coteries in which he moves, and writes for them in the language they have come to appreciate. His voice and his word do not reach the much larger public, and, if they happen to reach this public, they are not understood. Is it surprising that Hindi and Urdu books have restricted sales? Even our newspapers in Hindi and Urdu barely tap the great reading public . . .[36]

Nehru was always more critical of Hindi writers than those writing in Urdu, but this was both a linguistic or literary appraisal and a political tactic. We recall that Nehru usually referred to the form of the language he spoke as Urdu rather than Hindi, and his Allahabad-based Hindustani would have had more Persianisms in it than the Hindi of, say, Varanasi. In truth, 'Urdu' was for Nehru both a language and an icon: a symbol of Hindu–Muslim harmony and a secular India in which religion was no longer an issue men would die for. Nehru was always far more deeply committed to the ideal of a secular India than Gandhi, who was more of a Hindu reformer than a champion of the kind of secular India Nehru fought for all his life. It is this commitment to Urdu as icon of secular tolerance in a largely Hindu society that misleads Nehru into making suspect generalizations both about Hindi and Urdu and about language change:

> And this leads us to the real difference between Urdu and Hindi today — Urdu is the language of the towns and Hindi the language of the villages. Hindi is, of course, spoken also in the towns, but Urdu is almost entirely an urban language. The problem of bringing Urdu and Hindi nearer to each other thus becomes the much vaster problem of bringing the town and the village nearer to each other. Every other way will be a superficial way without lasting effect. Languages change organically when the people who speak them change.[37]

Whatever the level of its linguistic sophistication, Nehru's essay accomplished at least temporarily what Gandhi and he had hoped for: a reduction in the level of acrimony in the Hindi–Urdu confrontation. Rajendra Prasad, a Hindi proponent, and Abdul Haq, an Urdu proponent, met on 28 August 1937 in Patna and issued a joint statement of agreement:

> We are agreed that Hindustani should be the common language of India and should be written in both the Urdu and Nagri characters . . . By 'Hindustani' we mean the largest common factor of the language spoken in North India . . .[38]

And Sarojini Naidu, long-time associate of Nehru's, poet, politician, and president of the Congress in 1925, wrote a letter in praise of 'The Question of Language' to Nehru on 7 September 1937:

> Your language pamphlet is a miracle worker. You should see the radiant satisfaction it has produced among the most disgruntled! Old Maulvi Abdul Hakk whose opinion counts for much in Urdu literary circles, to whom I had sent a copy, has since been in conference with Rajen Babu [Rajendra Prasad] and has returned glowing

with satisfaction . . . Could I have a dozen more copies . . . ? I want to send some to various places to people who have had discussions with me on this point, in the Panjab and elsewhere.[39]

It is clear why Gandhi chose Nehru for this task. It required someone who wrote well and persuasively. It required sophistication and wisdom about language. It required a cosmopolitan outlook; someone with a reputation for integrity, someone with knowledge of Hindi and Urdu yet tethered to neither side in this crabbed conflict. Was there another man in India at the time who could have written the essay that Nehru did? Not likely.

After 'The Question of Language' in 1937 Nehru wrote only one further essay on language per se, though *The Discovery of India* is filled with allusions and observations that grew out of his extensive reading and experience. Language was never far below the surface of *The Discovery of India*, and we recall that Nehru devoted a major part of the preface of *Discovery* to language (cf. Chapter 6, 'The Private Nehru', Jail Time).[40] However, in 1949 he published an essay of moderate, length to which he unaccountably gave the same title 'The Question of Language'.[41]

'The Question of Language' (Reprise)

In substance this essay contains little that he had not dealt with earlier in the essays of the 1930s. 'The Question of Language' in its latter version is not, however, devoid of interest, for the perspective of the author is Nehru as prime minister rather than prime minister-in-anticipation. The first sentence of the essay seems to deny this — 'I am writing this article not as prime minister but as an author and as a person intensely interested in the question of language' — but it soon becomes clear that the reason he had put pen to paper was to sort out his confused feelings on the intensity of the language disagreements that were preoccupying him after two years of Independence: 'I am interested in [the question of language] because of its political and, unfortunately, communal aspects.'

His first impulse is to place language where he thinks it belongs, which is to say outside the political arena: 'Though I am not a scholar in any language, I have loved the beauty of a language, the music of its phrases, and the magic and power that lies in words.' But language lies not only beyond politics and aesthetics; it is a summation of national character:

I believe that a language is a greater test of a nation's character than almost anything else. If a language is strong and vigorous, so are the people who use it; if it is rather superficial, ornate and intricate, the people reflect it. Of course this may be more correctly put the other way about, for it is the people who create the language. But there is some truth also in the language moulding the people.

And, hearkening back to the Whorfian theme of 'The Meaning of Words': 'A language which is precise makes the people think precisely. Lack of accuracy and precision in meaning leads to muddled thinking and, consequently, confused action.'

He then proceeds to discuss Persian and Sanskrit, and their simultaneous power for good — as icons of important strains of Indian intellectual history — and bad — as drags on the development of the Indian vernaculars. Sanskrit, as always, occupies a special place in Nehru's heart: '[Sanskrit] is a magnificent inheritance and so long as [the Sanskrit language] endures and influences the life of our people so long will the basic genius of India continue.'

The development of an all-India language is vitally important, he says, but it is a matter of most supreme indifference whether that language be called Hindi or Hindustani:

We must deliberately aim, I think, at a language which is [the opposite of restrictive and narrow] and which has therefore a great capacity for growth. The English language, probably more than any other today, has this receptiveness, flexibility and capacity for growth: hence its great importance as a language. I should like our language to face the world in the same way.

But — he is clear about this — English for all its advantages cannot take the place of a pan-Indian language of autochthonous provenance. This he presents as an apodictic observation beyond assault, though he is (as ever) not dogmatic about it.

Buried in the latter half of 'The Question of Language' (the second version) is the real reason that Nehru has language on the mind in the restless linguistic currents of 1949 and why he has tackled the problem in a public forum at this time:

I am distressed at the way this question of language is considered and debated in India today. There is little of scholarship behind this argument and less of culture. There is no vision or thought of the future. Language is looked upon more as a kind of extended journalese and perverted nationalism which demands that it should be made as narrow and restricted as possible . . .

A language will grow ultimately because of its inherent worth and not because of statutes or resolutions.

There it is: a relatively pure distillation of Nehru's thinking about language. Language should be considered in the refuge of quiet reflection and not in the hot arena of political disputation. The future of India in its parlous post-Independence existence will depend on much else besides language. 'Perverted nationalism; narrow; restricted.' This is purest Nehru; the essence, as it were, of Nehru as linguist. And above all: 'A language will grow ultimately because of its inherent worth and not because of statutes or resolutions.'

This replay of 'The Question of Language' written with all the benefits and disabilities of political leadership and political responsibility is a good summary of Nehru's growing awareness of the divisiveness of language in an independent India and his concern for where the release of linguistic passions would take his country. He would hew hard to these positions as he moved in the 1950s.

It was henceforth to be in his speeches and his conduct of government that Nehru's lifetime of experience in language and its uses would be expressed and find practical application in his role as prime minister of independent India.

Notes and References

1. Gopal, *Biography* 1: 191.
2. *Selected Works* I.6: 339–40.
3. Ibid., I.6: 439–42, 442–5, 450–6.
4. Ibid., I.6: 445–9.
5. Ibid., I.6: 448.
6. Thakur, *Jawaharlal Nehru: The Man and the Writer*, pp. 60–2, touches on it.
7. *Selected Works* I.6: 445.
8. Ibid., I.6: 445–6.
9. Ibid., I.6: 446.

10. Ibid., I.6: 420–7.
11. There are arguments whether what I am calling the 'Whorf–Sapir Hypothesis' should more accurately be called the 'Sapir–Whorf Hypothesis', the 'Whorfian Hypothesis', or the 'Linguistic Relativity Hypothesis'; but these are disputes within the scholarly guild about intellectual pedigree and precedence and need not detain us here. The literature on this hypothesis is extensive: J.B. Carroll (ed.), *Language, Thought, and Reality; Selected Writings of Benjamin Lee Whorf* (Cambridge: MIT Press, 1956); J.B. Carroll, *Language and Thought* (Englewood Cliffs: Prentice-Hall, 1964); R.L. Cooper and B. Spolsky (eds), *The Influence of Language on Culture and Thought; Essays in Honor of Joshua A. Fishman's Sixty-Fifth Birthday* (Berlin and New York: Mouton de Gruyter, 1991); J.A. Fishman, 1960. 'A Systematization of the Whorfian Hypothesis', *Behavioral Science* (1960), vol. 5, pp. 323–39; J.A. Fishman, 'Sociocultural Organization: Language Constraints and Language Reflections', in *Language in Sociocultural Change* (Stanford: Stanford University Press, 1972), pp. 286–305; J.A. Lucy, *Grammatical Categories and Cognition: A Case Study of the Linguistic Relativity Hypothesis* (Cambridge: Cambridge University Press, 1992); R. Pinxten (ed.), *Universalism versus Relativism in Language and Thought; Proceedings of a Colloquium on the Sapir–Whorf Hypothesis* (The Hague: Mouton, 1976); I. Werlen, *Sprache, Mensch und Welt: Geschichte und Bedeutung des Prinzips der sprachlichen Relativität* (Darmstadt: Wissenschaftliche Buchgesellschaft, 1989).
12. R. Darnell, 'Personality and Culture: The Fate of the Sapirian Alternative', *History of Anthropology* (1986), vol. 4, pp. 156–83; R. Darnell, *Edward Sapir: Linguist, Anthropologist, Humanist* (Berkeley and Los Angeles: University of California Press, 1990); D. Mandelbaum (ed.), *Selected Writings of Edward Sapir in Language, Culture and Personality* (Berkeley: University of California Press, 1949).
13. B.L. Whorf, 'The Relation of Habitual Thought and Behavior to Language', *in* J.B. Carroll (ed.), *Language, Thought, and Reality; Selected Writings of Benjamin Lee Whorf* (Cambridge: MIT Press, 1956), pp. 134–59.
14. B.L. Whorf, 'Some Verbal Categories of Hopi', *Language* (1938), vol. 14, pp. 275–86. Rptd. *in* J.B. Carroll (ed.), *Language, Thought, and Reality; Selected Writings of Benjamin Lee Whorf* (Cambridge: MIT Press, 1956), pp. 112–24.
15. Ibid., p. 158.
16. Sapir, *Language* (New York: Harcourt, Brace & World, 1921), pp. 217–18.

17. The classic work on colour terms is B. Berlin and P. Kay, *Basic Color Terms: Their Universality and Evolution* (Berkeley: University of California Press, 1969).
18. W. O'Grady, M. Dobrovolsky, and M. Aronoff, *Contemporary Linguistics* (New York: St. Martin's Press, 1993), pp. 243–4.
19. *Selected Works* I.6: 449.
20. *Seven Types of Ambiguity* (New York: Noonday Press, 1955).
21. *Selected Works* I.6: 449.
22. *Autobiography*, p. 72.
23. Quotations are from the reprint of 'The Question of Language' in *The Unity of India* (*Unity*, pp. 241–61); it is also reprinted in *Selected Works* I.8: 829–45.
24. *Selected Works* I.6: 442–5.
25. *Unity*, p. 241.
26. Ibid., p. 245.
27. *Selected Works* I.8: 826–9.
28. 10 July 1937, *Collected Works of Mahatma Gandhi*, vol. 65, pp. 380–1.
29. *Selected Works* I.8: 159.
30. *Collected Works of Mahatma Gandhi*, vol. 66, pp. 7–8.
31. 4 Aug. 1937, *A Bunch of Old Letters*, pp. 247–9.
32. *Collected Works of Mahatma Gandhi*, vol. 66, p. 7.
33. Dittmer, *Die indischen Muslims und die Hindi–Urdu Kontroverse in den United Provinces*, pp. 160–4.
34. Ibid., p. 163.
35. *Unity*, pp. 248–9.
36. Ibid., p. 251.
37. Ibid., p. 248.
38. Dittmer, *Die indischen Muslims und die Hindi–Urdu Kontroverse in den United Provinces*, pp. 163–4.
39. *A Bunch of Old Letters*, p. 101. The date given for this letter in *A Bunch of Old Letters* is 1931, which is a misprint, cf. Dittmer, *Die indischen Muslims und die Hindi–Urdu Kontroverse in den United Provinces*, p. 163n.
40. On 12 February 1949 Nehru addressed in Hindi the Gujarat Vidya Sabha at its meeting in Ahmedabad. The speech, though quite long, is not exceptional. Its major purpose seems to have been to shore up his Hindi credentials and to deflect the incipient criticism of Nehru's 'Westernness' and affection for the English language: '[S]ometimes some people say, "See, Jawaharlal is on one side. We can take a decision about Hindi and all that, but Jawaharlal says Hindustani, Hindustani. He speaks his own kind of language and has become like a mountain in our path and does not allow anyone to march forward." Well, in certain matters I do want to

stand like a rock. On the other hand, you know that this question is not of recent origin . . .' (*Selected Works* II.9: 119–29).

41. *National Herald*, 13 Feb. 1949, *Selected Works* II.9: 129–34.

Chapter 7

Summing Up

I said in the preface to this book that Nehru has not been given high marks for his handling of the language problems India faced during his stewardship of its affairs, which lasted from the achievement of independence in 1947 to his death in 1964. I myself am not in the least disposed to criticize him in this. I think, on the contrary, that he did a good job — and an incomparably better one than anyone else could have done — in grappling with the linguistic problems of the country.

There seems to be a tendency among Nehru observers to feel that it would have been better if he had recognized early on that the movement towards linguistic provinces was going to come to be something of a juggernaut and had got out of its way. This would certainly have been a good thing to do 'politically' in one of the least attractive senses of the word 'politics' — politics as the art of winning votes. I am certain, however, that this would not have been a good thing for the future of India. It would have required on his part, and during the critical formative period of India's nationhood, concession of major areas of principle. It would have represented a compromise with regionalism, a retreat from the vision of the oneness of India, all of which would have been very bad, especially at that sensitive time.

I know of no one in 1947 anywhere, neither in India nor in the West, who was clear on the complex web of relationships that bind language to society, to class, caste, and religion. Its role in defining nationalism was not widely understood. The use of language as surrogate for baser demands was unfamiliar. There had not been enough time and experience of new-nation formation to have acquired the requisite wisdom in such things.

There are some situations so complicated, so delicate, so full of snarls and traps and potential for disaster, that the best course a wise political leader can follow is the classical British method of 'muddling through'; muddling through gains time, if nothing else. Language, in the India of the first decade and a half past Independence, was such a situation. Had India been led by someone eager to reorganize the country into linguistic provinces early on, say within months of Independence, as so many demanded so stridently, that would have boded ill for national unity. Regional nationalisms could easily have overwhelmed the nationalism of the centre — of India.

If India had had the bad luck to have been led at its birth either by an English-hater resolved to rid the land of the English language at all costs or by a weakling not firm about the retention of English, then we should have today an India isolated from much of what is good and useful in a world where English has become the international language. Today's India would be an inward-dwelling, neurotic backwater. More than likely we should not be speaking of a single India at all, if English had been eliminated, for Dravidian India would not have tolerated second-class linguistic status, which is what the forced imposition of Hindi as national language would have entailed. There is no serious question about that. If English had been denied official status and Hindi mandated as the sole national language, then we should have today not one India but at least two: 'Dravidistan' in the south and some other kind of '-stan' in the north, probably 'Hindustan'. We may recall that there had been mention of a 'Pathanistan' in the negotiations leading up to Independence.[1] Balkanization, a byword of the earlier half of the twentieth century, was a much greater threat to India in 1947 than it was in 1957 or 1967.

In Chapter 3, I quoted Percival Spear to the effect that the two principal language issues — linguistic provinces, Hindi versus English — were connected.[2] The drive by Hindi imperialists to make Hindi the national language strengthened not only the movement for English but the demand for local administrative units where the regional language could be used. If you force Hindi on us for national use, then you cannot deny us the right to establish a state in which we use our own regional language. I could go further and say that the linguistic states would not have succeeded nearly so well as they have if Hindi instead of English had been cudgeled through as the official language of the centre. The use of regional languages for regional state purposes works best when the language of the centre is *not* one of the state languages. English was, so to speak, equally distant from every regional Indian language and thus was fortuitously available as a neutral language of central administration. Nothing, no law, no guarantee or multitude of guarantees, would ever have convinced a non-Hindi speaker that he would get a fair stake in a country whose national language was Hindi.

India is a many-centred country. Its great cities are centres — Delhi, Bombay, Calcutta, Madras, Hyderabad. Its regions are centres. Its religions are centres. In India, and to another Indian abroad, the answer to the question 'Where are you from' would be: 'I am from Kerala, or Maharashtra, or U.P.'; 'I am a Bengali, or a Tamil.' A villager would name his village as the place he is from. These centres on the map and in the heart are sublimely significant in India. 'North India' is a centre; 'South India' is a centre. India has, I say, many 'centres', and recognition of its various 'centres' in all their size and complexity and history is essential to the well-being and good governance of the country. Recognition of what I am calling 'centres' can assume various forms. One of the easiest, and in the twentieth century most natural, ways of recognizing a 'centre' is to recognize its language, if it has one.

I think, therefore, that it was inevitable that India would reorganize itself linguistically after Independence and would do so according to language and culture, which in practical terms means according to language since culture is notoriously so difficult to pin down. Linguistic reorganization was inevitable, but linguistic reorganization worked out for the best by being delayed. And that is all Jawaharlal Nehru ever said he wanted to do — to delay the reorganization of the country according to linguistic states until other more pressing concerns had been resolved.

Another, and in my opinion even better reason for delay, was that India gained eight years, from 1947 to 1955, to prove that it could be a viable country; to prove that there was something concrete and not merely metaphorical and mystical in the idea of the 'unity' of India; that the partition into India and Pakistan was not the presager of inevitable further partitions along other fault lines of the subcontinent. The India of 1947 had no experience of governing itself. The India of 1955 had had eight precious years to show that it could govern itself and function not as warring fiefdoms but as a nation. Division into linguistic states after 1955 caused problems, and I cannot minimize them even if I wished to, but they did not have the effect I believe they would have had if states reorganization had taken place in 1947 with no experience of self-government. Division into linguistic states in 1947 would have been seriously destabilizing and might have crippled India at birth. By 1955 the country had matured enough to withstand the effects of linguistic reorganization of the state boundaries. If states reorganization had been undertaken in India's infancy, in 1947, then the goal of Indian unity might well have been strangled in its cradle.

I feel, with Joseph Schwartzberg, that the reorganization of Indian states along linguistic lines has, paradoxically perhaps, preserved the unity of the nation rather than balkanized it, as many had predicted:

> In creating a system of essentially linguistic states, India has provided a local political milieu that is conducive to the flowering of many linguistically-rooted cultures and thereby evolved a system which greatly enriches the cultural life of the nation as a whole. Further changes along purely linguistic lines are not likely to be great.[3]

The key to the art of good government in India has always been light government in strong hands. This was true in Asoka's reign, it was true in Akbar's reign, it was true in the British Raj, it was true in Nehru's India, and it is true today. It is the Indian Paradox: if you do not decentralize you will balkanize. If the many centres of which India consists have control at least of their culture and language, they fret less about the culture and language pretensions of the national centre. The linguistic states provide the means through which the regional cultures maintain their traditions and orient their citizenry towards their history.

Nehru's way was to make haste slowly in all matters linguistic. His way was to emphasize always that language in all its manifestations was important — linguistic provinces were important, the national language was important — but so were many other things such as national security, economic growth, and international relations. Everything in good time, nothing precipitately. The end result of the Nehru Raj in matters linguistic is an India in which language is important but not all-consuming. India's linguistic policy today is by default a policy of benign neglect, and that is, I submit, the best policy any language-troubled country can have. That sophisticated way of treating language is more Nehru's legacy than anyone else's.

As the twentieth century draws to a close, we do not find that language is becoming less important as icon. Quite the reverse. Language in the Middle East and in the countries of the former Soviet Union is as explosive an issue as it ever was in post-Independence India. Consider the following Reuter's dispatch of 21 March 1995:

CHISINAU, Moldova (Reuter) — Some 10,000 students protested Tuesday in the capital of Moldova against a government decision to reform school history lessons.

The government recently introduced the history of Moldova as a new subject in secondary schools and higher education institutions. It replaced the History of the Romanians, taught since Moldova gained independence from the Soviet Union in 1991.

The students, in the second day of protest, stopped traffic in the centre of Chisinau and chanted: 'Romanian is the official language' and 'We are Romanians.'

Most of what is now Moldova is land seized from Romania in 1940 by Soviet dictator Josef Stalin under a secret pact with Nazi Germany.

Ethnic Moldovans, who form 65 per cent of the former Soviet republic's population, share a common language and culture with their ethnic kin in Romania.

But the pro-Romanian bloc in parliament lost its majority last year to the pro-independence Agrarian Democratic Party, whose leaders are mostly former communist officials.

'The students were pushed by certain political forces who do not want stability in the country,' Moldova's vice premier, Grigore Ojog, told national radio.

The students said their protest was open-ended and threatened to go on strike until the decision was reversed.

Monday about 5,000 students gathered in front of the government building and burned their new textbooks.

This dispatch bears a depressing similarity to the accounts that appeared regularly in Indian newspapers during the great language battles of Nehru's time. What lay behind the events in

Moldova will be familiar to the student of Indian linguistic history in the post-War era.

The Moldavian SSR of the Soviet Union comprised most of what was earlier called Bessarabia. Russia had laid claim to Bessarabia since 1812. The ethnicity of the majority of the inhabitants of Bessarabia was Romanian, and the region voted for unification with Romania in 1918 upon dissolution of the Austro–Hungarian Empire; but Moldavia came under uninterrupted Soviet rule after 1941 as a result of the infamous Soviet–German pact that preceded the outbreak of the Second World War.

The language of the majority of people of the Moldavian SSR was Romanian. The differences between the Romanian of Romania and the Romanian of the Moldavian SSR (Moldova) are dialectal and minor, as trifling as the differences between British and American English. However, official Soviet policy was to deny that Romanian and 'Moldavian' were the same language, the better to drive a wedge between the Moldavians and their ethnic brethren in Romania and put paid to any future hope of rapprochement or reunification between the two groups of Romanians. Since 1936 the Soviets had required that the Romanian language of the Moldavian SSR be written in the Cyrillic alphabet used for writing Russian. This was a consequence of a general Stalinist policy laid down that year of mandating Cyrillic orthographies for all the languages of the USSR. The difference in script between the Romanian of Moldavia and the Romanian of Romania underscored, of course, the general point the Soviets wanted to make, namely that Moldavian and Romanian were different languages and the Moldavian SSR a different cultural and historical entity from Romania. It was and is linguistic tommyrot. In a hierarchical arrangement the reverse of that of Hindi and Urdu, at the highest literary levels there are no differences between Romanian and Moldavian; the differences are greatest at the 'bazaar' level, as it were, among farmers and the simple folk.[4]

In 1979, before Gorbachev and glasnost and perestroika, approximately 65 per cent of the population of the Moldavian SSR was ethnically Moldavian. There were minorities of Russians, Ukrainians, and Gagauz.[5] Russian was to all intents and purposes the official language of the MSSR. Though the Moldavian language was quasi-officially recognized and tolerated, it was discriminated against in the schools and elsewhere to the benefit of Russian.

In August 1989 hundreds of thousands of ethnic Moldavians demonstrated in the capital Kishinev (now called Chisinau) demanding adoption of their language, Moldavian (now called Moldovan), as the official language of the Moldavian SSR. Soon thereafter the Moldavian legislature voted 300–43 in favour, and the law went into effect on 30 August 1989. As of 1995 all official business was to be conducted in Moldovan. A return to the Latin alphabet went into effect immediately, and has remained in effect ever since. Edinstvo, an anti-separatist group of Russians, Ukrainians, and Gagauz, staged a counter-demonstration in August of 1989 in opposition both to separatism and official language status for Moldovan.

On 24 April 1990 Mikhail Gorbachev, recognizing that the language issue in Moldova and elsewhere was rapidly getting out of hand, declared Russian to be the official and international language of the Soviet Union. By conferring on Russian the status of official language of all parts of the Soviet Union Gorbachev actually accomplished the reverse. His proclamation fanned the fires of linguistic separatism to even higher temperatures, and where language goes, ethnicity and politics are never far behind — again, a situation sadly familiar to the student of Indian language politics and of language as icon. The battle lines were thus drawn up, and a language — Moldovan — was being used as a weapon against the central government in Moscow.

This then was the background of the demonstrations by students in Moldova in 1995 reported by Reuters. Stories like this can be multiplied many times over throughout the former Soviet Union. The former Soviet Union, like India, is a vast panorama of languages. A far-from-exhaustive listing of languages of the former USSR includes Russian, Estonian, Latvian, Lithuanian, Belorussian, Ukrainian, Armenian, Georgian, Polish, Korean, Azerbaijani, Chuvash, Kazakh, Kirgiz, Volga and Crimean Tatar, Uzbek, Tajik, Circassian, Kabardian, Abkhaz, German, Yiddish, and Romani. Language families and subfamilies include Indo–European, Caucasian, Turkic, Finno–Ugric, and those are only the major ones.

Since 1989, when the then Soviet Union set out on a path of

restructuring its society (perestroika), it has experienced turbulent inner strife, particularly in its outer republics. Religion adds another dimension to this unstable equation since many of the central Asian republics are largely Muslim and often have ethnic and linguistic allegiances that do not respect the historical state boundaries. Almost any one of these language–ethnic situations can at any time light a fuse that will eventually set off a very great explosion. The language conflict in Estonia, for example, has been especially bitter. Estonia has almost as many ethnic Russians as it does ethnic Estonians. Most of the Russians who live there do not speak Estonian, and many of them have lived in Estonia for over a generation. Estonia has passed legislation requiring knowledge of the Estonian language as a prerequisite for Estonian citizenship and as a prerequisite for work permits, education, and much else. Lithuania, upon gaining independence, restricted the use of Polish. These cases can be multiplied several times over. The former Soviet Union, clearly, is a mass of language–culture–religion tinderboxes any one of which can blow up at any time.

The peoples of the former Soviet Union — indeed, of any language-troubled country — would be well-advised to learn from India's experience of language. Nehru had taken to heart the early Leninist theory of tolerance — *laissez-faire*, what I call benign neglect — of language. It was one of the factors that made him refuse to join the rush to linguistic separatism and linguistic chauvinism, as we saw in Chapter 4 ('Nehru at the Helm'). The Nehru policy — or the Nehru no-policy — served his country well. As India under Nehru's leadership was wise to look north to its neighbour, the Soviet Union, for lessons in language tolerance, the countries now emerging from Soviet domination would do well to look south to the India of Nehru's making for current lessons in nation-building and language policy. The one lesson that should be learnt, but almost never is, is that the best policy a language-troubled country can have is no policy, or at worst a policy of benign neglect.

The Final Act

The Official Language Bill was brought before the Lok Sabha and debated in the early months of 1963. The purpose of the Official

Language Bill was to extend beyond 1965 the use of the English language for official purposes of the union. Nehru was then seventy-three years old. His health was not good. His spirit had never recovered from the war with China, which had been for him, as for his country, a deeply humiliating experience. Corruption in government was becoming an issue. Relations with Pakistan were bad. Kashmir was a boiling mess, as it always had been. Hindi enthusiasts were bitterly opposed to any delay in the imposition of Hindi as the sole official national language of India. 'Echoes of the events and the speeches of the first months of India's freedom returned in the last months of Nehru's life and darkened his last days.'[6] The Duke of Wellington had said that 'Next to a battle lost, the greatest misery is a battle gained.' What did Nehru think in 1963 about the battles he had fought — had he won or lost most of them?

In spite of all that weighed on him and in spite of his advanced age, Nehru rose in the Lok Sabha and delivered what I regard as the most remarkable and certainly the most wide-ranging speech he ever gave at any time on the subject of language.[7] But Nehru's speech on the Official Language Bill covers far more territory than the matter at hand — the continuation of English as an official language. It draws upon the knowledge of a lifetime's study of language and the uses of language. He cites facts and statistics about language that few leaders of any country have ever had at their disposal. This is a linguistically mature Nehru speaking; a man in possession of profound understanding of the uses, iconic and otherwise, of language, and of the terrible things that language could do. This speech is a perfect summation of Nehru's life with language, a valediction almost.

He begins by calling the attention of the house to 'a most extraordinary, disgusting and disgraceful spectacle' that had taken place when the bill was introduced (cf. Ch. 4), which was the disruption of President Radhakrishnan's speech by members who demanded that the President deliver it in Hindi and had then walked out in protest when he refused to do so (18 Feb. 1963):

> That [incident], I submit, raises more basic questions than even the question of language. Therefore, I am referring to it because language, after all, does represent some of the deepest urges of human beings and is the vehicle of all our business.

There then comes an exchange with Frank Anthony, a leader of the pro-English forces, concerning the use of the word 'may' in the bill, which as written provided that English 'may' continue to be used past 1965, in addition to Hindi, for all official purposes of the union and in parliament. The critics of Hindi, notably Frank Anthony and Rajagopalachari, had demanded more by way of statutory recognition in perpetuity of the rights of English — wanting to replace 'may' in the enabling legislation by 'shall' — but this assurance Nehru refused to give:

> As for the words 'may' and 'shall' — I would again say that when people get excited they do not see that the word 'may' is the most ordinary word, always used in this connection in the English language . . . [T]he question is one of removing a restriction, a restriction which would have prevented the English language from being used after a certain date. For removing this restriction, we say that this 'may' be used afterwards. It is quite absurd to say that the word 'may' means also 'may not'.

It is, as Nehru saw it, a pitiful point, this business of 'may' and 'shall'. But, in refusing to concede the point of 'may' versus 'shall' to the pro-English forces, he reminds them that he is partial to English because of his upbringing, though again he observes that 'any real awakening of the people cannot take place through the English language'. From his earliest involvement in politics he has:

> [B]elieved that it is through the [regional] languages of India alone that we could reach the people. This does not mean that we should discard English . . . ; English is likely to remain in India for a long, long time. I do not know exactly what form it will take, but the mere fact of its being there will serve as a vitalizer to our languages . . .
>
> Our languages are fine languages. They are old languages. Most of them, certainly the big languages — Bengali, Gujarati, Marathi and the southern languages like Tamil, Telugu, Kannada and Malayalam — are great languages from any point of view. They have produced great books which are rooted in the minds of the people . . . So far as Tamil is concerned, if I may say so, it is as old as Sanskrit, and all our languages, northern languages, apart from the four southern languages, are daughters of Sanskrit and have grown out of Sanskrit.
>
> The other languages also, to some extent, have grown from that

root and have been closely associated [with] and affected by Sanskrit. In fact, one may say with confidence that Sanskrit has represented broadly all the thought, culture and traditions of India . . . I am an admirer of Sanskrit . . . I think it would be a great pity if Sanskrit became a completely dead language in India at any time. That would do great damage to all that we stand for in India.

Unfortunately, we cannot make Sanskrit the working language of India today . . . It ceased to be a language of the common people 2,000 years ago . . . and gradually Prakrits developed.

What knowledge of the history of the English language, or of dialects of the English language, or of the role of Latin in the development of the English language, would a Roosevelt or a Churchill have been able to summon from memory in a legislative debate? Who, sitting as a deputy in the Lok Sabha on 24 April 1963 or as an observer in the gallery, would have had even a fraction of these linguistic facts on call?

Nehru then looks to other countries with more than one language. If India had only two or three languages, as Switzerland and Canada do, then he says that he would favour adopting them all as official languages. He cites Finland, where Finnish is the majority language but where Swedish is spoken by a minority, as an example alongside Switzerland (French, German, Italian) and Canada (English, French) — and he even gets the percentage of Swedish speakers in Finland's population correct, namely about 10 per cent. He then returns to his most constant theme of a lifetime:

In these matters of language one has to be very careful. One has to be as liberal as possible and not try to suppress a language. We should not try to coerce anybody into using a language, as far as possible. Whenever an attempt has been made to suppress a popular language or coerce the people into using some other language, there has been trouble . . .

[T]he makers of our Constitution were wise in laying down that all [the regional] languages were to be languages of equal status. There is no question of any one language being more a national language than another. I want to make that perfectly clear. Bengali or Tamil is as much an Indian national language as Hindi.

Hindi, he points out, has grown very much since Independence, as have all the regional languages of India. Growth of a language cannot be measured by its use by government clerks: 'no Government departments have ever made a language grow.' Use makes a language grow, but so does contact with other languages:

I do submit that even now, although they have grown and they will grow, further impact of English on our languages will be good for our languages . . . It is good to be in contact with foreign languages . . .

I think one of the most harmful things that has happened in India, not in regard to language only but also in other matters affecting our whole lives, is that we have lived for hundreds of years in a closed circle . . . This may have happened because we are an introspective people. Anyhow, we became self-centred and we lost these contacts . . . That affected our language, too. Language is a medium of the thoughts of the people, and our languages became static because our lives were static. The changes that came with the British invasion of India administered a shock and this had its effect on our languages also. It made them more dynamic — brought new forms, the novel, short stories, a new kind of drama, science and technology and so many other things.

At the present moment, we have to realize that India is a multilingual country. This is a new situation. We must realize that. Some Hon. Members opposite went on talking about 44 crores [440,000,000] of people knowing Hindi. It is not a fact.

There are always quibbles about what it means to 'know' a language, but Nehru was right about his numbers: no unbiased census of the time would have shown that 44 crores of Indians spoke Hindi anywhere near natively.

Nehru then returns, as he so often had before in public forums, to a theme always close to his heart — Urdu — and its importance to his secular, universalistic ideal of India:

[U]rdu is a dynamic language . . . [H]indi will get vitality from Urdu while retaining its own genius and nature. Urdu is vital. I shall tell you why. It has a strange capacity for adaptation and drawing from other languages. Urdu has drawn more from English than Hindi, strictly speaking. Urdu has drawn from Persian, from Arabic and from the Turkish language . . . It is this adaptability that makes a language strong. The other attitude weakens it . . .

Urdu itself is an amalgam, a synthesis of various languages; it is about 75–80 per cent Hindi and about 25 per cent of the words come from other languages [such as] Persian, Arabic and Turkish. It is quite clear that when two languages come together, they strengthen each other. The idea of pulling down a language and thinking that your language will profit by it is utterly wrong.

This is a thinly disguised criticism of the narrowness of Hindi zealots and hearkens back, as so much in this speech does, to Nehru's experiences of the mid-1930s when he was criticized by Hindi writers and journalists for his cosmopolitan outlook on language and, in particular, for his defence of Urdu. The tendency of Hindi purists to Sanskritize the language is also wrong, Nehru maintains, 'because these words which you have coined have no reality behind them, have no emotion, have no history'. And this takes him to the difficulty of translating from one language to another — the subject of his 1935 essay 'The Meaning of Words':

It will become impossible for you to really translate from one language to another [by introducing too much Sanskrit into Hindi] . . . You may translate, of course, simple words like 'chair' or 'table'. But as soon as you get a slightly more complicated idea, you cannot translate it with coined words.

Of course, as regards translating into or from Chinese, it is almost an utter impossibility to do it. Because the whole background of the Chinese language is quite different. It is not even an alphabetical language. It is a picture language.

It is not surprising that Nehru brings up Chinese out of nowhere and without preamble here — the Chinese invasion did not lie far in the past; but it is a revealing feat of memory that he should remember enough of his Firth and *The Tongues of Man* to conjure up the image of Chinese as a 'picture language' (see Ch. 5, 'The Private Nehru', Influences).

Nehru then proceeds to observe that:

We all know that standards of the English language are going down in India. This is not because of conflict between Hindi and English but because of the rising regional languages and English. English standards are going down and may further go down. But I think English would be more widely known in India in the future than now; though it will not be known for better quality.

As regards the spread of Hindi, there really is not much more the government can do about it:

If I may say so, all the steps that my Hon. friend the Education Minister may take in regard to the spread of Hindi do not go as far as the influence that cinema has had on the spread of Hindi. Any order that in a particular office Hindi must be used from tomorrow . . . would not spread Hindi.

And he brings his speech to conclusion by hammering once again on the theme that had been an invariant in almost every public utterance he had made on language since Independence in 1947:

I should like the House to consider the language issue not only in the limited sense in which we have been arguing it, but in the broader sense, in the wider context. We are passing through a difficult and delicate period of transition in many ways, and it requires wisdom and a capacity for flexibility in order to meet the demands of the times. Rigidity stops growth. The main question is of India's growth in every way, materially, intellectually and spiritually. We must view every step that we take from the point of that major question.

This was one of Nehru's last major speeches, and it is an extraordinary linguistic tour de force. It is eloquent, factually unassailable, informed by a lifetime of interest in language. It is urbane and cosmopolitan — elevated far above the rhetoric that has so regularly accompanied political debate on language in India and had so poisoned the wells of discourse on linguistic affairs at the time of the great struggles over language in the Nehru era. I cannot think of one other political figure in power in India in 1963 who could have delivered such a speech. I have never read any speech given by any other foreign head of state on language that approaches it in breadth of knowledge and sophistication.

With the passage of the Official Language Act, Nehru rendered his last service to the cause of progressive language policy in India — and a very great service it was. By delaying the execution of linguistic states and by securing the place of English in India indefinitely into the future, Nehru guaranteed a foundation for progress that will always remain one of his most enduring bequests.

Nehru understood the complexity of language and its disturbing power for bad as well as good far better than his contemporaries, whether by 'understood' we mean factually or intuitively is of no consequence. And why not, since he had been involved in language all his life to an extraordinary degree for a statesman. Also, he was an extremely intelligent man whose education and experience had elevated him to a height from which he could judge his country's problems without the regional prejudices and small-mindedness many of his fellow leaders brought with them when they assumed power in the wake of the British withdrawal.

He saw deeply into the nature of language and drew upon what he saw in both his private and public personae. The ultimate beneficiary of this his linguistic wisdom was India and its people with whom he was mystically attached. Here we must again observe how fortunate India was to have had Jawaharlal Nehru as its guide and preceptor during the years of the creation of independent India.

Notes and References

1. Campbell-Johnson, *Mission with Mountbatten*, p. 76.
2. *India*, pp. 440–1.
3. 'Factors in the Linguistic Reorganization of Indian States', p. 177.
4. My information on Moldavia/Moldova is taken from two articles by D.L. Dyer, 'Moldavian Part II', *in* H.I. Aronson (ed.), *The Non-Slavic Languages of the USSR, Linguistic Studies* (Chicago: Chicago Linguistic Society, 1989), pp. 93–105; and 'Russian and Romanian Intertwined: the Legacy that is Moldavian', *in* H.I. Aronson (ed.), *Linguistic Studies in the Non-Slavic Languages of the Commonwealth of Independent States and the Baltic Republics* (Chicago: Chicago Linguistic Society, 1994), pp. 65–77.
5. The Gagauz are Turkic-speaking Christians.
6. Gopal, *Biography* 3: 265.
7. 'The Official Languages', 24 April 1963, *Speeches* 5: 16–32.

Bibliography

SOURCES

The following sources are cited as follows:

NMML

Most of the Nehru correspondence and other materials dealing with language during the period covered in this book appear in one or several of the published collections cited below such as *Selected Works, Speeches, A Bunch of Old Letters, Letters to Chief Ministers, Freedom's Daughter, Two Alone, Two Together*, or *Nehru's Letters to his Sister*. Correspondence yet unpublished is found in the Nehru collection in the Nehru Memorial Museum and Library, New Delhi, and is cited by date and noted NMML.

Selected Works

Gopal, Sarvepalli (ed.), 1972–. *Selected Works of Jawaharlal Nehru*. New Delhi: Orient Longman/Oxford University Press; Jawaharlal Nehru Memorial Fund. This collection appears in two series. The first series covers the years 25 February 1903 through 2 September 1946 and comprises fifteen volumes. The second series (New Delhi: Oxford University Press; Jawaharlal Nehru Memorial Fund) commences with September 1946 and, when completed, will carry on down to Nehru's death in 1964. As referred to in the text the series number in roman numerals is succeeded by the volume number: for example *Selected Works* I.3: 167 indicates series I, volume 3, page 167; *Selected Works* II.4: 50 means series II, volume 4, page 50.

A Bunch of Old Letters

Nehru, Jawaharlal, 1960. *A Bunch of Old Letters*. Bombay: Asia Publishing House.

Letters to Chief Ministers

Parthasarathi, G. (ed.), 1985–8. *Letters to Chief Ministers 1947–1964*,

5 vols. New Delhi: Oxford University Press; Jawaharlal Nehru Memorial Fund.

Freedom's Daughter

Gandhi, Sonia (ed.), 1989. *Freedom's Daughter: Letters Between Indira Gandhi and Jawaharlal Nehru; Letters Between Indira Gandhi and Jawaharlal Nehru 1922–39*. London: Hodder & Stoughton.

Two Alone, Two Together

Gandhi, Sonia (ed.), 1992. *Two Alone, Two Together: Letters Between Indira Gandhi and Jawaharlal Nehru; Letters Between Indira Gandhi and Jawaharlal Nehru 1940–64*. London: Hodder & Stoughton.

Nehru's Letters to His Sister

Hutheesing, Krishna Nehru (ed.), 1963. *Nehru's Letters to His Sister*. London: Faber & Faber.

Speeches

Jawaharlal Nehru's Speeches, 1949–68. Publications Division, Ministry of Information and Broadcasting, Government of India. Cited by volume and page, for example *Speeches* 3: 143. A word of caution is in order here, for at least some volumes of *Jawaharlal Nehru's Speeches* have been reprinted ('Second Impression') in largely identical form to the original government publications but bearing a different pagination.

Autobiography

Nehru, Jawaharlal, 1941. *Toward Freedom*. New York: John Day.

Discovery

Nehru, Jawaharlal, 1946. *The Discovery of India*. New York: John Day.

Unity

Nehru, Jawaharlal, 1948. *The Unity of India*. New York: John Day.

Gopal, *Biography*

Gopal, Sarvepalli. *Jawaharlal Nehru, A Biography*, 3 vols. New Delhi: Oxford University Press (1975, vol. 1; 1979, vol. 2); London: Jonathan Cape (1984, vol. 3).

Selected Works of Motilal Nehru

Kumar, Ravinder and D.N. Panigrahi (eds), 1982. *Selected Works of Motilal Nehru*. New Delhi: Vikas Publishing House (issued under the auspices of the Nehru Memorial Museum and Library).

Collected Works of Mahatma Gandhi

Indian Government Publication, 1958–84. *The Collected Works of Mahatma Gandhi*. 90 vols. New Delhi: The Publications Division, Ministry of Information and Broadcasting.

Selected Speeches of Indira Gandhi

Indian Government Publication, 1971. *Selected Speeches of Indira Gandhi*. New Delhi: Publications Division.

Official Language Commission Report

Indian Government Publication, 1956. *Report of the Official Language Commission*. Delhi: Government of India Press.

Simon Commission

Indian Government Publication, 1988. *Simon Commission Report on India* (India Statutory Commission), 17 vols. Delhi: Swati Publications (rpt.).

SRC

Report of the States Reorganization Commission 1955. Delhi: Manager of Publications.

The quotations from the *Bhagavadgita* that occur throughout the text are taken from the translation of Barbara Stoler Miller, *The Bhagavad-Gita*. New York: Bantam Books, 1986.

SECONDARY WORKS CITED

Abdulaziz, M.H., 1971. 'Tanzania's National Language Policy and the Rise of Swahili Political Culture', *in* Wilfred H. Whiteley (ed.), *Language Use and Social Change*, pp. 160–78. London: Oxford University Press.

Abondolo, Daniel, 1987. 'Hungarian', *in* Bernard Comrie (ed.), *The World's Major Languages*, pp. 577–92. New York: Oxford University Press.

Akbar, M.J., 1988. *Nehru: The Making of India*. New York: Viking.

Alisjahbana, S. Takdir, 1971. 'Some Planning Processes in the Development of the Indonesian–Malay Language', *in* Joan Rubin and Björn H. Jernudd (eds), *Can Language Be Planned?*, pp. 179–87. Honolulu: The University Press of Hawaii.

Allan, John A. (ed.), 1934. *The Cambridge Shorter History of India*. Cambridge: Cambridge University Press.

Ambedkar, B.R., 1955. *Thoughts on Linguistic States*. Bombay: Ramkrishna Press.

Annamalai, E. (ed.), 1979. *Language Movements in India*. Mysore: Central Institute of Indian Languages.

Apsler, Alfred, 1963. *Jawaharlal Nehru*. New York: Julian Messner.

Apte, Mahadev L., 1976. 'Multilingualism in India and its Socio-political Implications: An Overview', *in* William M. O'Barr and Jean F. O'Barr (eds), *Language and Politics*, pp. 141–64. The Hague: Mouton.

Avineri, Shlomo (ed.), 1969. *Karl Marx on Colonialism and Modernization: His Despatches and Other Writings on China, India, Mexico, the Middle East and North Africa*. New York: Anchor Books.

Awasthy, G.C., 1965. *Broadcasting in India*. Bombay: Allied Publishers.

Balasubramanian, M., 1980. *Nehru: A Study in Secularism*. New Delhi: Uppal Publishing House.

Ballhatchet, Kenneth, 1990. 'The Importance of Macaulay', *Journal of the Royal Asiatic Society*, no. 1, pp. 91–4.

Bar-Adon, Aaron, 1975. *The Rise and Decline of a Dialect: A Study in the Revival of Modern Hebrew*. The Hague: Mouton.

Beames, John, 1966. *Comparative Grammar of the Modern Aryan Languages of India*. New Delhi: Munshiram Manoharlal (rpt.).

Beckett, James G., 1966. *The Making of Modern Ireland 1603–1923*. London: Faber & Faber.

Bennett, Charles J., 1980. 'The Morphology of Language Boundaries: Indo–Aryan and Dravidian in Peninsular India', *in* David E. Sopher (ed.), *An Exploration of India: Geographical Perspectives on Society and Culture*, pp. 234–51. Ithaca: Cornell University Press.

Berkes, Niyazi, 1964. *The Development of Secularism in Turkey*. Montreal: McGill University Press.

Berlin, Brent and Paul Kay, 1969. *Basic Color Terms: Their Universality and Evolution*. Berkeley: University of California Press.

Blanc, Haim, 1968. 'The Israeli Koine as an Emergent National Standard', *in* Joshua A. Fishman, Charles A. Ferguson, and Jyotirindra Das Gupta (eds), *Language Problems of Developing Nations*, pp. 237–51. New York: John Wiley & Sons.

Bloomfield, Leonard, 1933. *Language*. New York: Holt, Rinehart & Winston.

——, 1944. 'Secondary and Tertiary Responses to Language', *Language*, vol. 20, pp. 45–55, rptd. *in* Charles F. Hockett (ed.), *A Leonard Bloomfield Anthology*, pp. 413–25. Bloomington: Indiana University Press, 1970.

Brass, Paul, 1974. *Language, Religion and Politics in North India*. London: Cambridge University Press.

Breathnach, R.A., 1956. 'Revival or Survival? An Examination of the Irish Language Policy of the State', *Studies*, vol. 45, pp. 129–45.

——, 1964. 'Irish Revival Reconsidered', *Society*, vol. 53, pp. 18–30.

Brecher, Michael, 1959. *Nehru*. London: Oxford University Press.

Bretton, Henry L., 1976. 'Political Science, Language, and Politics', *in* William M. O'Barr and Jean F. O'Barr (eds), *Language and Politics*, pp. 431–48. The Hague: Mouton.

Brosnahan, L.F., 1963. 'Some Historical Cases of Language Imposition', *in* John Spencer (ed.), *Language in Africa*, pp. 7–24. Cambridge: Cambridge University Press.

Brown, Judith M., 1989. *Gandhi*. New Haven: Yale University Press.

Burrow, Thomas, 1973. *The Sanskrit Language*. London: Faber & Faber.

Butter, Peter H., 1960. *English in India*. Belfast: Queen's University.

Cambridge, 1922–53. *The Cambridge History of India*, 6 vols. Cambridge: Cambridge University Press.

Campbell-Johnson, Alan, 1986. *Mission with Mountbatten*. New York: Atheneum (rpt.).

Cardona, George, 1987a. 'Sanskrit', *in* Bernard Comrie (ed.), *The World's Major Languages*, pp. 448–69. New York: Oxford University Press.

——, 1987b. 'Indo-Aryan Languages', *in* Bernard Comrie (ed.), *The World's Major Languages*, pp. 440–7. New York: Oxford University Press.

Carroll, John B. (ed.), 1956. *Language, Thought, and Reality; Selected Writings of Benjamin Lee Whorf*. Cambridge: MIT Press.

——, 1964. *Language and Thought*. Englewood Cliffs: Prentice-Hall.

Chatterji, S.K., 1963. *Languages and Literatures of Modern India*. Calcutta: Bengal Publishers.

——, 1969. *Indo-Aryan and Hindi*. Calcutta: Firma K.L. Mukhopadhyay.

——, 1973. *India, A Polyglot Nation and its Linguistic Problems vis-à-vis National Integration*. Bombay: Mahatma Gandhi Memorial Research Centre.

Chomsky, William, 1957. *Hebrew — The Eternal Language*. Philadelphia: Jewish Publication Society of America.

Cohler, Anne M., 1970. *Rousseau and Nationalism*. New York: Basic Books.

Cooper, Robert L. (ed.), 1989. *Language Planning and Social Change*. Cambridge: Cambridge University Press.

Cooper, Robert L. and Bernard Spolsky (eds), 1991. *The Influence of Language on Culture and Thought; Essays in Honor of Joshua A. Fishman's Sixty-Fifth Birthday*. Berlin and New York: Mouton de Gruyter.

Corcoran, T., 1925. 'The Irish Language in the Irish Schools', *Studies*, vol. 14, pp. 377–88.

Crocker, Walter, 1966. *Nehru*. New York: Oxford University Press.

Darnell, Regna, 1986. 'Personality and Culture: The Fate of the Sapirian Alternative', *History of Anthropology*, vol. 4, pp. 156–83.

——, 1990. *Edward Sapir: Linguist, Anthropologist, Humanist*. Berkeley and Los Angeles: University of California Press.

Das Gupta, Jyotirindra, 1970. *Language Conflict and National Development*. Berkeley: University of California Press.

——, 1971. 'Religion, Language, and Political Mobilization', *in* Joan Rubin and Björn H. Jernudd (eds), *Can Language Be Planned?*, pp. 53–62. Honolulu: The University Press of Hawaii.

——, 1976. 'Practice and Theory of Language Planning: The Indian Policy Process', *in* William M. O'Barr and Jean F. O'Barr (eds), *Language and Politics*, pp. 195–212. The Hague: Mouton.

Das Gupta, Jyotirindra and John J. Gumperz, 1968. 'Language, Communication and Control in North India', *in* Joshua A. Fishman, Charles A. Ferguson, and Jyotirindra Das Gupta (eds), *Language Problems of Developing Nations*, pp. 151–66. New York: John Wiley & Sons.

Deshpande, Madhav, 1993. *Sanskrit and Prakrit, Sociolinguistic Issues*. Delhi: Motilal Banarsidass.

Deutsch, Karl W., 1942. 'The Trend of European Nationalism — The Language Aspect', *American Political Science Review*, vol. 36, pp. 533–41.

——, 1953. *Nationalism and Social Communication*. Cambridge: MIT Press.

Dimock, Edward C., Jr., Braj B. Kachru and Bh. Krishnamurti (eds), 1992. *Dimensions of Sociolinguistics in South Asia: Papers in Memory of Gerald B. Kelley*. New Delhi: Oxford & IBH Publishing Co.

Dittmer, Kerrin, 1972. *Die indischen Muslims und die Hindi–Urdu Kontroverse in den United Provinces*. Wiesbaden: Otto Harrassowitz.

Diwan, Paras and Pam Rajput, 1979. *Constitution of India*. New Delhi: Sterling Publishers.

Dua, Hans R., 1985. *Language Planning in India*. New Delhi: Harnam Publications.

Dube, Rajendra Prasad, 1988. *Jawaharlal Nehru: A Study in Ideology and Social Change*. Delhi: Mittal Publications.

Dubow, Fred, 1976. 'Language, Law, and Change: Problems in the Development of a National Legal System in Tanzania', *in* William M. O'Barr and Jean F. O'Barr (eds), *Language and Politics*, pp. 85–99. The Hague: Mouton.

Dyer, Donald L., 1989. 'Moldavian, Part II', *in* Howard I. Aronson (ed.), *The Non-Slavic Languages of the USSR, Linguistic Studies*, pp. 93–105. Chicago: Chicago Linguistic Society.

——, 1994. 'Russian and Romanian Intertwined: the Legacy that is Moldavian', *in* Howard I. Aronson (ed.), *Linguistic Studies in the Non-Slavic Languages of the Commonwealth of Independent States and the Baltic Republics*, pp. 65–77. Chicago: Chicago Linguistic Society.

Eastman, Carol M., 1983. *Language Planning: An Introduction*. San Francisco: Chandler & Sharp.

Edgerton, Franklin, 1928. 'Some Linguistic Notes on the Mimansa System', *Language*, vol. 4, pp. 171–7.

Edwardes, Michael, 1971. *Nehru*. London: The Penguin Press.

Embree, Ainslie T., 1985. 'Indian Civilization and Regional Cultures: The Two Realities', *in* Paul Wallace (ed.), *Region and Nation in India*, pp. 19–39. New Delhi: American Institute of Indian Studies.

Embree, Ainslie T. and Stephen Hay, 1988. *Sources of Indian Tradition*. 2 vols. New York: Columbia University Press.

Emeneau, Murray B., 1980. *Language and Linguistic Area, Essays by Murray B. Emeneau*, selected and edited by Anwar S. Dil. Stanford: Stanford University Press.

Emerson, Rupert, 1960. *From Empire to Nation*. Cambridge: Harvard University Press.

Empson, William, 1955. *Seven Types of Ambiguity*. New York: Noonday Press.

Encyclopaedia Britannica, 1946. 23 vols. Chicago: Encyclopaedia Britannica, Inc.

Fellman, Jack, 1974. *The Revival of a Classical Tongue: Eliezer Ben Yehuda and the Modern Hebrew Language*. The Hague: Mouton.

Ferguson, Charles A., 1962. 'The Language Factor in National Development', *Anthropological Linguistics*, vol. 4, pp. 23–7, rptd *in* Frank A. Rice (ed.), *Study of the Role of Second Languages in Asia, Africa, and Latin America*. Washington: Center for Applied Linguistics, 1962.

Ferguson, Charles A. and John J. Gumperz (eds), 1960. *Linguistic Diversity in South Asia: Studies in Regional, Social and Functional Variation*. Bloomington: Indiana University Research Center in Anthropology, Folklore, and Linguistics.

Finegan, Edward, 1987. 'English', *in* Bernard Comrie (ed.), *The World's Major Languages*, pp. 77–109. New York: Oxford University Press.

Firth, J.R., 1957. *Papers in Linguistics 1934–1951*. London: Oxford University Press.

——, 1964. *The Tongues of Man; and Speech*. London: Oxford University Press (rpt.).

Fishman, Joshua A., 1960. 'A Systematization of the Whorfian Hypothesis', *Behavioral Science*, vol. 5, pp. 323–39.

——, 1968. 'Nationality–Nationalism and Nation–Nationism', *in* Joshua A. Fishman, Charles A. Ferguson, and Jyotirindra Das Gupta (eds), *Language Problems of Developing Nations*, pp. 39–51. New York: John Wiley & Sons.

——, 1971. 'The Impact of Nationalism on Language Planning', *in* Joan Rubin and Björn H. Jernudd (eds), *Can Language Be Planned?*, pp. 3–20. Honolulu: The University Press of Hawaii.

——, 1972a. *Language and Nationalism: Two Integrative Essays*. Rowley: Newbury House.

——, 1972b. 'Sociocultural Organization: Language Constraints and Language Reflections', in *Language in Sociocultural Change*, pp. 286–305. Stanford: Stanford University Press.

Fishman, Joshua A., Charles A. Ferguson, and Jyotirindra Das Gupta (eds), 1968. *Language Problems of Developing Nations*. New York: John Wiley & Sons.

Freeman, Edward A., 1879. 'Race and Language', *Historical Essays*, 3rd srs. London: Macmillan.

Fromkin, Victoria and Robert Rodman, 1993. *An Introduction to Language*, 5th edn. Fort Worth: Harcourt Brace.

Frykenberg, Robert, 1985. 'State, Empire and Nation in South India: Demythologizing as a Scholar's Enterprise', *in* Paul Wallace (ed.), *Region and Nation in India*, pp. 60–84. New Delhi: American Institute of Indian Studies.

Frykenberg, Robert, 1986. 'Modern Education in South India, 1784–1854: its Roots and its Role as a Vehicle of Integration Under Company Raj', *The American Historical Review*, vol. 91, pp. 37–65.

——, 1988. 'The Myth of English as a "Colonialist" Imposition upon India: a Reappraisal with Special Reference to South India', *Journal of the Royal Asiatic Society*, no. 2, pp. 305–15.

Gallagher, Charles F., 1963. 'Language, Culture, and Ideology: The Arab World', *in* K.H. Silvert (ed.), *Expectant Peoples: Nationalism and Development*, pp. 199–231. New York: Random House.

——, 1968. 'North African Problems and Prospects: Language and Identity', *in* Joshua A. Fishman, Charles A. Ferguson, and Jyotirindra Das Gupta (eds), *Language Problems of Developing Nations*, pp. 129–50. New York: John Wiley & Sons.

——, 1971. 'Language Reform and Social Modernization in Turkey', *in* Joan Rubin and Björn H. Jernudd (eds), *Can Language Be Planned?*, pp. 157–78. Honolulu: The University Press of Hawaii.

Gandhi, Rajmohan, 1984. *The Rajaji Story 1937–1972*, 2 vols. Bombay: Bharatiya Vidya Bhavan.

Gopal, Sarvepalli, 1989. *Radhakrishnan: A Biography*. London: Unwin Hyman.

—— (ed.), 1991. *Anatomy of a Confrontation*. New Delhi: Penguin Books India.

——, 1992. 'The English Language in India since Independence, and its Future Role', *in* John Grigg (ed.), *Nehru Memorial Lectures 1966–1991*, pp. 197–212. Delhi: Oxford University Press.

Gould, Harold A., 1985. 'On the Apperception of Doom in Indian Political Analysis', *in* Paul Wallace (ed.), *Region and Nation in India*, pp. 287–99. New Delhi: American Institute of Indian Studies.

Green, Arthur, 1992. 'The Aleph–Bet of Creation: Jewish Mysticism for Beginners', *Tikkun*, vol. 7, pp. 45–57, 72–3.

Grierson, George A., 1967–8. *Linguistic Survey of India*, 11 vols. Delhi: Motilal Banarsidass (rpt. of 1st edn, 1903–28).

Gunther, John, 1939. *Inside Asia*. New York and London: Harper & Brothers.

Gwynn, D., 1928. *The Irish Free State, 1922–1927*. London: Macmillan.

Harris, Martin, 1987. 'French', *in* Bernard Comrie (ed.), *The World's*

Major Languages, pp. 210–35. New York: Oxford University Press.

Harrison, Selig S., 1960. *India: The Most Dangerous Decades*. Princeton: Princeton University Press.

——, 1985. 'An Overview: Region and Nation in India', *in* Paul Wallace (ed.), *Region and Nation in India*, pp. 300–8. New Delhi: American Institute of Indian Studies.

Haugen, Einar, 1966. *Language Conflict and Language Planning*. Cambridge: Harvard University Press.

——, 1971. 'Instrumentalism in Language Planning', *in* Joan Rubin and Björn H. Jernudd (eds), *Can Language Be Planned?*, pp. 281–9. Honolulu: The University Press of Hawaii.

Hertz, Frederick, 1944. *Nationality in History and Politics*. New York: Oxford University Press.

Heyd, Uriel, 1954. *Language Reform in Modern Turkey*. Jerusalem: Israel Oriental Society.

Hock, Hans Heinrich, 1992. 'Spoken Sanskrit in Uttar Pradesh: Profile of a Dying Language', *in* Edward C. Dimock, Jr., Braj B. Kachru, and Bh. Krishnamurti (eds), *Dimensions of Sociolinguistics in South Asia: Papers in Memory of Gerald B. Kelley*, pp. 247–60. New Delhi: Oxford & IBH Publishing Co.

Ireland, 1937. *Constitution of Ireland*. Dublin: Stationery Office (government publication).

——, 1965. *The Restoration of the Irish Language*. Dublin: Stationery Office (government publication).

Jannuzi, F. Tomasson, 1985. 'Land Systems, Economic Growth and Social Justice: The Permanent Settlement Region', *in* Paul Wallace (ed.), *Region and Nation in India*, pp. 183–96. New Delhi: American Institute of Indian Studies.

Jászi, Oscar, 1929. *The Dissolution of the Habsburg Monarchy*. Chicago: The University of Chicago Press.

Judd, Denis, 1993. *Jawaharlal Nehru*. Cardiff: University of Wales Press.

Kachru, Braj B., 1978. 'Lexical Innovations in South Asian English', *in* Ramesh Mohan (ed.), *Indian Writing in English*, pp. 80–100. New Delhi: Orient Longman.

——, 1983. *The Indianization of English: The English Language in India*. New York: Oxford University Press.

Kachru, Yamuna, 1987. 'Hindi–Urdu', *in* Bernard Comrie (ed.), *The World's Major Languages*, pp. 470–89. New York: Oxford University Press.

Kapoor, Purnima P., 1985. *Economic Thought of Jawaharlal Nehru*. New Delhi: Deep & Deep.

Katzner, Kenneth, 1986. *The Languages of the World*. London: Routledge & Kegan Paul.

Kelkar, Ashok R., 1968. *Studies in Hindi–Urdu*. Poona: Deccan College Postgraduate and Research Institute.

Kelman, Herbert C., 1971. 'Language as an Aid and Barrier to Involvement in the National System', *in* Joan Rubin and Björn H. Jernudd (eds), *Can Language Be Planned?*, pp. 21–51. Honolulu: The University Press of Hawaii.

Kennedy, Joseph, 1968. *Asian Nationalism in the Twentieth Century*. London: Macmillan.

King, Robert D., 1972. ' "Triuwe" in Gottfried's *Tristan*', *Canadian Journal of Linguistics*, vol. 17, pp. 159–66.

——, 1990. 'West from India: The Odyssey of Sir William Jones', *The Library Chronicle*, vol. 20, pp. 49–63.

Kishore, Satyendra, 1987. *National Integration in India*. New Delhi: Sterling Publishers.

Klaiman, M.H., 1987. 'Bengali', *in* Bernard Comrie (ed.), *The World's Major Languages*, pp. 490–513. New York: Oxford University Press.

Kloss, Heinz, 1968. 'Notes Concerning a Language–Nation Typology', *in* Joshua A. Fishman, Charles A. Ferguson, and Jyotirindra Das Gupta (eds), *Language Problems of Developing Nations*, pp. 69–85. New York: John Wiley & Sons.

Kluyev, Boris I., 1981. *India: National and Language Problem*. New Delhi: Sterling Publishers.

Koestler, Arthur, 1949. *Promise and Fulfillment: Palestine, 1917–1949*. New York: Macmillan.

Kohn, Hans, 1944. *The Idea of Nationalism*. New York: Macmillan.

——, 1967. *Prelude to Nation-States*. New York: D. Van Nostrand.

Koppelmann, Heinrich L., 1956. *Nation, Sprache and Nationalismus*. Leiden: Sijthoff.

Kulke, Hermann and Dieter Rothermund, 1986. *A History of India*. London and Sydney: Croom Helm.

Kumar, Virendra, 1975. *Committees and Commissions in India, 1947–73*. vol. II: 1955–7. Delhi: Concept Publishing Company.

Lenin, V.I., 1964. *Collected Works*, 45 vols. Moscow: Progress Publishers.

Lewis, Bernard, 1968. *The Emergence of Modern Turkey*. London: Oxford University Press.

Lieberson, Stanley, 1970. *Language and Ethnic Relations in Canada*. New York: John Wiley & Sons.

Lucy, John A., 1992. *Grammatical Categories and Cognition: A Case Study of the Linguistic Relativity Hypothesis*. Cambridge: Cambridge University Press.

Macdonnell, Arthur A., 1927. *India's Past*. Oxford: The Clarendon Press.

Macnamara, John, 1971. 'Successes and Failures in the Movement for the Restoration of Irish', *in* Joan Rubin and Björn H. Jernudd (eds), *Can Language Be Planned?*, pp. 65–94. Honolulu: The University Press of Hawaii.

Majumdar, R.C. (ed.), 1951. *The History and Culture of the Indian People*, 10 vols. Bombay: Bharatiya Vidya Bhavan.

Majumdar, R.C., H.D. Raychaudhuri, and Kalikinkar Datta, 1961. *An Advanced History of India*. London: Macmillan.

Mandelbaum, David (ed.), 1949. *Selected Writings of Edward Sapir in Language, Culture and Personality*. Berkeley: University of California Press.

Mannheim, Karl, 1936. *Ideology and Utopia*. New York: Harcourt Brace.

Mathai, M.O., 1978. *Reminiscences of the Nehru Age*. New Delhi: Vikas Publishing House.

Miller, Barbara Stoler, 1986. *The Bhagavad-Gita*. New York: Bantam Books.

Moraes, Frank, 1956. *Jawaharlal Nehru: A Biography*. New York: Macmillan.

Mukherji, Krishna, 1955. *Reorganization of Indian States*. Bombay: Popular Book Depot.

Narasimhaiah, C.D., 1969. *The Swan and the Eagle*. Simla: Indian Institute of Advanced Study.

Narayana Rao, K.V., 1973. *The Emergence of Andhra Pradesh*. Bombay: Popular Prakashan.

Nayar, Baldev Raj, 1969. *National Communication and Language Policy in India*. New York: Praeger.

O'Barr, Jean F., 1976. 'Language and Politics in Tanzanian Governmental Institutions', *in* William M. O'Barr and Jean F. O'Barr (eds), *Language and Politics*, pp. 69–84. The Hague: Mouton.

O'Barr, William M., 1976. 'Language Use and Language Policy in Tanzania: An Overview', *in* William M. O'Barr and Jean F. O'Barr (eds), *Language and Politics*, pp. 35–48. The Hague: Mouton.

O'Barr, William M. and Jean F. O'Barr (eds), 1976. *Language and Politics*. The Hague: Mouton.

O'Brien, Conor Cruise (ed.), 1960. *The Shaping of Modern Ireland*. London: Routledge & Kegan Paul.

O Cuív, Brian, 1969. 'The Changing Form of the Irish Language', *in* Brian O Cuív (ed.), *A View of the Irish Language*, pp. 23–34. Dublin: Stationery Office.

O Fiaich, T., 1969. 'The Language and Political History', *in* Brian O Cuív (ed.), *A View of the Irish Language*, pp. 101–11. Dublin: Stationery Office.

O'Grady, William, Michael Dobrovolsky, and Mark Aronoff, 1993. *Contemporary Linguistics*. New York: St. Martin's Press.

O Neíll, E., 1968. 'The Language Revival in Ireland', *in* F.G. Thompson (ed.), *Maintaining a National Identity*, pp. 54–63. Dublin: The Celtic League.

Ornstein, Jacob and William W. Gage, 1964. *The ABC's of Languages and Linguistics*. Philadelphia: Chilton Books.

Panikkar, Kavalam M., 1956. *A Survey of Indian History*. Bombay: Asia Publishing House.

Patra, S.C., 1979. *Formation of the Province of Orissa: The Success of the First Linguistic Movement in India*. Calcutta: Punthi Pustak.

Pinxten, Rik (ed.), 1976. *Universalism versus Relativism in Language and Thought: Proceedings of a Colloquium on the Sapir–Whorf Hypothesis*. The Hague: Mouton.

Polomé, Edgar C., 1968. 'The Choice of Official Languages in the Democratic Republic of the Congo', *in* Joshua A. Fishman, Charles A. Ferguson, and Jyotirindra Das Gupta (eds), *Language Problems of Developing Nations*, pp. 295–311. New York: John Wiley & Sons.

Polomé, Edgar C. and Clifford P. Hill (eds), 1980. *Language in Tanzania*. London: Oxford University Press.

Ram Gopal, 1966. *Linguistic Affairs of India*. Bombay: Asia Publishing House.

Redfield, Robert, 1967. *The Little Community and Peasant Society and Culture*. Chicago: University of Chicago Press.

Rosenthal, Franz, 1960. *The Muslim Concept of Freedom*. Leiden: E.J. Brill.

Roy, Ramashray, 1985. 'Region and Nation: A Heretical View', *in* Paul Wallace (ed.), *Region and Nation in India*, pp. 269–86. New Delhi: American Institute of Indian Studies.

Rubin, Joan and Björn H. Jernudd, 1971. *Can Language Be Planned?* Honolulu: The University Press of Hawaii.

Rubin, Joan, Björn H. Jernudd, Jyotirindra Das Gupta, Joshua A. Fishman, and Charles A. Ferguson (eds), 1977. *Language Planning Processes*. The Hague: Mouton.

Rudolph, Lloyd I. and Susanne Hoeber Rudolph, 1985. 'The Subcontinental Empire and the Regional Kingdom in Indian State Formation', *in* Paul Wallace (ed.), *Region and Nation in India*, pp. 40–59. New Delhi: American Institute of Indian Studies.

Rustow, Dankwart A., 1965. 'Turkey: The Modernity of Tradition', *in* Lucian W. Pye and S. Verba (eds), *Political Culture and Political Development*, pp. 237–86. Princeton: Princeton University Press.

——, 1967. *A World of Nations*. Washington: The Brookings Institution.

——, 1968. 'Language, Modernization, and Nationhood — An Attempt at Typology', *in* Joshua A. Fishman, Charles A. Ferguson, and Jyotirindra Das Gupta (eds), *Language Problems of Developing Nations*, pp. 87–105. New York: John Wiley & Sons.

Said, Edward (ed.), 1987. *Kim*, by Rudyard Kipling. Harmondsworth: Penguin Books Ltd.

Sapir, Edward, 1921. *Language*. New York: Harcourt, Brace & World.

Schwartzberg, Joseph E., 1985. 'Factors in the Linguistic Reorganization of Indian States', *in* Paul Wallace (ed.), *Region and Nation in India*, pp. 155–82. New Delhi: American Institute of Indian Studies.

Shiva Rao, B., 1966–8. *The Framing of India's Constitution*, 5 vols. New Delhi: Indian Institute of Public Administration.

Singh, Akhileshwar, 1986. *Political Leadership of Jawaharlal Nehru*. New Delhi: Deep & Deep.

Singh, K.S. and S. Manoharan, 1993. *Languages and Scripts* (People of India, National Series, vol. IX). Delhi: Oxford University Press.

Smith, Vincent A., 1923. *Oxford History of India*. London: Oxford University Press.

Spear, Percival, 1961. *India: A Modern History*. Ann Arbor: The University of Michigan Press.

Staal, J.F., 1972. *A Reader on the Sanskrit Grammarians*. Cambridge: MIT Press.

Stalin, Josef, 1940. *Marxism and the National and Colonial Questions*. Moscow: Foreign Languages Publishing House.

Steever, Sanford B., 1987. 'Tamil and the Dravidian Languages', *in* Bernard Comrie (ed.), *The World's Major Languages*, pp. 725–46. New York: Oxford University Press.

Strachey, John, 1888. *India*. London: Kegan Paul.

Thakur, R.K., 1989. *Jawaharlal Nehru: The Man and the Writer*. New Delhi: Bahri Publications.

Toynbee, Arnold J., 1927. *Survey of International Affairs 1925*, vol. 1. London: Oxford University Press.

——, 1934–61. *A Study of History*, 12 vols. London: Oxford University Press.

Van den Berghe, Pierre L., 1968. 'Language and "Nationalism" in South Africa', *in* Joshua A. Fishman, Charles A. Ferguson, and Jyotirindra Das Gupta (eds), *Language Problems of Developing Nations*, pp. 215–24. New York: John Wiley & Sons.

Varma, Siddheshwar, 1972–6. *G.A. Grierson's Linguistic Survey of India: A Summary*, 3 vols. Hoshiarpur: Vishveshvaranand Institute, Panjab University.

Wall, M., 1969. 'The Decline of the Irish Language', *in* Brian O Cuív (ed.), *A View of the Irish Language*, pp. 81–90. Dublin: Stationery Office.

Wallace, Paul (ed.), 1985. *Region and Nation in India*. New Delhi: American Institute of Indian Studies.

Ward, Barbara, 1959. *Five Ideas That Change the World*. New York: W.W. Norton.

Werlen, Iwar, 1989. *Sprache, Mensch und Welt: Geschichte und Bedeutung des Prinzips der sprachlichen Relativität*. Darmstadt: Wissenschaftliche Buchgesellschaft.

Whiteley, Wilfred H., 1968. 'Ideal and Reality in National Language Policy: A Case Study from Tanzania', *in* Joshua A. Fishman, Charles A. Ferguson, and Jyotirindra Das Gupta (eds), *Language Problems of Developing Nations*, pp. 327–44. New York: John Wiley & Sons.

—— (ed.), 1971a. *Language Use and Social Change*. London: Oxford University Press.

——, 1971b. 'Some Factors Influencing Language Policies in Eastern Africa', *in* Joan Rubin and Björn H. Jernudd (eds), *Can Language Be Planned?*, pp. 141–58. Honolulu: The University Press of Hawaii.

Whorf, Benjamin Lee, 1938. 'Some Verbal Categories of Hopi', *Language*, vol. 14, pp. 275–86, rptd *in* John B. Carroll (ed.),

Language, Thought, and Reality; Selected Writings of Benjamin Lee Whorf, pp. 112–24. Cambridge: MIT Press.

Whorf, Benjamin Lee, 1956. 'The Relation of Habitual Thought and Behavior to Language', *in* John B. Carroll (ed.), *Language, Thought, and Reality: Selected Writings of Benjamin Lee Whorf*, pp. 134–59. Cambridge: MIT Press, 1956.

Wolpert, Stanley, 1993. *A New History of India*. New York: Oxford University Press.

Yule, Henry and A.C. Burnell (eds), 1968. *Hobson-Jobson: A Glossary of Colloquial Anglo-Indian Words and Phrases*. London: Routledge & Kegan Paul (the 1968 edition of this famous linguistic simulacrum of Anglo-Indian life and language, first published in 1886, was edited by William Crooke).

Znaniecki, Florian, 1952. *Modern Nationalities*. Urbana: University of Illinois Press.

Index